Here We Go

Here We Go

A Summer on the Costa del Sol

HARRY RITCHIE

HAMISH HAMILTON · LONDON

HAMISH HAMILTON LTD

Published by the Penguin Group
Penguin Books Ltd, 27 Wrights Lane, London w8 5tz, England
Penguin Books USA Inc., 375 Hudson Street, New York, New York 10014, USA
Penguin Books Australia Ltd, Ringwood, Victoria, Australia
Penguin Books Canada Ltd, 10 Alcorn Avenue, Toronto, Ontario, Canada m4v 3b2
Penguin Books (NZ) Ltd, 182–190 Wairau Road, Auckland 10, New Zealand

Penguin Books Ltd, Registered Offices: Harmondsworth, Middlesex, England

First published 1993
10 9 8 7 6 5 4 3 2 1

Typeset by Datix International Limited, Bungay, Suffolk
Filmset in 11½/14 pt Monophoto Baskerville
Printed in Great Britain by Clays, St Ives plc

A CIP catalogue record for this book is available from the British Library

ISBN 0–241–13321–1

David Ritchie
born Kirkcaldy, 9 September 1895
died Arras, 12 May 1917

Here we go, here we go, here we go.
Here we go, here we go, here we go.
Here we go, here we go, here we go.
Here we go.
Here we go.

(Anon.)

Contents

Acknowledgements

I could not have written this book without the help of many people. Thanks, first of all, to all those who took the time on their holidays to talk to me, all the owners and staff who tolerated my solitary vice of hanging around their bars, and all the expatriate residents who told me about their lives on the coast. (To the holiday-makers who refused to be drawn into conversation, I hope that this book is some evidence that I honestly wasn't trying to sell them time-share.)

I am especially grateful to the following people who offered help and advice in many and varied ways: Anne Millman, Frederic Raphael, Edmund Swinglehurst at the Thomas Cook archives, George and Sarah at Bogart's in Calahonda, Mark Griffiths and Barry Hands at OCI Radio in Marbella, Gerry Brown, Gayle Davidson, Jane Holman, Edward Welch, Annemarie Rafferty, Julia Howlett, Elaine Paterson, Helen Fielding and, above all, Nigel Bowden. For further information on Jesus Gil's eccentric reign at Atletico Madrid I would recommend *The Secret Life of Football* by Alex Flynn and Lynton Guest.

I will be forever indebted to Paul Davis, Phil Smith and Margaret, Ken and Iain Mortimer, who all suffered my company and supplied invaluable companionship, in return for which I exploited and abused them. Cheers.

Large and guilty thank-yous are also due to John Walsh, Kate Carr and Andrew Neil, all of whom indulged, with worrying haste, my request for a leave of absence from *The Sunday Times*.

Finally, I'd like to add my enormous gratitude to my mother and father for first giving me the chance to worry about aeroplane wings, buy a bullfighter poster with my name below El Cordobes, and acquire a tan and a sombrero.

Introduction

As rules of thumb go, the one about honesty being the best policy is dafter than most. Unless, to be fair, you want to live a life of unemployed, friendless celibacy. However, I have to admit that this is one of the few occasions when candour is necessary. I really don't want to give you the wrong impression about the pages that follow.

As its subtitle might indicate, this book describes a summer I spent on the Costa del Sol. How I didn't spend that summer was searching for nuggets of Andalusian folk poetry or traipsing through the Sierras. If you want that sort of book, try one with a title along the lines of *A Quest for the Real Spain* by some Sloane with a significant surname or two. Something else I didn't do that summer was compile lists of things to do, sights to see, restaurants to patronize. Top tips and handy hints for your own holiday on the Costa del Sol will be found in one of the many guide-books to the area, and these can be recognized by the fact that they have titles like *The Costa del Sol: A Guide-book*.

I also think it's for the best to offer this warning: if you want to get stuck into a proper travel book, you've already wasted a few paragraphs of reading time. Let me detain you no longer. No hard feelings, I hope.

Right, with that lot gone, I would like to explain why this is not a proper travel book. Basically, I am sick to the back teeth of reading the damned things, so there's no way I'm going to write one. Jesus. What is it with travel books? Not so long ago, in the sixties and early seventies, the travel book was thought to be as popular and exciting as starched wing-collars. How could travel writers possibly survive when travel was something done not just by the rich and odd but by many millions of normal people? But survive they did. Nay, prospered. The trend was set by the likes of Paul Theroux, Bruce Chatwin and Jonathan Raban, and then, by the early eighties, by just about anyone who could do lunch with a publisher. (Intriguingly, the starched wing-collar made an inexplicable comeback at about the same time.)

The travel bandwagon was soon jam-packed by vaguely talented people with glints in their eyes and Kendal mint cake in their rucksacks. Why? Because it looked such an easy ride. Writers, especially young writers, jumped aboard for the simple reason that they didn't have to do any of the boring tasks that are usually involved with writing non-fiction – working and thinking, to name but two. All that was required of them was to think of a different place to go and/or a different way of getting there. That's why remainder shops are now crammed with books about journeys by pushbike through Afghanistan, or across the Andes by pit pony . . . My favourite is one of the several dozen books on Eastern Europe which have appeared since the dismantling of the Berlin Wall – an account of travels through East Germany and so forth, with not only the author's aunt but his aunt's pig and the coffin of his uncle who has just been killed by the pig falling on top of him, as well. Oh, yes, and they all travel in – wouldn't you just know it? – a Trabant. Pity there wasn't a hot-air balloon on the go as well.

Like Coca-Cola, travel writers have covered the entire globe. Like the Labour Party, they've tried every gimmick going. So here's hoping our travel writers have exhausted the planet's resources of insight-laden adventures, and will have to turn to new careers, managing outward-bound centres, perhaps, or stoking boilers on the Chengdu–Chongqing express.

But they have left one place on Earth unvisited, one ploy untouched. These, by an extraordinary coincidence, were the very destination and transport gimmick I wanted to try – the Costa del Sol and the chartered plane. Inexplicably, publishers proved reluctant to accept my brainwave, but eventually, through the judicious use of bluff and blackmail, I persuaded one firm into paying me an advance, which I promptly blew on a family-sized pack of Maltesers.

So why has no one written a travel book about the Costa del Sol before? Reason number one: it is well nigh impossible, as my Maltesers wrapper went some way to proving, to convince publishers that the idea is not the scam it really is. Number two: I suspect that many writers, especially the significantly surnamed ones, hold the place and its visitors in fearful contempt. Number three: the idea of getting a plane from Gatwick to Malaga, a journey completed by a million Britons a year, and then hanging out having a holiday in one of the world's most popular tourist destinations, would appal them. It'd be like asking a yoga guru to be the midfield ball-winner in a shinty team. Travel writers hate, above any other category of humankind, tourists. About as much as I would hate researching a book that required getting saddle-sore and assaulted by sci-fi creepy-crawlies.

So, as all self-respecting travel writers will doubtless be the first to agree, this is not a travel book. A tourism book, then. I have to confess, however, that the task of writing a book that wasn't a travel book about travelling somewhere confused me at first, leading me to some dreadful errors of judgement in my first fortnight. (Why was I the only person on his or her own in Fuengirola? Well, Colin Thubron doesn't hike across China with some chums, does he? Jonathan Raban doesn't set sail in a boat packed with his pals.)

And another thing that this book isn't. It isn't, or certainly isn't meant to be, snooty. May I suffer emasculation by blunt secateurs if I ever use that superbly self-deluding irregular verb, 'to go on a foreign holiday', the comforting plural of which declines thus: we savour the ambience of another country; you go abroad for a couple of weeks; they book an ignorant package tour and ruin the coastline.

The third person plural applies particularly to the Costa del Sol, which, ninnies who've never been there will readily avow, is frequented by young louts who deserve only condemnation. Actually, since the late sixties, when it became one of the first and most popular destinations for package tours from Britain, the Costa del Sol has attracted a wide variety of holidaymakers, of all ages, types and socio-economic strata – which is why I chose to go there rather than anywhere else. (Time for another pre-emptive strike. The Costa del Sol is said by some to stretch for 300 kilometres east and west of Malaga, but for my purposes – those dictated by convenience and sloth – I kept to the most popular and socially varied stretch, the forty miles between Malaga and Marbella, or rather Puerto Banus, to the west.)

Anyway, holidays, especially holidays in the sun, on the beach and at the bar, are tremendous things, are they not? Even as a child, I appreciated the superb replacement of fortnights in Llandudno by package tours to Majorca and Ibiza. Going for a swim no longer merited a Duke of Edinburgh Award, wearing trunks was not a daftly ceremonial uniform but a necessity, enjoying yourself suddenly seemed a natural part of the holiday deal. And you *flew*, at excitingly early times in the morning, or glamorously late at night, on precarious planes (was it okay to walk down the aisles?), which whisked you to places that greeted you with an unbelievable heat, places where you could swim all day and learn about new foodstuffs like peaches, places where you could stare up at the night sky and realize that the Milky Way meant something more than a bar you could eat between meals, then fall asleep under a single sheet that felt like eight blankets, to wake up and step on to your balcony (a balcony!) and start another day in paradise.

The wonderfulness of holidays abroad may seem a rather obvious topic to describe, but the very few bits of writing on the subject indicate that this is, bafflingly, a contentious issue. Take, for example, a highly regarded book called *Abroad*, by Paul Fussell. It was an educative experience to lie on a beach in Torremolinos and read about the way tourists have been sneered at. There's a quote in the book from some fool lambasting the contemptible project of one Thomas Cook who was offering organized trips down the Nile in the nineteenth century, one of the first package tours. Then, in 1870, there's another writer announcing, 'Of all noxious animals, the most noxious is the tourist.' Osbert Sitwell is quoted as describing tourists as 'locusts' and his sister Edith as complaining about 'the most awful people with legs like flies, who come in to lunch in bathing costume – flies, centipedes'. (Of all writers to use a look-ist justification for her snobbery, Edith Sitwell, who had the body of a stick and the face of one who was fed, when young, by catapult, was not the best equipped.)

That was bad enough, but then Fussell himself goes on to lament the passing of travel writing. (This perked me up for a moment until I realized that the book was published in 1980, the first year of a decade which witnessed the appalling boom in travel books; the author might as well have lamented the demise of the Conservative Party that same year.) The argument goes that travel writing is impossible because travel is impossible because travel means being independent and free, and tourists are herded together to go to places that are, says Fussell, 'pseudo-places' – like the Costa del Sol.

Tourists go to airports which all look the same nowadays and then go on planes which are all just flying cigars which whisk them joylessly to their pseudo-destination where they ape the rich by buying things in places where muzak is designed to make them into consumerist zombies, 'fantasists': 'The resemblance between the tourist and the client of a massage parlour is closer than it would be polite to emphasize.'

Thanks for sparing my feelings. This is a highly intelligent man, but he is imbued in a highbrow tradition whose knee-jerk reaction has always been to despise the masses, and 'mass tourism', like 'mass culture', is a rallying call to defend the last bit of the ivory tower from the barbarians busy knocking down the library to install an amusement arcade. This tradition demands that there was always a time when things were different, when people sang folk-songs rather than pop tat, read books rather than watched telly, made their own entertainment, grew their own food, knew their own minds. It has been calculated that most people date their good old days thirty to forty years before the present – for Fussell in 1980 it was between the wars and, later still, 1957.

A terrible year. (I don't know – it's when I was conceived, though I do hope that's got nothing to do with it.) Fussell points out that 1957 was the year when international jet planes were introduced and – no prizes for guessing the other awful novelty – radio was overtaken by television. Thus creating masses of zombies, you see. It's all part of the dreadful decline of real things being replaced by artificial stuff: 'coffee-cream by ivory-coloured powder, silk and wool by nylon, or glass by lucite, bookstores by "bookstores", eloquence by jargon, fish by fish-sticks, merit by publicity, motoring by driving, and travel by tourism.'

It's such a familiar sort of lament that there was a delay before I realized two things: that I used to take

this attitude as read, in both senses, and that, now that
I've come to think about it, I don't agree with a truism
crucial to almost every pontification about Western civilization I have ever come across. Since I was a child I
have assumed that things are, in general, much better
than in the old days, that I am really lucky to be alive now
rather than before. Thank God for anaesthetic. That in itself is enough but here are some more reasons for me to be
cheerful. My grandfather had to go over the top at the
Somme; I wasn't even required to do National Service.
Like many, many people of my age, I was the first person
in my family to take for granted the following: dental
care, health care, automatic schooling to sixteen and
beyond, the reasonable prospect of a university education,
my own bedroom, my own clothes, a family car, a home
with a telephone, fridge, central heating and carpets.

This air-punching gratitude at being born in 1958
rather than 1895 or even 1928 was also occasioned,
Professor Fussell might be horrified to learn, by the
quality of the culture I enjoyed. Television, for example
– obviously better than radio. I felt sorry for my parents
who'd only had *Listen with Mother* whereas I had *Andy
Pandy*. They'd grown up on tripe like *ITMA* and *Round
the Horne* but I was fortunate enough to be weaned on
The Likely Lads and *Fawlty Towers*. And if anyone born
after 1950 thinks *The Goons*, fine though they could be,
were better than *Monty Python*, he or she is a clot. No
doubt children now regard me with sympathy because I
was too old for *Postman Pat* – they're right to do so. (It
was a shattering experience to see re-runs of old favourites
like *Crackerjack* on a recent TV retrospective; compared
to programmes now, they were all crap.) And have you
seen the toys around these days? Robots and everything.
For the moment, for most people, despite recessions and
depressions and the worst efforts of appalling Tory govern-
ments, the ordinary fabric of living now, compared to
twenty years ago, is more colourful, stronger, better.

So there I was, on a beach in the pseudo-place of the Costa del Sol. Born after the cut-off point of 1957, raised on fish-fingers and Angel Delight, clothed in Bri-Nylon, brought up on a housing estate, glued to the telly since I can remember, taught in State schools, subjected to childhood holidays on package tours to Majorca, Ibiza and Yugoslavia, having experienced an adolescence fuelled by mass-produced cigarettes and mass-produced keg beer, and now experiencing an adulthood spent in flats converted from what were once very large Victorian town-houses. And, to make matters far worse, I'm so stupid, with sensibilities so stunted by modern mass production, I'm sobbingly grateful. I should be put down.

This is not the boasting CV of a working-class hero. That housing estate I was brought up on? It was a Wimpey estate deemed pretentious enough to earn the nickname 'Hungry Hill', because, went the jibe, to afford the pretension of owning their homes the residents had to forsake all luxuries – such as food. And those package tours in the late sixties, early seventies, marked my family as pretty damned prosperous. That I can be automatically thought of as one of them by cultural elitists proves to me just how barkingly elitist they are.

One more thing about those package tours which made foreign holidays possible for us: I wasn't the first person in my family to have gone abroad. My mother and father had been to Paris once. My uncle had been in the RAF in Singapore. The generation before that had been the real globetrotters, though. Three great-aunts emigrated to Milwaukee under the aegis of the great travel scheme that was the Depression, and my grand-father and his younger brother before him had seized the chance to visit foreign fields in the first world war. So the honour of being the first of my ancestors to travel abroad goes to my great-uncle David. I never met him because he died in northern France in 1917. He was in the machine-gun corps, where a soldier's life expectancy was slightly less than a mayfly's.

Where was I? Yes, what this book is not. You may well wonder what, if anything, this book is. The more cynically inclined among you may well be assuming that it can be nothing more than an extended version of that primary-school essay, 'What I Did On My Holidays'. The strange thing is, you're absolutely right.

I

Fuengirola

Passport, tickets, traveller's cheques, currency, camera, suntan oil (just in case they didn't have any out there), smalls, T-shirts, socks, shorts . . . I'd forgotten the shorts. Another rummage through a once carefully packed suitcase and holdall proved that they were indeed there, snuggling safely between some ironed and folded shirts and a jersey, items, like the Spanish dictionary, the phrase-book and the suntan oil, never mind the bloody socks, which belonged only in the luggage of a fool.

The suitcase and holdall had to be packed yet again and sat on yet again. The doorbell clanged, announcing the arrival of the mini-cab. A final pat of the jacket pockets (yes, my wallet, tickets and passport had not leaped out and made a bold bid for freedom), a daredevil refusal to recheck the contents of my suitcase, an old man's shuffle to the door, arms extended with the weight of my two bags, and I was off. It was Sunday, it was five-thirty in the morning, I'd been up since four, and I felt very dodgy.

We drove through a London deserted apart from a few shift-workers and a clutch of ravers making their weary progress home. The sky was as grey as my face.

Fifteen minutes later, after a journey that at any sensible time would take three-quarters of an hour, I was in an extremely short queue at Victoria. A couple of minutes and a couple of strained arms after that, I was on the train for Gatwick. I slumped into a sticky seat and thought about the three things I needed desperately: sleep, coffee and an unexpected yet substantial legacy.

The Gatwick Express scuttled through drizzle and a brown and moist south London which looked as though it had had its last heatwave in 1947. Checking first that the compartment was still empty, I muttered to myself that soon I would be sitting under blue skies and a fierce sun, with a chilled lager in one hand and a golden sex goddess in the other. Nope. My imagination was still fixated on a cup of coffee and the embrace of a clean, warm, cosy duvet. We passed through Norbury, Earlswood, Horley . . . These aren't the names of real places, surely? They're what towns are called in comics, towns with teams that challenge Roy and the Rovers for the Cup.

Did you know that when Gatwick opened as an alternative to Heathrow in 1958 it carried 219,000 passengers and that it's now Britain's second-biggest airport with 175,000 flights and 20 million passengers a year? (No? I suggest you note these figures down – I may be asking questions at the end of this chapter.) However, Gatwick at a quarter to seven on a Sunday morning, even at the beginning of July, was far from teeming with hordes of people. The place bore as close a resemblance as grim reality will ever allow to an airport as envisioned in architects' drawings. Large spaces with prominent design features held but a few human beings clipping on their purposeful way. It was odd to see that the humans were in three-D and were wearing clothes rather than fuzzy crayon. In the whole terminal, activity was to be found in only two queues. I didn't need to look up at the Departures board to know where I had to check in – it was at the desk hosting the much larger queue, the queue 200 yards long and getting longer by the second because there was no one at the check-in desk to check anyone in.

I took up my position a stone's throw – were the stone to be thrown by Geoff Capes or the Iraqi supergun –

from the queue's start. It was not yet seven and the flight
was at nine. How come I was the last to arrive? I was
going to be on a plane of swots. The self-control of a Zen
master, and three cigarettes, helped me to endure the
queue without cracking under the pressure of boredom.
It was half-eight when I went through the security arch,
triggered the alarm (of course) and was frisked by a man
with (of course) a tailor's devotion to the inside leg.

There were hundreds of people at the gate for the
Monarch flight to Malaga. Hundreds. I wondered how
many of them were booked for my hotel in Fuengirola and
prayed that the two boys in front of me, fat, loud shits who
were bullying their much younger sister, would be spending their fortnight bawling and brawling elsewhere.

After another era in queues outside and inside the
Airbus, I fell into my seat among the naughty smokers at
the back. It was time, at last, for that most extraordinary
of modern moments, when the plane finishes its taxi-ing
and you are pressed back into your seat, completely at
the mercy of a great feat of technology – the safety video.
Bag storage, oxygen masks, emergency exits, yeah yeah
yeah, and then, at last, the inflatable jacket with – there
it was on the screen now – a whistle. You plummet into
the Bay of Biscay from 30,000 feet, calmly inflate your
jacket and then, to attract attention, blow on a bloody
whistle. Of course.

Wet-palmed from take-off, I gripped with difficulty
my cigarette and the first of several duty-free whiskies. It
did feel odd drinking at half past nine in the morning
but, hey, it was effectively two in the afternoon. My
fellow-passengers obviously took the same attitude, so
there was a party atmosphere as we crossed the Channel.
They were drinking champagne two rows in front but
most of us stuck to beer or Bell's. The two girls next to
me were on orange juice, although that was forgivable
since they were only fifteen. As Nantes and then Bordeaux passed by to our left, outbreaks of bonhomie

became more frequent and jolly, particularly amongst the champagne set who'd embarked on a riotous game of cards.

The in-flight partying was a welcome distraction from worrying about the changes in engine noise, the thickness of the windows, the bolts on the wings, the question of whether or not, when the hold imploded, one would abruptly die of heart failure or live through the long dive to the whistle-less end. But, apart from the fact that it's fearful, flying is brilliant. Forget the drivel about ocean liners and gold-embossed flunkies on the Orient Express. *This* is the golden age of travel, when, for the cost of a pair of shoes, you can sip from a fistful of clinking Bell's as you and the whisky hurtle along at 500 mph, six miles above the planet's surface. Imagine thawing some deep-frozen Victorians and letting them see what clouds looked like from above. They would faint with ecstasy at a sight familiar now to 83 per cent of the British population. (That figure might be wrong, because I made it up. Anyway, millions and millions of people.)

Soon, too soon, we made landfall over Bilbao. I forsook the chance of snapping up booze, jewellery or a competitively priced 'Pilot Duck' soft toy from the duty-free trolley, concentrating instead on gazing down on the russet heartland of Spain. It wasn't long before russet turned to khaki and my ears began to pop.

'Welcome to Malaga, where the local time is half past noon and the outside temperature is thirty-four degrees. We hope you have enjoyed . . .' Blah blah blah. This is no time for corporate patter, let's go, Spain awaits. At least, Malaga airport awaits. A brand-new Malaga airport, a large, caramel-coloured structure, cosily monumental in the new vernacular style. It looked like it had been designed by Albert Speer in consultation with Prince Charles. We hundreds descended on Baggage Reclaim in a cool, cavernous hall where the ceiling was yellow, the walls and pillars cream and the marbled floor butterscotch. We were waiting for our luggage in an air-pocket in a sci-fi helping of Instant Whip.

Out in the crème caramel arrivals area, we were greeted by a phalanx of reps. The wonderful thing about a package tour is that you don't have to worry about how to work a foreign country; you don't need to get anxious about where to find the train or how to pay the bus-driver, because it's all taken care of. The Thomson woman pointed me through the door to another Thomson woman who pointed me to a bus ten yards away. In case we'd been fazed by the heat or, against all odds, found the wrong bus, there was a name-check of the two dozen or so of us on the coach by a third Thomson woman, the one who would be guiding us through the pitfalls of being driven to the hotels of our choice.

The hotel I had chosen was last on the itinerary, so I was to gain the full benefit of our guide's commentary, which had kicked off with an extensive welcome speech, followed by many words of warning about time-share touts and then by a full weather report. Meanwhile, the coach swung out into the race-track of the N340. Extensive improvements and the construction of subways and bridges for pedestrians have transformed the main thoroughfare of the Costa del Sol. It used to be the most dangerous road in Europe, with an annual average of thirty accidents per kilometre. Now it's merely one of the most dangerous roads in the world. As we careered along towards Torremolinos, I tried to forget that the most dangerous stretch of all is between the airport and Torremolinos. (Because of Brits, fresh from the car-rental office, driving patriotically on the left.)

Outside, there were surprising mountains in the background and a foreground cluttered with billboards in fields. The adverts of a consumerism which is supposed to be blandly international all proclaimed that we were Abroad – Ducados, Whisky *con musica*!, Zumo, San Miguel. Inside, there was the relentless monologue of our guide, who was now pointing out objects of interest with an enthusiasm for detail usually reserved for legal documents.

'Obviously, *on* the left, another hotel and some very badly parked cars. And *to* the right, you will see some blocks of flats as we enter the famous town of Torremolinos. Lots of shops, and lots of people, *as* you can see, many of them Spanish, who all take *to* the beach *on* a Sunday and park their cars very badly. Now, past the souvenir shop *on* the left and *down* the street we'll be coming to our first stop, so *all* of you who are booked *for* the Don Pedro, get ready to disembark *from* the coach and your hotel rep *will* be waiting for you.'

It was the badly parked cars that were our eventual undoing. Somehow, our driver had manoeuvred up a side-street for the fifth drop-off. I suppose the two people booked there could have walked the small distance to their hotel from the main street, but that must be against regulations. Thus we found ourselves making a ninety-degree turn in a lane where deft double parking would have made it hard for a tricycle to change direction. Something like a fifty-seven-point turn later, the driver conceded defeat, and one of the four passengers left on the coach, a short man in his fifties, lost his rag.

'Seventeen pounds surcharge I paid to get an earlier flight,' he told me through clenched teeth, 'and what's happened to my extra bit of time? It's gone down the bloody toilet. Seventeen pounds for the privilege of being stuck in a bloody coach going no bloody where.'

'Still, it's only getting on for an hour we've been here,' I replied brightly. 'And we've got a whole fortnight to look forward to.'

'You might. I've got a bloody week. I was hoping for a swim this afternoon.'

My expressions of sympathy only stoked his ire. The next time he spoke, fury got the better of his syllables.

'Stuck on blood bus. Blood diculous.'

The other two passengers were a couple in their late teens who were evidently here for a fortnight. They were content to look on with slack-jawed exhaustion as our driver climbed down to remonstrate with the owner of a double-parked van. Finally, the van-owner reversed down the street, allowing us to move off and out towards Fuengirola, as our guide launched into an extensive attack on thieving gypsies for whom we had to be on the look-out.

Apartments followed hotels that followed time-share blocks that followed restaurants and villas. The only empty parts of the coast appeared to be those that defied development or had been turned into golf-courses. Some constructions proclaimed their seventies' vintage, but the majority were ten years old at most. Many were unfinished: the grey concrete of half-built low-rises whose stairs led only to the sky soon became a familiar sight, as did that of unmanned cranes drooping over rows of incomplete flats appending a hillside.

My map suggested that we had passed through Torremolinos, Benalmadena and Torreblanca, but it was impossible to know where one resort ended and another began. Then, as the coach flew downhill, I caught a glimpse of dense development on a curve of the coast ahead. 'Long blood last,' muttered the furious man. So that was Fuengirola. We joined a traffic jam as soon as we hit town, and jerked our way slowly forward. The furious man shook his head in disbelief. Some time later we had made it to the seafront, where we inched towards a large, red hotel, the destination of the furious man who beetled off to check in and prepare for what would now be his evening swim. Three wasn't enough of an audience for our guide, it seemed, and we crawled the last few yards to the final hotel in silence.

It was a grey–beige amalgam of two buildings shaped like threepenny-bits and joined by a two-storey base. One building rose eight storeys above the two-storey base, the other sixteen. It had looked intriguing in the brochure. In real life, it was ghastly.

I didn't feel disappointed. Scared is nearer the mark. How was I going to spend two weeks here on my own? Would the view compensate for the vertigo if my room was on the sixteenth floor? Why were the young couple still slack-jawed? Did they share some nasal complaint? Preoccupied by queries and doubts, I was ushered into reception behind the young couple who, with the exertion of carrying their suitcases, were not so much breathing as snoring.

I checked in and received a jolly leaflet telling me that a 'welcome guestogether' for new arrivals would be held tomorrow in the Ceramic Bar on the first floor at midday. I was then led to my room by a porter who listed precariously to his left as he strained to carry my suitcase. Fortunately, we climbed only a couple of flights up a spiral stairway before the porter lurched to the right. He was taking me to the emergency exit. No. There was a white wooden door on the left. The porter ushered me in and promptly ran away.

My first reaction was to laugh. My second was to wonder when exactly this room had been converted from a store cupboard. It didn't even reach to four walls. It was triangular, with a loo tucked into the cone. I was going to stay for two weeks in a slice of pizza. The loo itself was minute but it seemed as spacious as the veldt compared to the bedroom. That contained two walk-in wardrobes only a very thin toddler could have walked into. A bedside cabinet nicked from a doll's house. A chair. And a bed – a bed shorter and narrower than the one I slept in when my room at home had Noddy and Big Ears wallpaper.

It was clean, though, and the floor was done in marble. And the decor wasn't bad – plain white walls added to the rustic touch of the wooden door. A less rustic touch there was the lock, of such bulk and ferocity it wouldn't have disgraced a flat in Harlem. In addition, I saw, after parting the curtains (period pieces from the seventies these, all beige blobs and lime-green circles), there was a small balcony which afforded a view of the adjoining rust-coloured fire-escape and a noisy back-street.

I lay on my bed and recalled how I had ended up here. Booking this fortnight only last weekend had been the result of my clever ruse to get a place on the cheap but, as young Nikki at my local travel agent's soon found out, there were no last-minute bargains. And precious few single rooms. Several hours at her computer yielded a room in something like the Hotel International Splendide in Marbella, a snip at £1500 for two weeks. Or the Hotel Dreck along the coast, understandably under-booked since not even the brochure could conceal its resemblance to a prison with awnings.

'Of course, it's more difficult to find a place for just . . .' Nikki had said. 'But since you're going on your . . . And there's usually a supplement if you're . . .'

'What supplement?'

'Well, any hotel will charge at least £50 or £60 a week extra for . . . For those who don't have . . .'

'For singles?'

'Well. Yes. Singles. And naturally there aren't many single rooms.'

'Can you give it one more go?'

She did, and struck lucky with this place. 'It's very reasonable, really,' Nikki assured me. 'Three stars, which means it'll be all right, and half-board at £563, which includes your £7 a day single supplement.'

'Blood in sand.'

'Well, it's either that or the International Splendide. Or the Dreck.'

'I'll take it.'

There were other supplements as well. A supplement for travel insurance. A flight supplement. A supplement for having a surname starting with R. A supplement for wearing specs . . .

I realized that during this reflection I'd been staring

at a notice on the door. 'Prohibido, Forbjudet, Kielletty, Forbidden, Verboten, Interdit, Forbudt,' warned the slogan that accompanied a sketch of some object with a red cross through it. But what was the object? Silly with fatigue, I decided that it was prohibited to use a hearing-aid attached to an egg-whisk. Or that curlers were banned. I had unpacked and showered by the time it dawned on me that the object was a portable heating-ring. I wasn't allowed to warm up food in my room.

Just as well there was a restaurant. That was on the second of the hotel's two communal floors, I discovered on my initial wander round the place. Dinner would start in half an hour, according to the noticeboard out-side, which also sported cartoon instructions. In the first drawing Mister Cartoonperson (bald, with a moustache) and Missus Cartoonperson (a bit of a floozie with long blonde hair) were seen being welcomed by another couple whose arms were flung magnanimously wide: 'Share Your Table!' urged the caption. Beside that were more drawings, the first showing Mister Cartoonperson in a flamboyant top hat and tails: 'It is not necessary,' it claimed. The next revealed Missus Cartoonperson saucily disporting herself in a green bikini: 'It is not correct,' that one admonished. The 'It is correct' drawing showed the Cartoonpersons arm-in-arm in the proper dress – hiking kit, apparently.

Thankful that I wasn't wearing a tuxedo, I went down the circular staircase, past a musty lounge on the first floor, to the reception area, where I found a shop, an exhibition of vivid landscape paintings, a pool table, a bar, and another lounge packed with semi-circular armchairs all facing a stage. There were also more posters of the Cartoonpersons to advertise coming attractions on the hotel's nightly cabaret shows – Isabel Marquez, Jockey, Miss Elección – which were incomprehensible.

After a much-needed beer, I climbed the stairs again to the restaurant, which had just opened. It was a large room, slightly chilly from the air-conditioning and made even chillier by the sign with a cigarette with a red line through it. Ah, well. There was a self-service buffet in the middle, with main courses explained by silhouettes of the relevant animal above each tray. I devoured my unspecifiable fish in solitude, then sprinted out for a smoke. Things would be different tomorrow when, no doubt, I'd be sharing my table and making new friends.

So where now? A stroll was the answer. The sun was setting but it was still very warm. I made a short detour to the alleyway my room looked out onto and saw why it was so noisy – in the space of twenty yards there was Teo's Hollandse Bar, Posers video bar, The Yorkshire Rose and a fourth pub called Pat and Adrian's Scots Corner. Resolving to explore a little further, I spurned that quartet and sauntered back through the crowds along the seafront to the west. The promenade was lined by six-storey apartment blocks above a procession of pubs and restaurants: Maxy's, Tahiti, Roxy, Scoffers. I chose Scoffers, lured there by the offer of a coffee and brandy for 190 pesetas. Just over a quid? Not bad. I felt a bit lonely, to be honest, sipping coffee and brandy and watching people go by, but it was my first night and I'd had a long, tiring day. It'd be better tomorrow.

I came to at half past nine. It was the longest sleep I'd had in years and it left me feeling not full of zip and go but as sluggish as a drugged captive. In TV movies and the like, drugged captives spend a maximum of fifteen seconds regaining consciousness, then rub their eyes, shake their heads, untie knots, immobilize guards, and make good their escape. At a quarter to ten, I was still practising the parting of my eyes and lips.

A ten o'clock deadline for breakfast forced me out of bed and on to the floor. Using the bed as leverage, I pushed myself upright. The Earth's gravity had increased appreciably overnight. With cowed back and stiff ankles I hobbled the tiny distance to the bathroom, where a series of slow and trying ablutions signally failed to provide me with vim or verve. Three minutes to ten. With the ease and grace of a Dalek on the parallel bars, I yanked on a T-shirt and hopped into jeans.

I scampered excitedly downstairs like a small boy on Christmas Day. That's a lie, but somehow I made it to the restaurant by ten. The place was chock-a-block with couples and families.

I was thirty-four, there was no alternative, I could handle this . . . Oh God, oh God, oh God.

There were – how could it be otherwise? – no empty tables, so, heeding the enjoiner of the Cartoonpersons, I attached myself to the end of a table occupied by a family, all of whose five members had, I soon guessed, just had a row. Nobody was having eye contact with anybody, especially me. I sat down and toyed awhile with my napkin to demonstrate that I was happy and comfortable with my lot before realizing that breakfast, like dinner, was entirely self-service. I slunk out of my chair and joined the queue at the buffet.

Huge jugs of fruit juice. Rows of cold meats. Rows of thin rectangles of yellow cheese. Rows of senile hard-boiled eggs. A shambles of diced frankfurters. Heaps of bread and rolls. Hillocks of cornflakes and muesli. Eating first thing in the morning, I don't get it. You're just out of bed, for goodness' sake. A normal person's breakfast is two very strong cups of coffee and two cigarettes and, if needs be, a second course of a very strong cup of coffee and a cigarette. However, having queued on automatic pilot, I found I was carrying a plate, so I decorated it with two slices of salami and a rectangle of yellow cheese. Coffee. I had to have coffee. And to have coffee I had to join another queue, at a machine that skooshed out hot, coffee-style liquid.

Back at my table, each member of the family was still

inspecting shoes, plates and middle distances, so my best jerk's ingratiating nod-and-smile combination was to no avail. I played with my plate of things, if only because I had to do something while I waited for my coffee-style liquid to cool. Having swigged that down, I paused for as long a time as I could manage, then got the hell out of there. In the safety of my room, I sucked mightily on a cigarette, then sighed heavy sighs while contemplating the loneliest number, then slumped on to the bed where I sat, rocking backwards and forwards, groaning and swearing into my hands, just in time for the maid to barge in.

Encouraged by her presence standing guard at my door and the prospect of more coffee, I left my room and the hotel. The outside world was bright and hot and full of people. A minute's walk away I discovered an attractive café where I set about regaining my composure and ordered in my best − in fact, only − Spanish a *café solo*. There followed the highly unlikely event of someone greeting me as if they knew me.

'Hello again.'

I swivelled round to see that the table behind had been taken by the furious man from the coach. What luck! A chum!

After we had exchanged pleasantries, I thought it an opportune moment to indulge in a little banter. 'Glad to see that you've recovered your temper,' I said with a smile.

'What?'

'It's just that the last time I saw you . . .' My voice trailed off as his previously sunny expression was replaced by that of a staunch defender of the faith, goaded beyond endurance by heretics.

'I must say, it's a lovely day, makes a change from rainy old Blighty, don't you think, here's hoping it stays like this for the fortnight, I should cocoa.'

The babbling seemed to work to the extent that he replied to it.

'I'm only here for a week,' he said.

'Of *course* you are. This your first holiday here, is it?'

Apparently contented again, he settled back into his chair. 'Oh, no. Been coming to Fuengirola for the past ten years. We loved it down here.'

I noted the pronoun and tense he'd just used while taking my first sip of coffee. That turned out to be black and viscous and apparently laced with cocaine, and the furious man turned out to be a widower of only three months' standing. He admitted to having trouble sleeping but was astonishingly stoical about his bereavement, so I risked asking him if he didn't mind coming back to a place permeated with painful reminders of his wife.

'Oh, no. I've got only happy memories of Fuengirola. Very happy. And I've got friends here as well. Just been to have my haircut from the barber I always go to up the road there. Had a good conversation, him in Spanish and me in English, like, but we got by. And I'll be seeing my drinking buddy tonight. He's Spanish as well, but he's got a bit of English, especially swearing, and what more do you want, eh?' His laugh burbled with nicotine then gave way to a cough.

I asked if he had any tips about things to do here, excursions, for example. A mistake.

'They're a bloody rip-off, that's what they are. You take that trip they advertise to the market and then Mijas. Nineteen hundred pesetas, is it? Bloody rip-off, more like. The market's only ten minutes' walk up the bloody road and you can get the bus to Mijas your bloody self and it'll only cost you fourpence bloody ha'penny.'

Aha! Something to expose! I thanked him for this inside information while he paid for the coffee that he'd drunk in one fierce go. He was off to the beach, he announced. Another bloody rip-off there, he could tell me, charging for the sun-loungers and parasols, bloody rip-off. I was to watch out. With that, he marched off,

leaving me to drink three more *café solos* that gave me a
strange, buzzy sensation and the heart-rate of a television
newscaster.

It was approaching midday when I remembered that
the welcome guestogether reception was being held at
twelve. I ran back to the hotel where I sprinted up the
stairs, down the stairs and up the stairs again. Did first
floor mean ground floor or the floor one above the
ground? And did the mezzanine count? I ran round the
floor one above the ground until I came across a room
that contained a large display of ceramic fish, ceramic
crustaceans, ceramic mermaids . . . Perhaps this was the
Ceramic Bar.

Inside there were ten pale people waiting in pairs. I
was sure I'd heard voices from the corridor but silence
fell as I rushed in. I sat down next to the slack-jawed
couple and smiled. Almost imperceptibly, they shifted
away. No one said a word. Time wore on. A middle-
aged woman fiddled noiselessly with her handbag. More
time wore on. This was now the most excruciating silence
I had experienced since Miss Muir demanded to know
which of us in Primary Three had done that dirty
drawing on the blackboard. I wiped the sweat from my
hands. Mental strength was required to survive this. I
embarked on the task of recalling the nicknames of all
the clubs in the Scottish Second Division. I had reached
number eight (Stenhousemuir, the Warriors), when the
silence was broken. A middle-aged man opposite started
to whistle softly through his teeth. The tune he was
whistling was 'Please Release Me'.

In the fullness of time, a sturdy rep bustled in with an
armful of brochures.

'Hello, everyone,' she said with great breeziness. 'Everyone settling in okay? . . . That's great. Right, then.
Could you pass round these brochures, please? Right,
then. My name's Jane and if I could just tell you that I
won't be your rep, that's Trevor, but he can't be here

today, and he'll be happy to deal with any queries or
problems that you have, all right? Fine.'

True to form, Jane proceeded to warn us about time-
share touts and explain everything to us. Where the
restaurant was and how to work the buffet. Where the
telephones were and how to call home. How to change
money and how to post postcards. Which buses to take
and from where. That Trevor could be found every
morning at his desk in the lobby and that we'd to be nice
to Trevor because he was new. That we could haggle at
the market but not in the shops. That there were lots of
excursions to choose from, but that, since our hotel was
nearby, we should avoid the organized trip to the weekly
market and Mijas and save money by going on our own.
Bang went my scoop.

With that Jane wished us a happy holiday and bustled
out. I had planned on exchanging a few words with the
slack-jawed couple but they had moved an appreciable
distance away by the end and had, in any case, now fled
the room. I was also ready to give my other fellow-guests
my most chipper nods and smiles. No chance. They'd
all scooted off, some of them chatting and laughing. I
lingered long enough to wonder if this was how lunatics
felt when they travelled by bus.

Ho hum. It was a perfect day for a little wander about
town. Well, what else was I going to do? Pop out for
lunch with some pals? Throw a party? I walked thoughtfully down to the lobby and out again on to the promenade. I decided to head east this time. I set off with the
air, I trust, of a man with a mission, or at least an appointment.

To the left was a marina and then the beach which
held large groups of Spaniards, some pink Britons, and
volleyball nets. At regular intervals there were also restaurants, all of which had rowing boats outside, rowing
boats filled with sand and topped by small fires grilling
sardines impaled on sticks. To the right were hotels and

then pastel-coloured apartment blocks whose ground floors were occupied by eateries and drinkeries: the Waterfront Bar, Ronnie's Café Bar, the Montego Ice-cream Parlour, El Bogavante (*cocedero de mariscos y freidura*), the Restaurante Chino La Suerte, Steve 'N' Kate's, Bonnie 'N' Clyde's. And how cheering it was to see that the Skandinaviska Turist Kyrkan's neighbours were something called the English Manila Bar and Bunters self-service carvery bar.

The most prominent feature of all was the heat. I slipped off my T-shirt and was pleased by the absence of catcalls. (My legs were sticking to my jeans but that I'd have to put up with.) About a mile east of the hotel, I decided I had grown bored with the going-for-a-walk-for-no-particular-reason game so I turned round, to walk, for no particular reason, back in the direction of the hotel. I told myself I was doing myself some good (exercise, ozone), a theory lent credibility by the tedium this jaunt involved.

To feel that I had earned my lunch, I went beyond the hotel and Scoffers – as far, you will be impressed to learn, as Ladybirds live music bar. This was adorned by boards urging me to come in and relax, and boasting that Ladybirds was 'as featured on Grampian Television' and that it offered 'burgers curries scampi salmon'. Other boards announced that appearing tonight was 'the one and only Rochdale cowboy, Mike Harvey', that tomorrow's act was 'Direct from Blackpool, the Colyers' and Thursday's 'Mister Personality, Dave Ellis'. However, these were all evening performances, and Ladybirds at one-thirty in the afternoon was as empty as my diary.

The danger with having so many places to choose from was to reject them all. I didn't like the seat covers in one pub, another had a waiter I didn't much like the look of, a third I spurned because there was a lovey-dovey couple at one of the tables. Finally, I plumped for Sam's English Breakfast Bar, a curious name for several

reasons, one being that almost all the British places I'd
seen so far made a big point about serving a full English
breakfast all day. (Why? Search me.) Hoardings here
advertised 'The Best Tea By The Sea (All Served In
"Pots" With Biscuits)', Cream Teas, and Sinful Pancakes.
Another hoarding claimed, 'There's only two places to
eat – Sam's and your Mum's', so I had to suppress
another attack of loneliness as I selected my table, which
was soon covered in a plate filled with a Sinful Jamaican
Pancake (stuffed with banana, jam and Tia Maria – I
can recommend it) and a glass of San Miguel.

Replete and refreshed, I settled down to study the
brochure Jane the sturdy rep had handed me. It was, the
cover said, my 'complimentary resort guide from Thomson', and it was full of interesting and valuable pieces of
information. I now knew, for example, that the Costa del
Sol normally enjoys 326 days of sunshine a year. And
that the Spanish for bank is *banco*. I also learned how to
say 'Good morning', 'Good afternoon' and 'How much is
it?' in the native tongue. Excellent. The list of translations
of Spanish signs meant that I could now go, with complete confidence, through an open door at an entrance,
find a lift and ascend to a lavatory, know which one
was the gents, and recognize if it was vacant or engaged.
Great stuff.

The brochure also carried various adverts, one of
them for a coach-tour outfit calling themselves Parody
Tur. I was quite taken with that but much less with the
rest. In the Hertz ad, for instance, there was a woman
with a sun-hat topped by a bubble that read: 'We're
having a fantastic holiday exploring with the freedom of
our Hertz car.' (Ah, the mysteries of the copywriter's
art.) The drawback was that 'we' were, inevitably, a
perfect nuclear family: mummy with her sunhat and
bubble, daddy in his Hawaiian shirt and knitting-
pattern-model's hairstyle, and two grinning kiddy-
winkles. Other slogans read: 'Tivoli World – for the whole

family'; 'Aquapark – toboggans, slides, parrot show and children's area'; 'El Elefante – traditional roast Sunday lunch, children's menu, kiddies' rides, large family bar'. Was there no ad that displayed a single man with a bubble above him saying, 'I'm having a fantastic holiday exploring the firm golden flesh of young women with the freedom of not being burdened by a wife and two veg'? No. There wasn't.

I paid up and walked slowly back to the hotel where I passed some time in the shop by reception, admiring its selection of paintings (dramatic sunsets, coal-black steeds galloping through the silvery brine, moonlight-shim-mered seas) and soon acknowledging that a fellow can spend just so much time pretending to window-shop for dolls, belts, ornaments and ashtrays. Pacing myself, I climbed the stairs to my single room, that's to say, room for sad lonely fuck with no wife or kids. There I ate up more time by neatly arranging my shirts in their drawer and matching and carefully bunching my redundant socks. Even they were in couples. There was nothing for it but to fall on to the bed and into a profound slumber.

My early-evening shower was something of an event, particularly because the shower-head proved to be non-detachable. As a result, rinsing involved adopting a series of muscle-man poses under the trickle of water which was as much as the shower granted. Ten minutes of contortions washing myself and twenty minutes of psyching myself up meant that I was ready to face another meal in the restaurant. This time it would be far easier. I'd get to know some people.

Wrong. I felt as popular as a sex offender. A waiter conducted me, pityingly, to an empty table, whence I looked on as mums bantered with sons and husbands joshed wives. I had the cow and chips, since you ask. And a glass of beer, which could only have stigmatized me further since no one else was drinking. Oh, there was a bottle of wine at one table, shared among six adults.

Only twenty-three more meals here to go.

The long hours before that night's cabaret (flamenco by Isabel Marquez) I whiled away in a supermarket, where I bought a bottle of much-needed brandy for bedside consumption, and in a couple of cafés where I watched the world, his wife and his children go by. After a time, I joined the procession of people for an evening stroll. It seemed to be the thing to do. And, if you were Spanish, the thing to do in an extended family group with toddlers strewn strategically across the width of the pavement, and at a maximum speed of one mile an hour.

The slowness of the collective pace condemned each pedestrian to be at the mercy of the vast population of haranguing street traders. Because they only preyed on couples or family units, I was distinctively immune from the terrible pest of the time-share touts, and I was evidently too old for the disco leafleteers, but even I didn't escape the pitches of the caricaturists, the painters of soft-focus portraits, the beggars and the youths who specialized in weaving beads through hair. Nor was there any escape in the bars, where shoe-shine men would be on patrol, ready to buff and polish your espadrilles, where women would try to sell you fans or rugs or shawls. Then there were the young African guys who were reputed to live in ruins outside the town and just about kept body and soul together by selling belts and bangles and fake Rolexes. (Some of them, I was to discover, had been adopted by British bars, where they were invariably known as Chalky.)

I arrived back at the hotel early enough to catch the finale of the cabaret's preamble, a youngsters' elimination game that required them to put a hat on their heads, then pass it on, and whoever was wearing the hat when the music stopped was out. The elimination games of my childhood always ended in acrimony and tears, and sometimes fisticuffs, but this one was conducted in a spirit of hilarity. I dunno. Kids these days . . .

The winner having been decided and warmly applauded by her rivals, it was time for the big show. The lights dimmed and the speakers belted out a tape of flamenco music, but the large audience had to wait. From my vantage-point at the back I could make out, at the emergency exit that doubled as the artistes' entrance, a costumed person in deep argument with a party who remained hidden from view. All was obviously not well with Isabel Marquez.

When the argument was finally settled, Isabel Marquez took to the stage. It transpired that Isabel Marquez was actually two men and two women, all four of them dressed in black hats, black jackets and tight, very tight, trousers with cummerbunds. And off they went, snapping their fingers, stamping their feet, throwing back their arms, twirling about in an almost-synchronized routine. This was followed by a solo performance – by, quite possibly, Señora Marquez herself – of a dance that mimed some catastrophe, I assumed, from the way she sped about the stage looking for help, stretched out her arms to fend off a terrible fate and then succumbed to same by collapsing in a decorous heap. Perhaps an aficionado would appreciate some wonderful significance in all this, but to me it looked like the dance equivalent of the kind of song Nana Mouskouri used to sing after giving a brief translation: 'I am but a little shepherdess and my village has no water, and the gods they are cruel, and see, now the bull gores me.'

After fifteen minutes of this, I knew that flamenco, or at least Isabel Marquez's performance of it, was one of those activities, like collecting stamps, horse-racing and coprophilia, in which I would never have the slightest interest. I repaired to my room and a companionable session with my bottle of brandy.

I'd missed breakfast. This time I was suffering from a hangover as well as too much sleep. It had, I must stress, required tremendous powers of concentration not to wake up irretrievably for the final two hours of my marathon snooze, which had been regularly attacked by noise. First there had been sporadic assaults by cisterns, which were loud enough to have worried me at first about my room being flooded. These were followed by the frequent PING–PING–PINGs of the lift and the steady clomp of those who preferred to walk to breakfast. Then I'd had to dismiss a surreal invasion from the alley below; it was too early for Posers and its neighbours to start up their jukeboxes but prime time for an old biddy who kept calling out, 'Ocki ocki ocki ocki.' When I'd heard her yesterday I'd assumed that she was calling a domestic animal; when she started up again today I blearily reassured myself that this was a traditional Andalusian chant to greet the dawn. (It was only in the second week, when I saw her in action, that I realized what she was up to. She was a fabulously old crone who spent her days selling lottery tickets, so 'Ocki ocki ocki ocki', I reckon, must be Spanish for 'Come and buy my lucky numbers.')

All these I'd survived to return to haunted sleep. But even with ear-plugs and padded helmet I couldn't have slept through the maids. When they weren't road-testing the next room's flush, or hoovering my door, or carrying out what sounded like impromptu carpentry in the corridor, they were talking to each other. Talking at a pitch and level that qualified them to perform microphone-less dialogues in the Albert Hall. 'HOLA, MARIA!' one would bawl. 'HOLA, ANA!' her colleague would reply. '*Paracaracaracaros!!*' Ana would jest. '*Paracaracamente!!!*' Maria would yell in jolly riposte. I saw them later that morning, still hollering at each other. They were a yard apart.

I was to come across a fact that made me rethink my initial theory that these ambulant megaphones were having a rare old time deliberately waking people up at

the crack of ten. The fact is this: according to a United
Nations survey, 80 per cent of Spaniards are constantly
exposed to noise of eighty decibels or more, fifteen decibels above the UN's safety limit. And 20 per cent of
Spanish youth suffer from hearing damage. That'll be
because of their mums crooning them to sleep. That
morning I checked my dictionary for the first and only
time of the summer. Strange to tell, there are Spanish
words for 'quiet' and 'whisper'. No doubt there are also
Inuit words for 'surfing' and 'heatwave'.

Thanking heaven that I had somehow managed to
wake up too late for the restaurant, I shoved beach stuff
in a bag and made my way out to a nearby British pub
where I ordered a coffee. Idiot. I should have gone to a
Spanish place where I could have had my fix of *café solos*
rather than a mug of milky Nescafé. I sleep-walked to
the beach for a much-needed rest.

I idled along the promenade, wondering which bit of
taupe sand should be mine. The bits to avoid were those
the furious man had warned me about, the bits with the
straw parasols – coolies' hats on wooden legs – covering
the psychedelically patterned mattresses of the sun-loungers. The few people who'd bothered to stump up the 500
pesetas for these seemed to be exclusively British, couples
busy reading bulky paperbacks or just dozing.

The open sand was populated mainly by Spaniards,
clans of them, eight, ten, twelve strong, spanning three
or four generations and large stretches of beach. Towels,
mats, deckchairs and umbrellas advertising San Miguel
or Fortuna or Ducados marked each family's territory. It
was not so much a beach as a shanty-town, with the
difference that no shanty-town dweller would ever possess
such quantities of food and drink as these Spanish families
had carried to last them a day at the seaside.

Teenagers had been consigned to the outskirts of the
shanty-town. Near the waves they disported themselves
with frisbees and footballs. On the strip of beach between

the encampments and the promenade they conducted elaborate courting rituals – chasing games, teasing games (steal the lighter, twang the swimsuit), energetic volleyball performances, languid displays of prowess at smoking. All these courtship routines seemed unnecessary since the teenagers were wearing very little. Why not just cut out the flim-flam and get down to the nitty-gritty of foreplay on a beach-mat? Odd.

In contrast to the tranquillity to be found under the straw coolies' hats, life in and around the Hispanic shanty-towns maintained the decibel count of the rest of the country. Conversations meant shouting, courtship meant squealing and yelling, being a child meant shrieking without cease. Just in case the racket was in any danger of subsiding below acceptable levels, there was a battalion of blokes armed with ghetto-blasters. Waves pounded the shore twenty yards away from where I stood on the prom and I couldn't hear them.

After some delay, I found my patch of sand, not too near the sea, not on shingle, not on litter, not near a rubbish bin, not too close to a ghetto-blaster. I laid down my beach-mat, secured the corners with my espadrilles, a bottle of water and the bag itself, and undressed.

Exposure on the beach is a strange thing. People who would no more be seen in public without three layers of clothing than deal in crack suddenly strip off, in front of hundreds, thousands, to their underwear. Slightly reinforced underwear, granted, and often with many a cheery pattern, but underwear – knickers, bra, teddy – none the less. As I lay on that beach, trying to spot someone else as untanned and unfit as me, I remembered from my childhood vivid and entirely understandable scenes of traumatically gauche undressing at the seaside. The strands of Bournemouth and the like were bordered, as I recall, by huts where parents would sit, *in their clothes*. Only a real heatwave might eventually persuade them to hitch frocks or trousers up a fraction. More adventurous stripteases were confined to the under-twelves and took place behind windbreaks or four bath-towels. After a hectic session of hopping and clutching, combined with constant surveillance, the young heliophile would emerge, decked out, if male, in trunks Stanley Matthews would have worn with a sense of happy recognition, or, if female, protected against the elements and rapacious looks by one-pieces so sturdy they could have fought fires dressed in less.

Try telling that to youngsters nowadays and will they believe you? Will they fuck. The days of the demure, nerve-racked sunbather, like Spangles and sidecars, are gone. Of course, it's all changed now. You can't peer through your binoculars on a beach here without coming across some melon-breasted strumpet wearing only a thong and sun-factor five, shamelessly exposing her full, round, bronzed, oiled breasts, her taut, smooth stomach, and her full, round, bronzed, oiled bottom.

I can't understand how some people can say sunbathing is boring. Or why people who are sunbathing don't spend all their time looking at one another. I tried to be mature about being surrounded by the more-or-less-nude and, using the great asset of self-knowledge, realized that there was no point. If you come from a culture where undoing the top three buttons of a shirt can be construed as a heavy come-on, the spectacle of a hot Spanish beach is no cause for nonchalance. It was the lighter-stealing, swimsuit-twanging adolescents who really got to me. Not the boys, you understand, although I must say that their lean, lithe, firm bodies were shown off to splendid effect as they gambolled and frolicked, those sloe-haired young scamps. One could so easily imagine them exercising with a medicine ball in a Roman gymnasium, or wrestling, naked and oiled, by a hearth whose firelight would flicker and gleam on their lean, lithe firmness. Oh, yes.

What was I saying? No, no, of course, I mean *obviously*, it was the young girls I was really interested in. A painstaking survey that day allowed me to conclude that Spanish women are at their womanly best when they are sixteen. If Fuengirola's beach population is anything to go by, it has to be said that the Spanish are not, sloe-haired scamps excepted, a thin race. Although lagging way behind Americans in the obesity stakes, the Spanish – a lot of Spanish, a significant proportion of Spanish – are . . . fat. So, just as your average Midwesterner reaches a fitness peak in the womb, whence it is a roly-poly tumble downhill to a vast arse and the ability to pinch an inch on the feet, many Spanish women seem to pass the gawkiness of adolescence at the age of eight and blossom into brief but wonderful curvaciousness in their mid-teens.

The parade of teenage gorgeousness was a great incentive to continue with my beach experience until it was gone three and my knees had gone pink. It was time for a spot of lunch. It was also high time I talked to someone. If I couldn't start a normal conversation, I'd pretend to be a reporter. Wisely, I selected a pub some distance from the hotel and up a side-street. Sadly, its location explained why there were no customers in it. Stupidly, I persevered and tried to chat to the man behind the bar.

'A San Miguel please. And a cheese sandwich.'

'Okay. Three hundred and fifty pesetas.'

'There you go . . . Oh, that lager's good. You work up a real thirst on the beach, don't you?'

'I suppose.'

'That's one hell of a hot day out there.'

'Yes.'

He was a big man but he moved with surprising nimbleness to polish some glasses at the far end of the counter. The contingency plan swung into operation.

'Excuse me?'

'Aha?'

'I was wondering if I could ask you a few questions.
I'm writing something on the British out here, you see,
and was wondering . . .'

'What kind of questions would those be?'

'Oh, nothing really, just a bit of general background.'

'I don't think so.'

'Just general things. By the way, my name's Harry.'

'Ah. My name's, umm, Tom.'

'How d'you find life out here, Tom? Enjoying it?'

'I suppose.'

'And how long have you been here?'

'Nah.'

'Sorry?'

'Nah. Not answering that. Can't be too careful.'

Shaking his head and excusing himself, 'Tom' hurried
off into a back-room, mumbling something about checking the beer barrels. I stared blankly at the gantry that
held the magnificent array of one bottle of gin, one
bottle of brandy and one bottle of whisky. I munched
my sandwich. I drank my drink. There was no sign at all
of 'Tom'. Nonplussed, I left.

I walked back to the hotel, but, preferring not to
spend the rest of the afternoon in my pizza, I dodged
round to Pat and Adrian's Scots Corner in the alleyway.
It was a pub with several noteworthy touches. The
tartan upholstery of the seating, for example. The Celtic
team photograph on a wall. A montage of snaps of
Scottish sporting heroes, Dalglish, Shankly, Johnstone,
Baxter . . . There was also one of those comic announce-
ments in vivid lettering: 'Teenagers, If you are Tired of
Being Hassled by Unreasonable Parents/Now Is The
Time For Action!!!/Leave Home And Pay Your Own
Way/While You Still Know Everything!'

That and the middle age of the handful of customers
indicated that this was not a place where a young blade
should be hanging out. Even so, I ordered a pint from
Pat, who obviously had no dark secrets. She talked to

me. What joy. She and Adrian had come here from
Bo'ness five years ago, having been to Fuengirola once
on holiday. They'd run a bar back home so it hadn't
been too difficult to set up, and yes, they had to put in
the hours, and yes, I wouldn't say no to another pint.

Supping that, I flicked through Pat and Adrian's
visitors' book which was lying on the counter in front of
me. The acclaim was universal: 'Pure dead brilliant'
(Janette and Scott, Kilmarnock); 'Thanks for making
our holiday a great one' (Doreen and Mel, Wolverhamp-
ton); 'Fourth time here. We'll make it a fifth' (Cath and
Syd, Bridlington) . . . Couples, couples, couples. I ordered
a whisky, a chaser to chase away loneliness.

Two men joined me at the bar. Very shy men, I soon
found out, but men I could still have some sort of
conversation with. Peter and his even quieter friend – I
never did learn his name – were in their early forties,
unmarried, worked as engineers, and had been coming
to the same flat in Fuengirola for the past seven years,
usually three times a year. Attempting to hide any tone
of desperation, I asked them what they found to do here.

'We relax,' said Peter. 'Walk. Play a bit of golf,
maybe. Eat. Sleep. I've been known to sleep all day.
Brilliant. Back home, I go to bed late and have to get up
at six. God, the sleep's brilliant. And the drink, of
course.'

We chinked glasses at that and Peter's friend got in
another round, using words to do so. By the time late
afternoon had become early evening, Peter had told me
that there were far more Spanish in Fuengirola these
days, and I'd told him the story of my life. Some words
of which I'd had a little trouble pronouncing. Having
assured, or warned, Peter and his anonymous friend that
I'd see them around, I wove over to the hotel and up the
stairs to the restaurant. After an escalope of pig with
chips and a resolute glass of beer, I went back down to
the hotel bar to watch the kids' elimination game. They

had to pass a hoop round, you see, after putting it over themselves, and when the music stopped, whoever was caught in the hoop had to throw a big bouncy green dice which then gave the number to be counted from the person in the hoop to the person who was then out. I think. The kids seemed to know what they were doing, at any rate.

At half past ten the kids were ushered off before the cabaret started. The poster in reception said that tonight it would be 'Jockey'. The name of an artiste? A game involving amusing balloons and some sexual shenanigans? The bilingual mistress of ceremonies gave an explanation in Spanish which lasted a long time while, to great applause, four guests dressed as jockeys took to the stage. The backdrop was a large, multi-coloured snakes-and-ladders-style board, with squares marked from 1 to 49. I still held out hopes of sexual shenanigans.

The mistress of ceremonies' English spiel made everything clear. The idea was to progress up the multi-coloured board which, as we could see, was marked with some red squares, landing on which meant a forfeit whereby the jockey would perform some act, such as jiggling a hula-hoop or singing a given song, for five seconds. And how was progress up the board to be achieved? Simple. By throwing this big bouncy green dice.

The front-runner had reached 23, a square that required him to find and fetch a blue shoe worn by any woman in the audience, when the thought of a large brandy in my room became irresistible in its appeal.

Once upstairs, I squeezed out on to my balcony to watch the diminishing crowd in the alley below and listen to the dull thud of muffled dance music, courtesy of the disco in the basement, and Rod Stewart's greatest hits, courtesy of Posers. It was 'If You Think I'm Sexy' that sent me to bed, where I lay, squiffy and with pink, hot, itchy knees, waiting for the onset of another ten hours' unconscious.

*

Nikki's embarrassment at my solitary state had been slightly unnerving but I'd had no idea that coming here alone would be this bad. A challenge, for sure, but that was part of the deal of being a travel writer, was it not? The only companions a proper travel writer should have are a survival kit, Turgenev in French and a honed sensibility. I mean, how are travel writers supposed to refine their insights or meet the nomads who give them camel's milk if they're accompanied by relatives and friends? What kind of travel writer is it that gets homesick after three days and wants to go back to his pals? The kind of charlatan and big jessie who can't handle two weeks in a pizza in a 316-room hotel, that's what kind.

I'd assumed there would be other singles in the hotel. I'd rather anticipated being the object of someone's unslakable lust. A holiday crush at the bare minimum. As it was, I was beginning to think that I was the first person in the hotel's history stupid enough to have paid £7 a day extra to be on his own. And, after three days, I had to admit that Fuengirola was the hotel with streets added – a very respectable venue for families who'd maybe go to the aquapark or on a day trip to Ronda but otherwise have a really good fortnight just mucking about together. There was a night-life, with discos like the London Underground or the Paradiso in the hotel's basement, but they were for teenagers whose parents would be waiting up for their return. There was as much likelihood of someone chatting me up here as at my mum's sewing bee.

Social intercourse was difficult enough. I'd seen myself forging friendships with fellow-guests, who'd exchange addresses with me at the end of the fortnight. Back home, we'd meet once but somehow it wouldn't be the same and we'd settle for a rather guilty exchange of Christmas cards. Not much chance of that. I had already given up on my tentative nods and smiles. A bloke in his mid-thirties and on his own? Tendency to smile and nod? If I was in one of those families, I wouldn't talk to me.

'Hi!'

'Hello?'

'Hi! It's me!'

'Oh, it's you.'

'What? You'll have to shout. The line's really crackly.'

'Sorry? Hold on for a minute, I'll just go and turn down the stereo . . .'

'What? What was all that? I can't hear a word now.'

'Back again. This is a surprise. I didn't expect to hear from you until the weekend.'

'Eh? It's a surprise. So how are you?'

'Fine. Pretty busy. Is it really boiling down there?'

'Shit. The machine's rejecting the coin. I've only got another hundred pesetas left.'

'Oh, dear. It's my turn to have the crackles. You've got what?'

'The machine's counting down. It's down to a hundred. No, ninety.'

'The temperature's ninety?'

'No, the telephone. Oh, God, it's, no, it's just changed *again*. Seventy.'

'What's heavenly?'

'Oh, *fuck*. The beeps will be going soon.'

'Sorry? Where?'

'All I wanted to say was that I . . . *Damn*. That's them going now.'

'Does that noise mean we're being cut off?'

'No, the cut-off tone.'

'What? Oh, no. Well, take care of.'

After a couple of days I felt qualified to make a reasonable estimate of the mean age of the hotel's guests. It was fifty-five. Not counting the staff, there was one person of my age, a father of three. There were some adolescents but the slack-jawed couple were noticeable in themselves as being unmarried and unescorted by their parents. And some of the guests were very, very old indeed. I kept an eye out in the restaurant for one aged and unfathomable threesome, a dapper little man, never without his cream cap and clip-on shades, who was accompanied by two triangular ladies with arthritic hips the width of a seagull's wing-span. Because he always went in first and always chose a table as far as possible from the entrance, the ladies had to blunder and sway their massive and painful bulk through a long gauntlet of tables and chairs and children.

That trio must have had a combined age not far off 250, but they were as lambs compared to one tiny old boy, a Spaniard, who was greeted each mealtime with some reverence by the head waiter. Presumably he was just grateful to see him up and about and not causing an unseemly parade of ambulances outside the hotel. All credit to the old boy, I thought, not just for being alive but upright. He couldn't walk, though. Rather, he tottered as he made his breathtaking way to his table with the speed of a tectonic plate, despite maintaining a steady three or four pitty-patty steps a second. I nurtured a fantasy that he'd led a life of riotous decadence, of fags and beer and wild, wild women, and that he was really only forty years old, but he must have received his telegram from Juan Carlos at least two World Cups ago.

I created, as you do, biographies for various other guests, in default of actually being able to get to know them. The slack-jawed couple, I decided, were first cousins whose incestuous love had banished them from their Cornish hamlet. The 'Please Release Me' whistler had been a backing vocalist until, drunk one night on *Top of the Pops*, he'd made an ill-judged career move by lunging at one of Pan's People. Another middle-aged man, whose distinguishing characteristic was a moustache that would have been the envy of many a Castro

clone, seemed to be spending most of his holiday in Pat
and Adrian's; drinking away the sorrows, I reckoned, of
what was a marriage in name only. Then there was the
Morose Muscleman, a grim, five-foot-four cube whose
lumpy calves bulged beneath shorts held up by braces
that emphasized the magnificence of his chest. His petite
wife never exchanged a word with him that I could see,
and no wonder, with his bizarre sexual quirks.

I looked back at the end of that first week and found
that, in addition to those conversations with the furious
man, 'Tom', Pat, and Peter and his unnamed friend,
and not counting that phone call, buying things or
mumbling to myself, I'd used the power of speech on
only two occasions. Once, in Scoffers Bar, to one of the
owners, a young guy called Scott who'd told me the
results of some football friendlies. And once to John and
Kathy, a couple from Kinross; over several San Miguels,
I learned that John was a fifty-nine-year-old semi-retired
printer-cum-folk singer who'd just appeared on Radio
Scotland, and that Kathy was sixteen years younger
than him and taught in a primary school. They were
driving around Spain and having a superb time staying
and eating in cheap places recommended by their trusted
Rough Guide. Kathy said she thought that Fuengirola was
rather lovely, though lacking in excitement, and I said I
couldn't agree more. My hopes began to rise of Christmas
card-exchanging friendship, but, alas, they had to get to
bed early that night because they faced a long drive the
next day. That's what they said, anyway.

These were real highlights of a week which mainly
passed in a soporific routine. I'd wake just in time to
brave a quick breakfast, potter in my pizza, hit the
beach at eleven or twelve, sunbathe till two, lunch on a
beer and a sandwich or Sinful Pancake (having swum for
a minute to work up an appetite), then, exhausted by
the day's events, shuffle back to the hotel for a little lie-
down. Then, after some bodybuilder's posing in the

shower, a drink in the always deserted hotel bar before braving a quick dinner. Thence to Pat and Adrian's or Scoffers for a coffee and a brandy before returning to the hotel for the night's cabaret. Thence to my pizza, where I'd listen to the thudding beat of the basement disco. Kids were down there, shouting into each other's ears, dancing in smoky rooms lit by strobes. Foolishness, really. How much better to enjoy a little nightcap and then head off to bedfordshire for a good long sleep. A week of this and the thought of even part-time employment seemed absurd, as unimaginable as the thought of food after a large meal, or sex after sex.

These were typical days for someone holidaying in Fuengirola. I was just unfortunately spending mine by myself. There were two consequences of this solitary state. One was that I became prone to semi-drunken self-appraisals wherein my life became nothing but a catalogue of evasions and failures. Another was that my status in the hotel changed. I was no longer merely shunned, I was giggled at. Just as the Morose Muscleman, the slack-jawed couple and the rest had become part of my private fiction, so others had apparently created a character for me. God knows what reputations I'd acquired, but the backing-vocalist whistler obviously thought they should lock me up and throw away the key, and their nudges and splutters whenever I passed them suggested that the slack-jawed couple had come up with a particularly hilarious biography.

As I hope you will understand, I'd come to dread that bloody restaurant, the increasingly traumatic site of two of my three daily public appearances in the hotel. The third was the lounge, where darkness and my regular position at the back helped conceal my solitary shame during the nightly cabaret. The jockey evening and the flamenco display had been followed by shows of varying quality. Posters for 'Miss Elección' and 'Noche Chino' had transpired to be announcements for more elimination games in which the handful of guests uninhibited enough to do so would have to dress up and do some mild clowning about, dancing demure can-cans and the like.

There was also 'Sketch Night', starring the mistress of ceremonies, her sidekick and the bloke who was often the DJ. This was, by some way, the least successful show. After long delays the trio would appear in some home-made costumes and do mimes. One act demanded the MC's sidekick to be a secretary tapping, faster and faster, at an imaginary typewriter. A second act was an incomprehensible affair involving the MC wearing a succession of hats and saying '*Si, señor*', which I hope is a side-splitting catchphrase in Spain. Another had the three of them in white overalls and cycle helmets walking as if underwater to the Moonshot theme tune from *Also Sprach Zarathustra*. The climax came when, unfurling a flag, they claimed the Moon/stage for Spain. The natives in the audience went wild at that, but so good-natured were all the guests that they applauded each non-act, every non-punchline, with great enthusiasm.

Other events of that first week? Well . . . I changed my brand of cigarettes to Royal Crown, the favoured make for Brits in Spain. And I went to the local snooker hall to see Alex 'El Huracán' Higgins. Several hundred people had paid to see this cueing legend not pot balls and fail at trick shots. Some of the locals almost beat him. Alex 'Intermittent Drizzle' Higgins. I also made my one visit of the fortnight to the hotel's rooftop swimming-pool, the only place I've done the breast-stroke while suffering from vertigo. That phobia, together with the pest of screaming, dive-bombing pubescents, forced me out and down the stairs, where I read with interest a notice that claimed: 'It is forbidden – the violent games or jump'. One other adventure was a day trip to Gibraltar. That was, I confess, against my rules, being well beyond my limit of Marbella, but I can plead two mitigating circum-stances: I was bored and the trip lasted as far as the hotel lobby, where Trevor told me it was cancelled, owing to a week-long, multi-miled tailback caused by 45,000 Moroccans queuing for the ferry home at Algeciras.

Saturday night, I looked back on the week and thought, what, so far, have I done on my holidays? Answer – bugger all. It was time for a new, Stakhanovite regime and it was going to start first thing the following morning.

And it was the Sabbath.

And he did not rest but decided, after breaking fast on this the Lord's Day, to check out an evangelical service, as advertised in the hotel foyer, all welcome, favourite songs and hymns, at eleven.

And he *was* an unbeliever yet *went* to the Ceramic Bar, where the service *was* held.

And twelve disciples were already gathered there, in front of a man of God and another on the piano, and surrounded by graven images of fish and mermaids showing *their* bosoms.

And the elderly women in the front row did raise their hands aloft from time to time to break the fall of the Holy Spirit should It descend from Heaven.

And the others were not so keen on any charismatic shit but still knew the tunes, whereas the unbeliever, even though he had been to Sunday school where he had acquired a book full *of* stickers for regular attendance, recognized none of the favourite songs and hymns.

Yea, and these were all in a book with *a* nice sunset on the cover.

And the unbeliever did his best to join in, guessing the next note and sometimes getting it badly wrong.

And he was not the thirteenth disciple but, sad and lonely though he was like all Christians, he denied the existence of God, saying unto himself, 'Yea, it is all a gang of bollocks.'

Yet the mark of Satan was upon the unbeliever for the

godly men had shaved and put upon their feet socks and sandals.

And they were smooth men but he was an hairy man and wore dirty espadrilles and was sockless to boot.

And after some favourite songs and hymns, the man of God, who wore the costume of scrupulously clean and ironed short-sleeved shirt and a nice red tie, launched into a sermon, *which* involved picking good bits out of the Bible.

And the man of God took as his sermon some story in the Gospels about finding treasure in a field, interspersing that with homely nonsense about a bloke in Norfolk who had come across an aged and valuable trove, about the man of God himself finding God after reading some religious nutter's tract and then finding that finding God meant he lost all his friends, which came to the unbeliever as no fucking surprise, and about Saul going to Damascus and other people who found God, yea, though they *did* not seek Him.

And there was another bit about the treasure – i.e., the treasure found in the field in the Gospels story – being God's treasure, which was worth untold millions of pounds, especially compared to the worthlessness of worldly goods when possessed by a spiritual bankrupt, the likes of whom would be certainly condemned to an eternity of hellfire and torture.

And he smiled benevolently as he said this, but it was all right for him because he had been born again and *was* therefore saved.

And the sermon meandered along pleasantly enough, although, the threat *of* eternal violence notwithstanding, the spiritual bankrupt in the espadrilles was getting bored and desperate for a smoke.

And there followed a final rousing song which included a line about the burning heat of the noon.

And that was only appropriate.

And during the final song one of the women from the front row came round with a hat.

And yea, not only was the sinner spiritually bankrupt but when *it* came to his turn for the collection, all he had to put in was a 1000-peseta note, so he was well and truly skint and had *to* go to the cashpoint.

Having risen at the ungodly time of nine-thirty on a Sunday, I spent the afternoon recovering on the beach, gaining pink inroads into my bikini line. The God-be-with-yous I'd swapped at the end of the service hadn't really been enough. I needed to talk to someone. A therapist wasn't available but I did have one valuable telephone number, that of an English expat journalist who lived down the road in Marbella. One phone call later and the world was a brighter, friendlier place. I'd be meeting Nigel Bowden for lunch the next day. Shoot the breeze, have a few beers, you know how it is.

Celebrations took the form of a visit to a Spanish bar in the back-streets, where a massive brandy and a *café con leche* cost a more than reasonable 225 pesetas. The poorer by 1350 pesetas, I stumbled back to the hotel just in time for dinner and a laugh at the new arrivals – white and fazed by the buffet system – before returning to my pizza. There, with the help of a large bottle of Osborne brandy, I settled to appreciate an increasingly vivid sunset, so unrealistically spectacular it merited being framed for the hotel lobby. A splendid manner in which to finish off His day.

Although we'd never met before, I recognized Nigel Bowden in the bar because he'd appeared on a recent Alan Whicker programme about the Costa del Sol. He was clearly a frightening sort of journalist, one who had his ear to the ground and his finger on many a pulse. He was the kind of journalist who could do shorthand and everything. A pro.

Over a number of beers we exchanged work gossip – or rather, I told him things he knew last year, and he disclosed extraordinary scandals about . . . no, a sum of money has since secured my discretion. He also told me things about Fuengirola that had me performing a passable impersonation of the slack-jawed couple. This most respectable of resorts, where a beer at dinner was a bit iffy, had its dark side. A small red-light area by the bus station, for example. And that side-street with all the karaoke bars? Tin Pan Alley? Yes, I knew it – full of little pubs advertising singalongs with Ray Conway and Kim Allen; walk along there of an evening and you'd hear a dozen people belting out 'Nobody's Child' or 'Yew are theagh sunaaghshine of myeyeyeye life'. Well, go after midnight and you could see the town's junkies shoot up. Last year an English barmaid there was shot by her boyfriend over a drugs dispute. (She survived because her twelve-stone bulk pillowed the bullet.) And up the road there were a couple of British pubs it would not be advisable to visit unless you really wanted to muscle in on the hash gangs. I was stunned. It was like hearing about a heroin epidemic in Lytham St Annes. But Nigel's revelations about Fuengirola being the new capital for the Costa's crims did explain why 'Tom' had seemed a touch odd.

I have an inkling that we then had lunch. In a restaurant. Definitely a restaurant. I remember the squid.

I woke up at six to find Nigel long gone and my left ear in a basket of bread. Outside, it was shockingly bright. I stumbled towards the nearest pub for a pick-me-up beer. I felt so much better I had another, and then another. I felt so good I decided to tackle head-on something I'd been putting off for a week – the sightseeing train trip round the town.

The problem wasn't the town, though I couldn't think what sights there were to see, nor was it the stigma of being a sightseer, because we were all tourists here. The problem was the train. For a start it wasn't a train but a

van with a choo-choo painted on it, which hauled three
dinky carriages. It would have been barely acceptable in
a theme park – but in a town? And it couldn't even
pretend to be a proper train because on top of every
carriage were high placards reading 'Burger King'.

I managed to hand over my 300 pesetas and fell into a
seat. Lots of these were available since just four children
and two parents were aboard. Directly above me was a
tannoy relaying music and ads from the local radio
station. Very jolly. I tapped a lively drum accompaniment on my knees as we sped off along the prom at five
miles an hour. We swerved out into the traffic and a
woman carrying her daughter tried to flag us down. No
way, bitch. Ain't no stopping us now.

To the best of my recollection, we simply toured the
town, ignoring any possible distraction like the old castle
on the outskirts, concentrating on back-streets and the
main road under the railway line. I imagine the other six
passengers were much more enthralled by the sight of
the chap on his own in the middle carriage, the chap
who sang along to all the adverts and applauded the
railway line.

It was all I could do afterwards to make it to the hotel
restaurant before it closed. It held no fears for me that
night. I smiled and nodded to all my fellow-holiday-
makers and relished another plate of unnameable fish
and chips.

My head ached and a drowsy numbness pained every
sense, so I had to forgo breakfast again. However, a
clutch of *café solos* at a neighbouring café set me up for
the day ahead, which, this being Tuesday, was to consist
of a trip to Fuengirola's weekly market and then to the
mountain village of Mijas. I joined the procession of
people going to the market, which turned out to be full
of people wondering why they had come here.

I walked up and down several long lanes of stalls

selling things I'd never thought of, far less thought of wanting. Beach-towels with signs of the zodiac. Decorative fans. Jim Reeves tapes. Leather belts (with holster) marked Costa del Sol. I quite liked the look of an imitation Louis Vuitton holdall, priced at 12,000 pesetas. By dint of haggling, I think I managed to beat down the snaggle-toothed stall-owner to 15,000. I had 1700 on my person so I made do with a decorative fan and a bar of chocolate which swiftly melted in my pocket while I walked back to the bus station, there to shove aside the old and the infirm, and thus get a seat on the local bus to Mijas.

It was a short journey remarkable for the steepness of the climb and the endlessness of Fuengirola's outskirts. We passed a steady roadside straggle of villas, car and furniture showrooms, restaurants and hotels, the Lew Hoad tennis village, more villas, then, with the bus grinding down the gears to cope with the climb, what seemed to be Mijas. At least, that's where the bus came to a final stop.

A (dated) guide-book I'd read extolled Mijas as an unspoilt, authentic, traditional Andalusian village. Together with the fact that there were special tours up here, that had led me to expect . . . something different. I'd also read somewhere that a leading Republican went into hiding in a cellar in Mijas after the civil war, only venturing out, thirty years later, during a political thaw in the late 1960s. Presumably, the man had managed to creep out now and again in the intervening period, otherwise the hilltop view of the coast – impoverished fishing hamlets being transformed by a series of building sites – would surely have induced a heart attack.

If his amnesty had been delayed by another twenty-five years, the sight of his own *pueblo* in itself would have guaranteed a major cardiac incident. Doubtless, back in 1936, when Franco seized power and Mijas's leading Republican had to exile himself in a local basement, the village was authentic. Now, though, the only people who'd agree with the tourist office brochure's claim that Mijas is a traditional Andalusian village work as art directors in EuroDisney. The brochure itself gives the game away by boasting about Mijas's 100 *urbanizacions*, golf-courses, apartment complexes, hotels and tennis courts. Attracting middle-class tourists who like the idea of avoiding tourist traps and don't quite know how to, Mijas has become its own theme park, as traditional an Andalusian village as Malaga airport.

The town's main square is flanked by a coach park and a row of donkey taxis on one side, and a car park on another. No doubt this was once the site of traditional Andalusian pastimes such as peasants listening to the local potentate decide just when he would exercise his right of shagging their wives. Now it's an extended tribute to the power of the souvenir. The miniature straw donkeys were endearing, but my heart was stolen by a variety of model houses. Perhaps if I bought, say, 500 of them, I could turn my sitting-room into a small-scale reproduction of Mijas's reproduction of itself . . .

It was but a short stroll from Patricia's souvenir shop, past a phalanx of bar-restaurants, to a promontory which boasted yet another bar-restaurant and a view that would certainly be fatal to any newly amnestied Republican. Villas with pools dotted the terraced hillside that fell away in the foreground to level out at Fuengirola, five miles away. Since I didn't have a twenty-five-peseta coin for the telescope, I could identify only two structures from this distance and height − the new bypass and the magnificently proud, thrusting, threepenny-bit-shaped erection that was my hotel.

Just past the telescope, there was an attraction that didn't require loose change − a kind of grotto affair that turned out to be half souvenir shop and half church. The holy bit was a cave-cum-small chapel, which, I guessed from a framed text, had been built to commemorate the

special occasion 400-odd years ago when two local children broadcast the delusion that they had been visited
by the Virgin Mary.

It was a very small chapel, accommodating only a
couple of short rows of pews, but still chock-a-block with
left-footers' paraphernalia – candles, flowers, pictures of
the Pope, bows, ribbons, and bits from Barbie's wardrobe
to represent afflicted limbs, as well as Photo-Booth photographs of loved ones, all tacked on to the walls. Judging
by the altar's centrepiece, which was protected against
the attentions of the faithful by strong glass, the
sixteenth-century urchins had been graced by the heavenly presence of one of the larger dolls in Patricia's
souvenir shop. According to her incarnation here, the
mother of the son of the supreme being of the universe is
two feet high, wears a wedding dress and has long, black,
polyester hair.

Reflecting that I had taken another wrong turning on
life's spiritual treasure hunt, I wandered back to the
centre of the village, climbed some dinky steps, declined
the offer of paying some no doubt exorbitant sum to visit
a bullfighting museum, and stumbled into Fred and
Barbara's Yorkshire Bar, for a refreshing pint of Youngers
Tartan Special (draught) and a cheeseburger.

The table next to mine was occupied by a – family
seems the wrong word – commotion from the other side
of the Pennines. I got chatting, when she had a moment
from quelling her two children, with the adult member
of the commotion. Lesley was thirty-one, from Manchester, and enduring her first foreign holiday, with Cath
(five) and Matthew (four). It seemed impolitic to ask
where Cath's and Matthew's father was, so I stayed on
tactful territory, agreeing that you needed a holiday now
and again to get away from it all, though the only way
Lesley was going to get away from it all was by dumping
the kids with Fred and Barbara and doing a runner.

Our chat was, perforce, brief.

''Scuse me,' she said. 'Matth*ewe*. *Stop* that. I said, *stop*. Eh, eh, Cath, there's no need for that. Yes, I know, but you shouldn't stab him back. You're going to be using that fork in a minute for your chips. Matth*ewe*. Come back here. If you don't stop being nawrteh, this man here will put you on the next plane back to Manchester.'

I nodded sternly, in the manner, I hoped, of a punitive immigration officer. To no effect. Matthew pronged my thigh with his fork.

Lesley seemed to be in a bit of a fix. She was miserable, fraught, crimson-skinned under a thirty-four degree heat, three-quarters of the way up a mountain in Spain and Matth*ewe* had just called her bluff. I anticipated that she'd only gain control of the mêlée with a heavy police presence and a semi-automatic weapon. But what she did next was a stroke of genius.

'Matthew. Cath,' she whispered with slow, controlled menace. 'If you don't. Start. Behaving yourselves. *Right* now . . .' (Pause.) (Longer pause.) 'You won't get any chips.'

The silence was like an instant cure for a raging hangover.

I crammed in what remained of my cheeseburger, swigged down the rest of my Tartan Special, paid and left. I said goodbye to Lesley but she didn't look up as she replied. She was too busy keeping guard on her kids, her eyes flicking from one to another, like a cowboy cornered in a shoot-out.

I'd gained the status of a regular at Scoffers the second time I went there, when I discovered that Scott was no mere waiter but the bar's co-proprietor, and one who had already, at the age of twenty-three, retired from professional football (he'd been on Arsenal's books for five years). Now, on my fourth visit in ten days, I was greeted like someone who has his own monogrammed tankard hanging from the gantry. Seeing Scott reading a newspaper, I asked him if anything exciting had been happening back home.

'Don't know. I've been reading this daft article about here.' He stabbed at a page of the *Independent on Sunday* which carried a feature about the plight of British bars in Fuengirola. 'And will you just look at that.'

He was pointing to a large photograph of a pub whose every seat was empty. There was one person in shot, a passing Spanish dotard. It was a wonderful image of a commercial catastrophe, made all the more stunning by the fact that the deserted establishment was the London Pub, a place I'd never been in, only because it had always been packed out.

'When do you think they took that photograph?' Scott asked. 'Seven in the morning? Same old story. Okay, there's a recession, but we have people sitting on the wall over there waiting for seats. And it's only quiet now because it's early evening. You watch it fill up. Jesus.'

He threw down another piece of bad publicity and went off to serve the early arrivals. I was engrossed in my San Miguel and the weekend's cricket scores when one of those early arrivals interrupted me. Chris had been my best friend at school. I hadn't seen him for seventeen years. Through amazed smiles, we asked each other how the hell we were and what we'd been up to for the missing halves of our lives. Then a little girl came up to us, a really pretty five-year-old, who called him 'Daddy'. I didn't even know he was married. Well, you know how it is, you move on, you lose touch . . .

Bumping into Chris in Fuengirola, I reasoned later, was not the most extraordinary of coincidences. Fuengirola was just the kind of place he, his wife and his daughter would want to go for their holidays. I joined the three of them for a drink and inferred a lot from the conversation. That he'd got his life sorted out while mine was a complete mess, for a start. And that Fuengirola was, for them, ideal. It was clean and unrowdy, there was the beach, and the aquapark for little Louisa, there were places like Scoffers with children's menus, good food, fine drink and friendly staff who spoke the same language as you, often in the same accent.

God, but you're kept busy on the beach. You have the constant struggle to keep your towel or mat from blowing up and away, for one thing. And the gusts of wind also mean regular spasms of brushing off sand which coats your oiled bits like harling. And then those bits have to be oiled again. There's also the business of finding the right position to lie in – not for comfort but for roasting the right bits. So you have to adopt the most awkward poses – flat on the back, say, with left knee bent in to get the outside left calf done, and arms extended palms upwards in the vain pursuit of tanning the underarms.

While you're lying there, before cramp, heat or more harling attacks make you turn on to your side (resting on the left elbow, with face twisted upwards and left knee still bent in to get the outside of the left calf done, and right underarm hoiked round towards the light), you have time to reflect on the mysteries of the suntan.

Mystery number one. Why are the Spanish brown all over? Is it genetic?

Mystery number two. Why, in the privacy of your own room, pirouetting on the bed to check yourself out in the mirror or pressing yourself to the bathroom wall like a police suspect, craning round to examine the colour of your back, do you look fine – though a bit red in some places, particularly the rim around your swimwear and, needless to say, your nose – whereas out here on the beach you're white and pink?

Mystery number three. Just why is it so difficult to tan your underarms? Plus the sides of your torso? Despite your best crash-position poses, and the most scientific applications of oils and creams, the result is always the same. Stand with your arms spanned out and you have, not the all-over, mahogany skin of the sex machines on the sun-lotion bottles but your very own homage to the Arsenal strip.

As my second week in Fuengirola progressed, I maintained a discreet surveillance of my favourite fellow-guests. The slack-jawed youngsters had acquired brick-red skin by now and become regulars at Posers, which meant I began to go on elaborate detours to reach Pat and Adrian's or The Yorkshire Rose. (There's just so much giggling a chap can take.) The Morose Muscleman had taken to wearing cap-sleeved T-shirts that highlighted his biceps, but he and his wife were still not on speakers. The Castro clone moustache had gone, so takings at Pat and Adrian's had, presumably, dipped significantly that week. The holidays were also over for the pitty-patty centenarian, much to the relief, I imagine, of the hotel staff and Fuengirola's intensive care units. But the dapper little man and his triangular ladies remained an intriguing fixture. He was still to be seen always five or ten yards ahead of them as they stumbled along in arthritic purdah. I'd spotted the three of them at Mijas, him admiring the view from a promontory, the ladies gamely heaving themselves up the long, long flights of stairs to join him. I bet he took them to the aquapark as well.

I also caught up with Peter and his friend again for a quiet drink – actually a drink that would have been entirely silent had I not been on wittily sparkling form, quizzing them about their sex lives, that kind of thing. And, I can proudly state, I talked to lots of other people. This was the result of my having concocted a variety of approaches to mount the obstacle of being, now that the furious man had gone, the only person in Fuengirola on his own.

The least successful ruse soon proved to be that of asking people if I could interview them for a book I was

writing. No one bought that for a moment. Quite understandably, they assumed this was the patter of a particularly wretched time-share tout. I had better luck with
the asking-to-look-at-the-day-old-newspaper ploy and the
hanging-around-the-counter-talking-to-the-barman-and-
muscling-in-on-someone-ordering-a-drink   scam.   Once
the conversation was under way I usually slipped in the
information that I couldn't stop for too long because I
had to go back to the wife. Cheryl and I had been
married for as many as seven years. Sometimes she'd be
suffering from sunstroke, sometimes tucking in young
Julia and wee Michael. I grew to love that woman.
We'd had our troubles, sure, our downs as well as our
ups, but you had to work at a marriage, and, when all
was said and done, she was a girl in a million.

Those conversations were enlightening as well as enjoyable. Given the nature of Fuengirola, it was inevitable
that most of the people whose newspapers I borrowed
were middle-aged and comfortably solvent, if not exactly
prosperous. (Some sociologist would probably be able to
identify them as belonging to the upper-lower-middle-
middle-lower-middle class or some such.) I found that
the majority of these salesmen and newsagents and nurs-
ery nurses in their forties and fifties had first ventured
abroad a few years before. Peter, for example, had first
been on a plane at the age of thirty-five, and had only
coped with the trauma by getting smashed on duty-free
gin. Brian and Karen, a friendly couple from Derby,
seemed to be quite well off, but had taken their first
foreign trip in 1986, when they'd found the Costa Brava
to be a great improvement on Skegness and Devon.
Graham and Pat, with whom I chatted in Scoffers, had
discovered the Continent in 1989. Even Kathy, the adventurous *Rough Guider* from Kinross, hadn't been abroad
until she went to Brittany when she was thirty-four.

My great thesis for this book stated that foreign holidays are a wonderful, recent phenomenon for most of us,

a chance to see abroad, which the not-stinking-rich of previous generations only managed to do in uniform. The accounts I'd read usually dated the rise of package tourism from the mid to late sixties, which tallied neatly with the fact that that's when my parents first whisked us off to Majorca. I'd forgotten, though, that the tan I cultivated in Yugoslavia in 1972 was considered pretty damned flash even then. Those conversations in Fuengirola made me appreciate just how recent, for so many people, the foreign-holiday phenomenon is.

Which explained several things. The fact that development on the Costa, although substantial in the seventies, had grown most rapidly in the eighties. Plus the persisting practice of brochures and reps of explaining the most obvious details, because it wasn't the cost that had prevented Graham and Pat and Peter and the others from going abroad so much as fear – a completely understandable fear of having two precious weeks' enjoyment ruined by the anxiety of coping with a different country for the first time.

Because I'd be spending the summer down here, I had also managed to forget how goddamned important holidays are. They are, after all, the weekend that lasts a fortnight, the highlight of everyone's year. So, unless you are a cretin, you don't want to cock it up by doing something you don't want to do. Therefore, to answer the jibes of those who condemn – and I quote from one especially dreadful shite – the 'fish-and-chippy' holidaymakers for not lapping up Spanish culture: why should we? The point of a holiday is to have a good time, and if that means sleeping, and drinking and eating in British bars, well, why the fuck not? Hmm? Are you supposed to earn a merit certificate for learning the lingo or checking out at least five art galleries? And if you are, then doesn't that also condemn many of the condemners who, in reality, visit a couple of Umbrian churches only because they think they ought to, and reach page three of their Italian phrase-book? Wankers.

Most of the people I met were perfectly content doing what they wanted to do, and that wasn't much. They were here to relax, and quite right too. The goals of Brian and Karen were straightforward and typical: 'We might go to Marbella for the day,' Karen reflected, 'and we're thinking of going to Seville, but mainly we just want to soak up the sun.' Margaret and Jack, a couple in their forties from Ayrshire, were revelling in their first holiday without the children, and were rigorously following a schedule much like my own: get up around ten, have a leisurely breakfast in their apartment until half-eleven, go out to the beach, maybe do some shopping, then go back to the apartment for lunch about four. They said they used to walk around in the afternoon, but were being pestered so much by the time-share touts that now they just had a siesta. Then it would be time for a shower and then dinner and after that a couple of drinks. Perfect.

Margaret and Jack were also representative in being regular visitors to Fuengirola, three times now they'd come in the past four years. A family I met from Limerick were on their ninth holiday here in nine years. Peter and his pal still took the biscuit, though, for being on their eighteenth visit in seven years. Why change a winning formula?

The veterans told of amazing changes in the town and the coast as a whole. A couple in their mid-fifties from Motherwell, with whom I watched the third round of the Open live by satellite in Posers, recalled their first visit to the coast fourteen years before when some resorts were still fishing villages. But five or six years ago, according to Peter's expert opinion, Fuengirola had been a lot busier. The place had become much cleaner since, said the regulars, and you didn't see drugs being sold on the street as you once did, and the marina had been built . . . But each year the number of Brits had gone down.

All the pub-owners knew why. The Spanish were pricing themselves out of the market. Food and drink were still inexpensive but they were even cheaper in Florida, which was where a lot of people were going instead. You could buy an ice-lolly for seventy-five pesetas a couple of years back and now what were they? Two hundred? One pound fifteen pee for a lolly . . .

By a neat twist of economics, tourism, which had taken off in Spain partly because the country was poor and therefore cheap, had helped the Spanish economy to boom, which meant that the country was far less cheap for foreigners than it used to be, but which also meant that the Spaniards themselves could now afford a seaside holiday. As a result, there were as many tourists on the Costa as ever, but the majority of them were now natives. In Fuengirola most estimates now settled for a proportion of 70 per cent Spanish, 25 per cent British, 5 per cent the rest. (It was about fifty–fifty in my hotel, which attracted Spanish who'd come here to escape the mid-forties heat of the high summer inland.) The influx of the natives didn't please many of the British pub-owners, who said the Spanish were tight – look at the way they took their own food and drink to the beach. More pertinently, the British wouldn't or couldn't do *tapas*, and the Spanish showed no desire for gammon steaks or shepherd's pie. The *Independent on Sunday* article had wildly exaggerated the problem, but the boom was over for the British bars here, and the owners knew it.

The conversation with Margaret and Jack had gone so well, I almost forgot about the hotel cabaret that night. I ran back to find that a small crowd had gathered outside the lounge to peer through the net curtains at tonight's show. Los Adams, according to the poster in reception, were a duo whose act involved Señor Adams holding his wife aloft in the palm of one hand. The word on the streets was obviously that Los Adams were something special. I'd never seen a crowd squinting through the curtains before. One middle-aged Spanish bloke was actually setting up his Camcorder. I hurried into the lounge and took up my regular position at the back beside one of the pillars. Lights flashed up and down the backdrop and then began to strobe as the DJ struck up the James Bond theme tune.

With a great flourish, Señor Adams, cutting a magnificent dash in pink flares, pink frilly blouse and panama hat, strode on to the stage. He acknowledged the applause from the packed lounge as he strutted back and forth before veering towards a big orange box. This contained, we learned after witnessing some ferocious posturing, a long wand which Señor Adams transformed, as if by magic, into a bunch of plastic flowers.

A period of more strutting later, he went back to the orange box which now yielded a sheet of newspaper. This Señor Adams fashioned into a cone. Unfeasible ceremony demonstrated that the cone was empty and that it now contained water poured from a clear jug. Abruptly, Señor Adams chucked the water at the nearest table. The two old dears seated there covered their faces – but needlessly. There was no water. It had disappeared.

The audience participation I had feared continued. Thanking the Lord it wasn't me, I watched in relief as a mother of several of the brats sprinting to and fro by the bar was persuaded on to the stage to wear a metal halter round her neck. Señor Adams thrust a sword through a hole in the halter. I waited for the sword to appear at the other side of the mother of several's neck. But no. The sword stuck. Señor Adams thrust again, with ostentatious force, and the mother of several let out a squeal.

This was more like it. So Señor Adams, for all his strutting and flares and James Bond music, was crap? Dangerously so, by the looks.

Then it happened. Another vicious thrust (various members of the audience, including me, gasping at its sudden, murderous force) saw the sword pass right through the mother of several's neck and out the other end. All credit to her for not squealing again. If that had been me, he'd have had to hose down the stage. As it was, I almost bit through my cigarette.

Some calm returned as the mother of several was led back to her gleeful table and Señor Adams turned his attention back to the big orange box. The James Bond music was replaced by the theme tune from *ET*. Some minutes later, an unconscionable amount of pointing and opening had established that the big orange box was completely empty.

Sure. So now he'd open it and produce another plastic fucking bouquet. Easy. He pulled down a few latches and the side facing us fell open.

And lo! The sequined assistant! A vision in fishnet tights and pink leotard conjured from nothing! Señora Adams, for it was she, celebrated her release into the limelight with a huge, immobile smile and a lengthy balletic display. The bit where she tiptoed towards the backdrop was especially good value for she was balletically clenching her splendid bottom. Great thighs as well. It was an extensive dance but no way extensive enough, to my mind.

Señora Adams' bout of buttocky prancing was brought to an abrupt end by another change in the music, to a soundtrack of high drama, of the sort used to announce the arrival of the High Priest in a Hammer film about Druid sacrifice. She skipped off to return a few minutes later in a more than fetching white mini-dress.

'*Usted paracaracaracos?*' Señor Adams asked us. 'Do you believe in hype knowsis?' he translated obligingly.

No one replied. I hid behind the pillar. Some poor schmuck would soon be munching an onion on that stage, or performing a flabby striptease, and it wasn't going to be me.

Brandishing his wand, Señor Adams swept the audience threateningly. I considered dropping a coin under the table and hunting for it. No need. The wand settled on Señora Adams. Her rictus grin was replaced by an oval of horror. No, no, she mimed frantically, but all her protests were useless. Señor Adams mercilessly dragged the proud beauty to the front of the stage, there to cast a deep spell on her by staring at her face and wafting a hand in front of her eyes.

With unquestioning obedience, Señora Adams, reduced to a plaything for her spouse's evil fancy, allowed herself to be balanced horizontally on three poles. Then, the pole under her feet having been whisked away, two. Drama graduated to crisis when Señor Adams then removed the main pole supporting his wife's muscly backside. Señora Adams was prone in mid-air, resting only her neck on one thin pole. Following the order signalled by his masterful hand, she raised her firm, fishnetted thighs aloft. She was a creature of rare loveliness. More to the point, she was the only woman in Fuengirola I could possibly take back to my room. I could have the bed and just suspend her in the bog.

Señor Adams spun her round so that we could marvel at his handiwork and I could marvel at Señora Adams' luminescent white pants. A final crunching chord blacked out the stage and the Adams family was gone.

Their next entrance, after a spell of even more sinister soundtrack, was astonishing. In place of his panama hat, Señor Adams now wore an executioner's hood. Having slowly stalked the stage, he lunged behind the backdrop curtain and, without pity or qualm, forced Señora Adams, still in the white mini-dress but with her hands now bound, face-down over a kind of globe. A quartet of septuagenarians at the table to the left of my pillar looked shifty.

What happened next I'm not sure. I saw the masked Señor Adams raise a sword over his wife's taut, helpless neck, lower the sword gently, then raise it again, but at that precise moment, a vast pensioner at the front of the audience regained her table and in doing so blocked out my view. In fact she was big enough to block out the light.

By the time her eclipse had passed, Señora Adams was being placed on another pole. Just the one this time, supporting the small of her back. By the miracle of hypnosis, she did some more balancing until her husband swiftly and brutally thrust her down. A spike came up through her stomach, we all gasped, and she lay limply impaled. Another crescendo of chords, then Señor Adams lifted his gored beauty up, up and free. We need not have worried. She was alive! See, her eyes are opening, she rubs her face in sleepy disbelief! The nightmare has passed!

Excellent news, especially because this gave Señora Adams the opportunity to rejoice at her rebirth with a wonderful amount of frenzied pirouetting and high kicks which showed off her luminescent white pants again.

'*Señoras y caballeros!*' yelled the DJ. 'Lazy jailmen! Los Adams!'

Back in his panama, Señor Adams marched along the stage's perimeter, one hand outstretched to receive our eager applause. Tragically, Señora Adams had stopped her high kicks to do the same. They climaxed with an embrace, formed a Y of farewell and sprinted off, then on again for some deep bowing, then off for the last time.

Great show. Great pants.

Okay, the second week had been a lot better than the first, but so would have been seven days of double shifts cleaning the oven. It was time to jettison any pretence of being a proper travel writer. There was no way I was going to spend the next two weeks in Torremolinos on my own. By Christ, the money I was getting for this book was paltry. I might as well enjoy the research.

Besides, hanging about with a chum would be more authentic, wouldn't it? The drawback was finding someone who could drop everything and have a holiday in Spain at two days' notice. There was only one candidate. My friend Paul, who was going through one of those barren patches freelancers get sometimes. A patch that, in his case, had now lasted something like four years. The man would have nothing to drop. He'd be on for it. Plus, by palling about with someone sporting such a stupid suede-head haircut, I'd look all the more chatuppable.

'It's me.'

'What?'

'It's me. From Spain.'

'Who?'

'It's me, you numbskull.'

'Oh.'

'What?'

'Christ, this line. Hold on a minute, I'll just go and turn down the stereo . . .'

'What? What? Are you still there?'

'So how's it going?'

'Fantastic. Really brilliant. You should see the women here. And you can get drunk for a quid.'

'You've got drunk on squid?'

'Yeah, the food's amazing too. Listen, what are you doing the next fortnight?'

'There might be a commission in the pipeline. And I've got to go for a trim soon.'

'Right, you're free. Come out to Torremolinos with me. I've rented a flat, all you have to pay for is the flight. Just tell me when your plane gets in and I'll get a taxi to the airport to collect you. Come on, it's wall-to-wall decadence there.'

'You been already?'

'Sure, I passed through it. Looked really great. We'll go mental.'

'So going mental is part of the research, is it? You said you were being a proper travel writer.'

'Fuck that for a game of soldiers.'

Sunday. The last day. At the unseemly time of quarter to ten in the morning, I said goodbye to my pizza and lugged my bags down the spiral staircase to the lobby.

Trevor the rep was there to make sure that we'd got everything and had had a good time. This didn't take him long because there was only me and the slack-jawed young couple – now crimson – for him to see off.

Fair play to him, he kissed the slack-jawed girl on the cheek (it was hard to miss) as he waved us on to the coach where the guide with the comprehensive commentary was waiting to hurry us aboard. She was strangely mute while we did a complicated tour of various hotels to pick up more passengers. Collecting these two dozen or so people demanded of the driver a repeat performance of laborious turns, finicky reversals and energetic gesticulations at anyone who would pay attention, but his limelight was stolen by the tragic entry at one of the hotels in Torremolinos of a nine-year-old girl dressed entirely in pink, who, despite or because of a smacker of a kiss on the forehead from the hunky rep, had to be pushed, crying uncontrollably, aboard.

Fortunately, her wails were drowned out – unfortunately, by the garrulous guide, whose bad mood had changed her into a gym mistress.

'Good morning,' she announced into her mike. She paused and turned round to face us. 'I *said*. Good *morning*.'

'Good morning,' came back our startled, diffident chorus.

'Have you all had a good holiday, then?'

'Yes, thank you. Oh, yes. Thank you very much, yes,' we replied.

'Have any of you been to Expo in Seville?'

Silence.

'*Shame* on you.' The guide looked at us as if we'd all

mucked up on the parallel bars. 'Well, you *all* missed a once-in-a-lifetime opportunity, I can tell you. There were pavilions from 102 countries. Britain, Spain, America, Canada, Australia, New Zealand . . .'

Even she wouldn't list all the countries, surely?

'. . . *even* some places from the Third World. Morocco, Algeria, Egypt, China, Mexico . . . Anyway, you all missed something special. But you'll be interested to know that it's been a very *damp* and *rainy* fortnight back home. They haven't had the weather too good at all there, so *that's* something. Now. We're beginning to approach the airport. Yes, that's the airport there on the left. With the planes. So. We'll be stopping the coach outside the Departures Lounge, where you can get trolleys for your suitcases, and you'll queue at the check-in, that's check-in desks 39 to 41, 39, 40 and 41, and *that's* where you hand over your tickets and your passports. Everybody got their tickets and their passports? Good. You need your tickets and your passports, *don't* you? Right, then, so you'll get a seat number *at* the check-in and if you want to smoke, say you want smoking and if you don't, say you want non-smoking. That'll be when you're given your boarding pass. Once you've put your luggage through check-in, except your hand luggage, which you'll be carrying on *to* the plane, go through *to* the security check and passport control and then you're through *to* duty-free, shops, toilet facilities, bar, self-service restaurant, etcetera. Then make sure you've got your boarding pass which will tell you the gate for your flight and that'll also be on the departures board on the TV screens you'll see. Now, you're all flying with Monarch, so look out for . . .'

Finally, we drew up outside the Prince Charles/Albert Speer memorial building.

'So it *only* remains for me to wish you, *on* behalf of all the reps here, Thomson Holidays, and the whole Thomson Group, a happy voyage home. So. *Hasta la vista.*'

'*Hasta la vista*,' we all replied.

'Oh, there's one more thing,' said the guide, as we rose from our seats. 'Your flight, unfortunately, has been delayed. Spanish air-traffic control, unfortunately. Anyway, hope to see you again soon.'

'How long?' asked a brave woman at the front. 'The delay on the flight, I mean.'

'Ooooh, four hours, I heard. Might be longer, you never know . . .'

Bye bye, then, gym-mistressy guide. Bye bye, coach driver. Bye bye, coach. Hello, check-in desks 39, 40 and 41. Hello, inexplicably long queue of fractious and peeling people heading back to damp weather and alarm clocks.

I, on the other hand, faced the trial of heading back on the train to Torremolinos to start another fortnight on holiday. How one has to suffer for one's art . . . I wheeled my trolley round and edged my way out and away towards the exit. Four hours later, I was settling into my second assignment, swigging lager on a balcony in a flat in Torremolinos, watching the planes zooming into the sky, wondering which of them I should have been on.

Now, what was the plan of action for tonight and tomorrow? So much to do, so little time. Go to laundrette, buy beer, potter, laze, have siesta, then go back to Malaga to meet Paul's late-night flight from Gatwick. Which reminds me. Make sure you have straight margins and write in pen. How many passengers travelled via Gatwick in 1958?

Torremolinos

We walked along neat alleyways, past discreet *bodegas*, whitewashed houses, a few small, appealing restaurants. Only occasional yells from unseen children broke the mid-afternoon hush. Glimpsing the sea to our right, we turned down yet another pristine, tranquil lane and arrived at a quiet promenade. The sea lapped gently on to a beach where some, but not many, Spanish families had set up their usual sunbathing encampments.

I couldn't believe it. Silence. In a Spanish town. And, of all Spanish towns, this one.

'Maybe if we came here in the evening it'd be really pandemonium,' said Paul.

He didn't sound convinced. He certainly wasn't convincing. It was easier to imagine orgiastic bedlam in Weybridge. Even by the most charitably elastic stretch of the imagination, this was not the site of the wild holiday I had sold to Paul on the phone and over eagerly gulped whiskies when he arrived late last night. It was, however, the town promised by the flat I had rented. This was, worryingly, eminently comfortable and respectable, in a well-kept complex with its own bar, supermarket and pool. Okay, okay, I'd assured Paul, it's nice enough here in Benyamina, but it's on the north-east outskirts. The suburbs, as such. Just you wait, I'd said, just you wait until we hit Torremolinos proper . . .

We'd been on this exploratory stroll now for at least two hours and it was becoming impossible to avoid the anxiety that Torremolinos was going to be as much fun

as window-shopping in Warsaw. We'd walked down
from Benyamina, past the Playamar complex – a complex
of over twenty eighteen-storey blocks, to be sure, but
well-designed, cream-coloured blocks set among quite
impressive, well-tended, sub-tropical gardens – along the
thronging but relatively peaceable beachfront, up a
knackering flight of rather pretty stairs, past a fairly busy
intersection and on to what I thought was the main
road. Indeed it was, the N340, distinctly run-down but
hardly jam-packed with jumping joints, or even traffic,
for the new bypass had clearly appropriated most of
that. In desperation we'd turned left down a quiet side-
street, back towards the beach, and found only this
haven.

There had been the sight of Onkel Willi's yellow
restaurant on the promenade, and a pub with a pool-
table destructively positioned outside, then a beautiful
blonde in a jeep, but none of these highlights, intriguing
in themselves, were intimations of crazed decadence. At
a pinch, Torremolinos seemed a bit busier than Fuengirola, perhaps a touch more downmarket, but hardly a
town that would have shocked the citizens of Gomorrah.

Dazed and confused, we continued on our walkabout,
spurning a succession of Spanish restaurants whence
wafted gut-rumbling aromas of tortillas and fried seafood,
and eventually seized on The Hartlepool Bar.

A charming waitress brought us two welcome pints.
We gulped them down, ordered a couple more, and
admired the view of the beach, the sea and a sixteen-
year-old girl of rare beauty languidly drying her long,
blue–black hair. At the table adjoining ours a muscular
bloke with a Geordies Rule tattoo considered the same
girl for a while before speaking to his burly mate.

'Do you use conditioner?'

'Not any more. That all-in-one stuff seems to be as
good. I mean, *maybe* it isn't, but for all the bother . . .'

'Aye, the wife just buys that as well now, like.'

'Anothah beeah?'

'Make it a hoff.'

The muscular bloke picked up his empties and walked inside to the bar, politely dodging the cue of a small boy playing pool with his dad.

I gulped down a good deal of my second pint and looked around. On the whole beachfront there were only two people clearly hell-bent on a wild time – a guy with a skinhead haircut and his iffy-looking pal, both of them drinking rapidly. Us.

Our next refreshment stop was Dubliners, back in the centre of town. The tables were set out in a square that was mildly dilapidated but decorated with trees in the centre, and that was – by now no surprise – subdued and noticeably underpopulated. The owner was an Irishwoman in, I estimated inexpertly, her lateish fifties, who wore a gypsy-style costume with slim grace. More to the point, she promised us really good cold Guinness.

She brought over our pints and we got chatting. She'd been living here for four years now, moved here with her husband when he retired, to fulfil their dream of running a bar on the coast. Within a few months of their arrival out here he'd died and she'd taken over the bar on her own. She missed him terribly but you had to get on with it, didn't you? And yes, Torremolinos was a very civilized place, not at all what they made it out to be. They? They were the press. Of course, it was different at night – very lively. Especially just round the corner, in what they called Combat Alley.

'Combat Alley? What's that in Spanish?' I asked.

'Combat Alley,' she replied.

'And whereabouts is it exactly?'

She laughed. 'Come here after midnight. You won't miss it.'

I hoped not. We were getting desperate.

*

The cue ball bagatelled around three cushions, cannoned off three of the four striped balls I still hadn't potted and came to rest a convenient three inches behind the black. As a snooker it had been less than successful. Paul dispatched the black with embarrassed aplomb.

'What's that?' he asked. 'Six-nil?'

'Eight-nil, but thanks.'

Yawning, I looked at my watch. Half past twelve. We'd been biding our time in Benyamina's local, Smudgers Bar, for two hours. Surely to God it was late enough now. The barman obviously thought so. He was yawning as well as he continued his tidying up but gave us a pleasant farewell, probably one of relief, as we let him close up early.

We flapped our T-shirts to fan away the sweat that had broken out immediately we left the relative cool of the pub. (It was still thirty degrees.) Arm in arm, a middle-aged couple passed us as they made their way home. We exchanged good-nights and Paul and I headed off in the opposite direction towards the middle of town.

We walked gingerly along the dirt-track which served as a pavement at this end of the avenue that would lead us into the centre. The headlights that dazzled us belonged to cars racing away from where the action allegedly was. No one was walking in our direction and the traffic which was going the same way as us consisted solely of empty taxis and overnight artics. Our quest for nocturnal revelry was, plainly, daft.

Having reached our reference-point of Dubliners Bar, we walked through a short, deserted shopping avenue, followed a few people marching purposefully, turned a corner and stopped.

Before us was a chaos of crowds and flashing neon.

The young Britt Ekland, wearing a bikini, roller-skated up to us and swivelled to a halt.

'Hey!' she announced. 'It's my lucky night. A pair of gorgeous men. So what are your names?'

We told her.

'Wild!' claimed the young Britt. 'Hey! Aren't you thirsty? Let's go in here and get a drink.'

While I wondered which of us it was she fancied, Britt whirled off into a nearby bar and soon whooshed back holding two pints of lager. 'Hey! There's room inside!' she yelled above the racket, handed over our pints, placed herself between us, guided us through a throng to a gloomy, packed bar, and showed us a miraculous space.

'So,' I said, casually but smoothly. 'What's your name?'

'Louisa.'

'Wild!' Paul claimed.

'Where do you come from?' I asked.

'Plymouth.'

'How long you been here?' Paul asked.

'Three weeks now.'

'Wild!' I said. 'Hey! I really like the roller-skates!'

'Yes. Anyway, that's 600 pesetas for the beer.'

'Oh.'

'Thanks, guys! Hey! Have a wild time!'

Britt/Louisa skated off to find some more complete schmucks. I looked around the bar. It was crammed with pairs of blokes sipping pints of lager pensively.

At these prices, the young Ursula Andress serving behind the bar was so underemployed that she was quite happy to chat to us. I soon learned that she was Danish, had a boyfriend, had worked here for two years, lived with her boyfriend, had an amazing night when Denmark beat Germany in Sweden, spoke Spanish because her boyfriend was Spanish, and that Britt/Louisa was a 'propper', someone whose job it was to proposition punters into a bar.

Having gleaned this much and asked her to pass on our regards to her boyfriend, we made to leave.

'Wait a minute!' she shouted above the din. 'Take these.'

Young Ursula handed over a bunch of tickets and leaflets offering free entry or discounts at various discos.

'The best is the Palladium,' she yelled. 'But don't go before three. Just go up Combat Alley, then turn left, you can't miss it.'

'And where's Combat Alley?'

'You can't miss that either.'

We squeezed our way outside, taking care to avoid an advancing threesome – the gliding Britt/Louisa sandwiched between two puzzled but smug blokes.

We stopped to take stock. We were in the middle of a long rectangle, flanked on either side by a line of bright, booming bars. The rectangle itself contained wide pavements on either side of a small park. I recognized this as a place we'd turned down this afternoon, only to turn back again after a few yards because it was so quiet.

It seemed absurd recollecting that now as we joined the milling revellers and resisted the efforts of beautiful young men and women asking if they could buy us more overpriced lager with our money. We inched past a group of teenagers listening to a dishevelled young guitarist playing the one song played by dishevelled young guitarists throughout mainland Europe. So it was with a plaintive chorus of 'Stairway to Heaven' drifting above the thudding beat from the bars that we saw a small break in the rectangle. It was a lane leading up to the main drag and it looked and sounded like a street party organized by Beelzebub.

Our progress up Combat Alley was, necessarily, slow since so many people were spilling out of the bars and milling around the tables that jutted into the dense parade in the lane itself. Someone came hurtling at us and held out his hand in a traffic cop's stop signal.

'Gentlemen, gentlemen. What's up? How you doing? Come into this perfect pub and drink a lager and a schnapps, all for 250 each. Come on, come on, come on, you know it makes sense, you know you have to do this, yeah? 'Course you do, come this way, follow me for a fucking great time, yeah? Trust me.'

He took about three seconds to say this. It was the most energetic prop we had had and it seemed churlish to refuse. He led us to two empty seats outside his bar.

'Wait there, gentlemen, yeah? Be back in a minute with your drinks, yeah?'

Clapping his hands to his own frenzied beat, he dashed inside and dashed back with two pints and two small glasses of what smelled like apple juice. All around us was a riot of bunting, neon, videos, people bustling around, laughing, shouting, being cool. Our pub was playing house music, the one on the left was belting out heavy metal, the one on the right was giving us the benefit of Bob Marley's greatest hits. I watched two teenage Aryan girls being suavely chatted up by a swarthy youth wearing a denim boiler-suit. It was almost two in the morning. In Fuengirola I'd have been asleep for two hours by now. I felt old, sensible and knackered. The adrenalin rush of entering the night-life of Combat Alley was wearing off fast.

A man suddenly appeared at my shoulder.

'Hash,' he said.

'Sorry? Oh, right.'

The last thing I needed was a relaxing joint but, for the purposes of research, I asked him how much he had. He frowned and pulled his hand out from his pocket to show me a block of dope the length, breadth and width of a cigarette packet. A Superduper Jumbo Mega King-size cigarette packet. More in amazement than refusal I shook my head. He disappeared.

Only to be replaced by the energetic propper who had stopped at our table to banter with some gawkily lanky chums. That's what I assumed at first, but their yelled conversation soon proved that they meant business.

'Come on, then, we got the pesetas,' said one of the lanky boys.

'Hang on, yeah?'

The propper's search for whatever he was supposed to have now involved tugging every pocket in his jeans inside out. He produced a tiny, wet ball of Kleenex and a couple of banknotes.

'Guys, guys, shit, look, they must have fallen out. Shit. Look, come back tomorrow, okay? Yeah, I'll have them then. Yeah, well go to Charlie, you know Charlie, yeah? He's down there, he's got them for sure, and ask for the *purple* microdots, yeah? Okay, yeah, see you tomorrow.'

When the lanky boys had sloped off, he punched his pockets back in and shook his head at us in disbelief.

'*Excellent* trips, yeah, excellent, must have fallen out. Took one myself yesterday, yeah? Jesus, then got on the train. Tell you something, those tunnels freaked me out. Freaky tunnels, yeah? Yeah. *Freaky*.'

'What are you on now?' I asked. 'Coke?'

'Nah. Fuck coke, yeah? For fucking yuppies, yeah, fuck it. Speed, speed, speed, speed, speed.' He drumrolled his hands with a flurry on the table top. 'Your drink okay, yeah? Great, great. Yeah, speed, amazing speed going about.'

'How much is it?' asked Paul.

'Yeah. Yeah. Three thousand pesetas a gram. But top-quality, tops, *excellent*. You want some, yeah? Right, right, go to the top of the alley, yeah? Opposite the Swedish bar, yeah? Couple of big guys there, one's a really big guy, really big, yeah? Wearing a football strip, yeah? *Big* stripes down it. Barcelona? Yeah, yeah, Barcelona strip. You want microdots, I'll have them tomorrow. Yeah, Oliver.'

'The guy in the Barcelona strip's called Oliver?'

'Yeah, yeah. No. I am. Smy name, yeah? Oliver.'

We shook hands, thanked him and headed off to find the man with the speed. Since Oliver's description was accurate he wasn't hard to spot.

He was too cool to speak at first but I bet myself he

was French from the way he answered our request with that shitty lip-curling the French go in for. Eventually he replied.

'Dee meenoot.'

'Okay.'

As soon as he'd sloped off, a small adolescent sidled up. 'Speed?'

'You got some?'

'Three thousand a gram. Really strong stuff that's going around.'

'Fair enough.'

We handed over three crumpled notes. He handed back a pack of Royal Crown cigarettes. I looked inside.

'It's empty,' I said.

'Stuff's in the silver foil at the bottom. Umm, you can take it out like that if you want but the police might think you're taking the piss.'

'What police?'

'The ones in the car two yards behind you.'

'Ah.'

'They don't really bother but still . . . Take one of these to keep you going. Slimming tablets.'

Crunching a slimming tablet apiece, we went in search of the Palladium. I opened my eyes as wide as they could go and gasped. Bloody hell. No wonder people went on diets.

Feeling very, very fine, we followed the crowd shambling along the main road and came to a stop outside a salmon-pink, floodlit building whose lime-green logo announced that this was indeed the Palladium.

Several things struck me when we went inside. One was that the sound-proofing must have been superb, since the distant throbbing we heard outside had suddenly become a sternum-vibrating assault; I noted with interest that the music was so loud it was shaking the calves of my trousers. Another was the crowd. Another was the swimming-pool separated from the dance-floor by a wall of glass. Another was the sight of a pert and nubile girl, who appeared to have been beamed here straight from starring in a lingerie ad, diving into the swimming-pool.

Paul, who had acquired possession of the packet of Royal Crown, shouted into my ear that he was heading off to the bog for a line of the speed. The pert and nubile lingerie model had executed three heart-breaking dives by the time he came back. He was smiling broadly and shaking his hands, like an athlete before a race.

'Oh, yes,' was all he said at first but he said it five times. I watched the lingerie model hoisting herself out of the pool again and wished I hadn't. Paul handed over the cigarette packet and discreetly bawled the helpful hint that, since the one cubicle lacked a lock, I should just take a pinch of it, like snuff. I headed off in the direction of the *servicios* sign. The *servicios* were cramped and packed with lads at the basins, throwing water over themselves. Two guys emerged from the cubicle, sniffing powerfully. I took their place and, leaning against the unlockable door, began the cautious fiddle of opening the silver foil. I took a couple of small pinches. Nothing. While I waited to change up several gears, I tried, with no success, to recall just how severe the speed hangover had been when I vowed long ago never to touch amphetamine sulphate again. Still nothing seemed to be happening. I took two larger pinches.

Minutes later we were both jogging on the spot on the dance-floor. The noise was deafening, the strobes were manic, dry ice was billowing around us and a guy wearing a Flowerpot Men hat was dancing on a table and blowing a whistle. We had set the controls for the heart of the bass. We could feel it in the air. We were ready to fly.

It was six when we left. Many of our fellow-dancers were heading towards Voltage, a club that opened at this hour and continued until nine or so. Good luck to them. We were heading home. The street was still busy with people, all of them entranced by a BMW's erratic progress westwards. The car jerked past us and stopped obediently at the lights. Which was fine except the lights were at green. They changed to red and the BMW hopped off, swerving madly at five miles an hour, tacking down the road to Benalmadena.

Our own progress was much more authoritative. At one point during our brisk march home I informed Paul that the speed had worn off by now.

'What makes you say that?'

'My scalp's stopped tingling.'

'So how do you explain the fact that you are gibbering and snapping your fingers all the time?'

'Fair point. True, yip, true, yes indeedy, true, true true,' I remarked.

'I mean, do you seriously want to go to sleep yet?'

'No way. Absolutely not. Not a chance.'

'We've got that litre of brandy back at the flat,' mused Paul.

'Brilliant idea.'

'There's no need to shout.'

'Sorry, I am really sorry, *shit*, I'm sorry.'

It was a brilliant idea, though. A little nightcap on the balcony. Actually, it was quite a large nightcap because we had to wait for at least an hour before the sun appeared above the mountains to the east. Below us, the town emerged from darkness into the milky light of the morning. To our left planes continued the procession of flights home, climbing above the sea before doubling back northwards to Dusseldorf, Helsinki, Glasgow, Gatwick. By Christ, say what you like about life but sometimes it could be just fucking wonderful . . .

By ten the planes and the brandy had begun to lose their appeal, so we skipped down the road to an empty bar. Only after a protracted session of *cervezas* and pool did it occur to us that sleep was no longer a ridiculous notion. The amphetamine sulphate was, at long last, beginning to wear off.

I woke up, damp and stunned. The alarm clock said 8.04. At least that was normal. Everything else felt very odd. Then I realized – it was 8.04 in the evening. And the seven-hour sleep had only replaced exhausted abandon with queasy dismay.

Unreasonably terrified, I got out of bed and padded carefully through to the kitchen where Paul was making coffee very slowly. He looked at me with the wide eyes of a man who has just been told by his surgeon that something went wrong with the circumcision.

We wandered round and round the small flat, sipping coffee, groaning quietly. I tried to think of the nice, pure things in life – the smile of my year-old nephew, waterfalls in leafy glades, the season when Raith held Rangers to a draw.

No. Health, normality and peace of mind were precious gifts we had scorned. All that was left was fear and despair. We were doomed. We belonged to the rank and vile.

The heat in the living-room was hellish but the thermometer reading of 102 only partly explained why I was sweating like the Michelin Man in a sauna. Paul tried to cool down by sitting out on the balcony. I knew the move had gone wrong when he hurried back in after a couple of minutes. We both slumped on the sofa, silent, in our pants. When Paul eventually spoke it was in a whisper.

'I couldn't handle it. Not with a sulphate hangover.'
'I know.'
'Not out on the balcony.'
'I know.' -
'Not with the bats.'
'Oh, sweet Jesus. Bats?'

'We're a long way up as well. Six floors. We could fall over.'

'I know.'

I tried to fight off the thought that down there, far, far below, was an alien world, 2000 miles from home.

'Paul?' I whimpered. 'I want my mum.'

Over the next four hours we tried every cure we could think of. Panadol helped but only a bit and not for long. Shaving was frightening, standing under the shower was ghastly, unburthening the bowels was horrifying. After that I resigned myself to fending off panic attacks.

There followed a long period of nervy, scared silence while I tried not to chain-smoke and Paul flicked through magazines.

'These seem to help,' Paul announced. 'Read this.'

He passed over from the magazine rack an ageing issue of *Woman's Journal*.

'Check out the recipe pages. Reassuring.'

'What?'

'Honestly. Try it. There's a good one here for lemon meringue pie.'

'Fucksake, Paul.'

I stared blankly into the middle distance. From an embarrassing recess of my mind came an image of a little fluffy rabbit hopping about forlornly in a nasty dark forest. He was lost and night had fallen. Was there anyone to rescue him? No, he was all alone. Poor little bunny. I swallowed back tears and turned to Paul for help.

He slapped his thighs decisively. 'Fuck it. There's only one way out.'

He jumped up, strode into the kitchen, taking with him the appallingly empty litre of brandy, strode back in with a folder of silver foil I recognized only too well, poured some powder on to his copy of *Woman's Journal*, amassed two long white lines, rolled up a yellow leaflet offering 150 pesetas' discount at the entrance of Piper's Monsterdisco and paused.

'Fancy a toot?'

Two hours later we were jogging on the spot in the Palladium. The noise was deafening, the strobes were manic, the dry ice was billowing around us and the guy with the Flowerpot Men hat on was dancing on a table and blowing his whistle.

'Fucking come *on*,' shouted the DJ. 'Make some fucking *noise*.'

That was like ordering paparazzi to take some snaps of a topless royal. Shrill yells wafted above the hammering beat as one house hit followed another. Floating around somewhere in the back of my mind was the thought that, since Paul and I had launched ourselves on Torremolinos forty-eight hours before, all we'd eaten was one small sandwich. A quivering in my stomach warned me not to think about food. Or about the morning − or afternoon − that would follow this night before . . .

Since we'd made a pact to take it easier this time, we left in search of a bar at around four. The places in Combat Alley were closed by then so when we were approached by a painfully thin, woefully dodgy character propping us to go to a girlie bar nearby, we hesitated for just a moment. The dodgy thin man seized on this slightest of hints of prevarication.

'You don't like the girls, no obligation. Just a drink is fine.'

'How much for a drink?' asked Paul.

'Two hundred pesetas for a beer, is all. Is cheap.'

'Okay,' I said. 'But drink only. No girls.'

'You want boys? Another bar I show you boys.'

'No, no. No boys either. We want only drink.'

'Fine,' said the dodgy thin man. 'You come with me I get you drink.'

He led us down a side-street to a bar called − my memory of all this is hazy − something like Can-Can or

Pussy Galore. He ushered us through the curtain that
served as a door to a room only twice the size of my
bedroom in Fuengirola, much of it occupied by a miniature bar, the rest of it by a sofa where two haggard
women were making the most of crossing and uncrossing
their mini-skirted legs. As soon as we ordered our beers
they joined us at our bar stools. We established that they
spoke only Spanish, so I performed a needlessly intricate
mime indicating that we meant no disrespect (see, the
hands held out in a gesture of well-intentioned hopeless-
ness, the friendly smile), but we had (pockets patted,
shoulders shrugged) no money to pay for them. The
woman assigned to Paul nodded and began to rub his
back. The woman assigned to me just looked at me with
bored contempt. I tried to act cool and poured my bottle
of San Miguel into a glass, like, you know, I could
handle this.

With a fixed grin, Paul turned to me and suggested
that we drink up fairly quickly.

'Why?' I asked.

'Apart from the fact that I am not enjoying this one
little bit, I think you also ought to know that we have
been followed in by two men who are standing behind us
and staring at us very intently and I am getting a bit
worried.'

Draining my beer was a problem since I had managed
to pour myself a glass of pure froth, but I inhaled as
much as I could and eased myself down off the stool. We
did a lot of smiling and nodding to the barman, the
prostitutes and then the two men who were indeed
staring at us in a way that would have been explicable
if we had repeatedly said dreadful things about their
mothers, and sidled out. It was difficult not to break into
a sprint but we managed, just, until we had covered most
of the fifty yards to the end of the side-street, where we
accelerated into a relieved trot.

'Gentlemen, gentlemen, what's the hurry, yeah?'

'Oliver.'

'Yeah, yeah, Oliver, smee. How you doing?'

'Fine,' I lied. 'How about you?'

'Cool, cool, *excellent.*'

'Did you get the microdots?'

'Microdots? Oh, yeah, yeah, yeah, easy, no trouble, yeah. You want some? I got a few left.'

'No, thanks,' said Paul. 'We're fine with the speed.'

'Good stuff, yeah? *Excellent* stuff.'

'A bit hard to come down from,' I reflected.

'Sure, sure, sure. What you need, yeah? A joint. Yeah, a joint.'

Oliver led us back down through a deserted Combat Alley to the park in the middle of the Plaza de la Nogalera, the rectangle where we'd been propped by Britt/Louisa. We sat down on a bench and Oliver produced a spliff the size of a respectable Havana. A couple of puffs and I could feel my whole body slump. It was only with a determined effort that I managed to talk.

'How, umm, did you end ... up here, Oliver?' I asked.

'Friend of a friend runs the bar I prop for, you know how it is.'

I didn't, but let it pass.

'And where ... where's ... where do you come from?'

'Beckenham, yeah? Yeah, but fuck Beckenham. Been out here, what? Two months? Something like that. Getting a bit tired of it.'

'What'll you do next?'

'Christ knows.'

It was a question to rank alongside the is-your-dog-still-dead query. Fortunately, my stoned investigations were interrupted by the arrival of someone I recognized after a while as the dishevelled young guitarist who had played 'Stairway to Heaven' the night before and an even more dishevelled young Spaniard who was completely out of his box.

'Nidge,' said the guitarist as he shook our hands.

'Heroin?' asked the Spaniard as he didn't.

Nidge, for that was indeed his name, settled down to share the joint and complain about the busker's lot in Spain. Nidge had, it transpired, forsaken the dole queue of his native Yorkshire for the minstrel's life and had spent the past five months busking his way through France and now Spain. He was thinking about Tangiers which he had heard was a pretty cool place to hang out. He was eighteen.

The pusher/junkie, meanwhile, was showing more interest in Nidge's guitar than the conversation or even the hash, indicating by sign language that he would like to strum a few chords. Nidge paused in his abuse of mean Spaniards and meaner tourists to pass his guitar over to the junkie, who, I noticed, was wearing that most unusual of garments in the Costa del Sol – a long-sleeved shirt. The junkie could have stepped out of a poster warning of the dangers of drug abuse. He looked an ill forty but was probably half that age. He was definitely ill, though. He tried to play a chord, failed to hit the strings and collapsed sideways and head-first on to the pavement.

'I suppose that's why it's called smack,' mused Oliver.

'He's with that bunch over there,' said Nidge, nodding behind us towards a cluster of shambling people about ten yards away. Suddenly, a fight broke out amongst them, an emaciated woman screaming at an emaciated man and then, screaming evidently not assuaging her anger, slapping him manically around his head and shoulders. According to Nidge's uncertain translation, she was somewhat peeved that he hadn't brought her her fix.

I thought of my guide-book which had given the impression that this place was a bit lively but jolly, like a party for mildly wacky Venture Scouts. I checked the write-up later: 'Late at night in the Plaza de la Nogalera, young people from all over the world band together and it isn't at all surprising to see a bottle of wine being passed around in a spirit of carefree camaraderie.'

Well, not quite.

'Heroin, jeez, never touch the stuff, yeah?' advised Oliver as he tried to lean the junkie against the bench. 'Me, I stick to speed, trips, maybe a bit of E if it's going.'

'Nothing serious, then?' I asked.

'Sright.'

'Every night?'

'For sure.'

There were two more questions I had to ask him. 'Oliver, how much sleep do you get?'

'Depends. Sometimes an hour, sometimes more, sometimes less. If I'm propping that starts about eight. In the evening, yeah? Finish three, four, splenty time to have a trip or something, get home, have a kip. Depends.'

'Uhuh. Erm, Oliver, how old are you?'

'Seventeen.'

Half my age, eight times my staying-power. Oliver seemed perfectly in control whereas I felt like I was recovering from an operation. It was time for bed.

We bid Oliver and Nidge good-night. We didn't bother with the junkie because he wouldn't have heard us. We stumbled off on the short walk back to Benyamina.

Surprisingly enough, there was the odd sign of life as we approached the entrance to the block of flats. Two preposterously drunk men staggered out of the darkness. As we staggered past them they were finishing off the elaborate process of parting.

'Nice one, Trev. See you in the morning, rye?'

'Rye. Inna fuckin pool.'

'Nine. For a rice.'

'No sweat.'

'Fih-ee lengce.'

It was half-five in the morning.

*

Waking up a mere two hours after noon seemed like the start of a new, fibre-filled, press-uppy regime of health and fitness. Save for the hangover and the nauseous weakness, I felt very well. And I didn't feel like bursting into tears – a huge advance. Having paced ourselves over the first coffees and cigarettes of the day, we were in a position, by four, to think about food. Rather as a workaholic must think about a laze on the sofa watching cartoons, but at least we were able to entertain the idea of eating. So, after some shilly-shallying, we set off down the road to a set of British pubs, and finally settled on a place that must, libel laws being what they are, acquire a fictional title.

'Monroe's' was not a happy choice. The TV was far too prominent and loud for a start, especially for a fragile pair such as ourselves. I tried to make sense of the Sky programme but gathered only that there are people in this world who consider balancing motorbikes at high revs atop muddy hillocks a challenging and gratifying – and broadcastable – sport. I also tried to make sense of the menu but had even less success with that. Who in the name of God would want to eat a Full English Breakfast? Or liver and onions? Or chicken curry and chips? I settled on a popular dish of the region, fried eggs on toast, and Paul on a restorative omelette and salad.

Perhaps we were unlucky. Perhaps 'Monroe's' is famed the length of the coast for its fine cuisine and scrupulous hygiene. I can only say that even if we had just returned from a fortnight at a health farm, the food would still have been nigh inedible. I mean, how do you fuck up an omelette? Or fried eggs on toast? Easy. By cooking both in yesterday's fat and ensuring that you burn everything on the outside, while, cunningly, making everything on the inside runny and gooey. Paul managed only to toy with his espadrille-flavoured omelette. By the time I had force-fed myself half my meal, the commotion in my stomach could be ignored no longer and I had to sprint to the (needless to say, revolting) loo.

Recovery back at the flat involved a strict diet of chilled beers. Come five we were in a fit enough state to shower. Come seven, we were able to discuss playing pool in Smudgers. Come ten, we were being hammered in a foursome doing just that. The victors were the barman and a guy called Tony who had been coming to Torremolinos two or three times a year since the early eighties. As an old hand he advised that, if we didn't do anything else of note while on the coast, we simply had to check out The Old Bailey, a pub where the karaoke was terrific and the minge was quality.

The Old Bailey would have to wait. There were discos out there that required inspection. It was dark and lonely work but someone had to do it. A small, precautionary line of speed back at the flat set us up for another night of gruelling research.

It was time for a little variety so we preceded our visit to the Palladium by popping into Piper's Monsterdisco, allegedly the largest dance venue in Europe, and one boasting, according to the proppers' leaflets, '22 years of world fame – 2400 square metres, 6 bars, 6 dance-floors, dance-floor surrounded wiht [sic] illuminated fountains, swimming-pool, cinema, rising dance-floors [yes, I know, and no, I have no idea], 40 people to serve you, the latest records and best sounds, 10 PM to 4 AM.'

Tonight's leaflets also advertised, not 150 pesetas' discount, but free entry, which partly explained why there was a twenty-yard queue outside. The other reason for the queue was that the bouncers were suffering punters to enter only a few at a time. Why? Because they could. But their whimsical exercise of absolute power did allow us to watch the television placed by the entrance to keep us amused. We queued long enough to admire most of a video of car crashes, amusing pile-ups of jalopies in demolition derbies, slo-mo re-runs of Grand Prix accidents, and, stunningly, what we slowly came to acknowledge were real-life fatalities.

It was just after a stock car had somersaulted over two others and burst into flames from which no one emerged that we reached the bouncers. We showed our leaflets promising free entry and, after an inexplicable delay, the bouncers showed us downstairs to the Monsterdisco. Or, more precisely, to a table at the bottom of the stairs where a girl claimed that we had to pay.

'No, no,' said Paul in a firm, hard, thrusting, masterful way. 'We've got these tickets for free entrance.' He gave her the smile that he always maintains is winning and held out a crumpled leaflet.

'Of course,' the girl said. 'You have the free entrance. Now you must to pay for the first two beers.'

'But what if we don't want to drink beers?' I asked, trying to look like a teetotaller.

'You must to pay.'

'What if we only wanted a glass of orange juice?' Paul asked. 'Or water? Tap-water?'

'You must to pay.'

Scunnered, we handed over our money, and made our way through to Europe's allegedly largest dance venue. It looked no bigger than the Palladium. We went to the bar to order the first of our obligatory beers and I realized that what I thought was a hall of mirrors wasn't. Beyond our bar were countless others, beyond the dance-floor in front of us were more dance-floors. In the distance we could make out a mural of Michael Jackson, several podiums topped by gyrating go-go dancers, a fighter aircraft of Second World War vintage suspended from the ceiling, and a wall from which jutted out half a Cadillac or Chevette – one of those – slightly battered but in far better condition than the vehicles we had just seen explode on video.

Having collected our beers, we essayed a tour of some of Piper's 2400 square metres, admired the illuminated fountains and agreed that the swimming-pool was something of a disappointment, since it was no more than a

big jacuzzi with a go-go dancer inserted. I did my best
not to look at that go-go dancer since she was, ostentatiously, a martyr to cellulite. As for the cinema, well, we
never did find that. Not our fault. In a disco so large it
could accommodate a Second World War fighter aircraft
as an incidental whim of decor, a housing estate might
have been successfully tucked away from all but those in
the know.

Which was the problem with Piper's. With a capacity
greater than many a semi-respectable football ground, it
required thousands of frenzied customers to generate
anything like an atmosphere. Several hundred teenagers
were doing their best to whoop it up, but the sight
reminded me forcibly of Queen's Park supporters celebrat-
ing a victory over the might of Forfar at Hampden.

Stinginess demanded that Paul and I stayed long
enough to swig down the second beers we had been
obliged to pay for, but we agreed to leave as soon as we
could. That communication involved a complicated
dumbshow of head-jerking and thumb-signalling since
the latest records and best sounds (i.e., constant repetition
of the two big hits of the summer, 'Rhythm Is a Dancer'
and 'Please Don't Go') were being played at a volume
loud enough to shame Concorde.

'Where next, do you think?' asked Paul when we
reached the street, without, strange to tell, paying for the
privilege.

'Palladium?'

'It's still only half-one. What about Picasso's or
Splash?'

'Splash,' I decided. I pride myself on having a nose for
the in place to be. Besides, I had overheard two hep cats
informing each other that Splash had been the in place
last year and had just undergone two months' refurbishment to challenge the Palladium as the in place to be
this year.

The voyage from Piper's to Splash was not arduous,

requiring, as it did, only a crossing of the main road. Our journey complete, we discovered that two months' doubtless extensive and expensive refurbishment had ensured that Splash was a splendidly chic disco with tastefully minimalist decor and an uncompromisingly minimalist population. There were two chaps at the bar, wearing identical black and white clothing. I don't suppose this was a going-steady outfit, because the two chaps were actually behind the bar and that was because they were barmen. And there was another, younger chap playing a solitaire version of pool. And that was it.

Splash looked good, the sound system was good, the latest records and best sounds were being played. So why had it become this year's place to bodyswerve? Because no one was going to it. And no one was going to go to it as long as no one was going to it. The DJ could play 'Rhythm Is a Dancer' and 'Please Don't Go' until the point where he would be led gently but persuasively away by orderlies to a high-security asylum and still no one would go to it. The free market can be a real bitch.

As I am sure the owner of the *Marie Celeste* – I'm sorry, Splash – would agree. As Paul and I dithered at the entrance, I imagined the scene at the owner's once proud home. Sweet little apple-cheeked Manuela Splash is raising her tear-brimmed eyes to her father's gaunt, haunted face. 'Papa,' mewls little Manuela, 'why is there no food for my kitten Fifi, whom I love second only to you and Mama? See, she is thin and weak and no longer plays with her ball of streeng.' Señor Splash slaps his forehead and turns his gaunt, haunted face to one of the cracked walls in his empty sitting-room. 'Because . . .' he says, his voice croaking with shame and misery, 'because there is no money for the food so you, Mama and I must to eat the Wheeskas ourselves.' 'But Papa,' flutes little Manuela, 'although I feel faint and eel, I will gladly share my Wheeskas with Fifi . . .'

The dithering-at-the-entrance lark didn't take up any

time at all. As every other prospective customer must have done, we turned round and got the hell out of there. An empty disco? Fuck you, Manuela. Eat Fifi.

If Piper's was Queen's Park at Hampden and Splash a Raith Rovers reserve game, the Palladium proved yet again to be Celtic v Rangers on New Year's Day. Even this early – it was only two in the morning – the Palladium was already going mental. We trotted in behind a wonderfully drunk girl who had managed to get past the bouncers only because she was being held up by her two pals. Rubber-legged, she somehow made it through to the dance-floor, where she abruptly transformed into a zippy raver. 'Leavis ellown,' I heard her tell her friends. 'Uh feel *grite*.' With that she climbed up on top of one of the tables and started dancing hip to hip with the guy wearing the Flowerpot Men hat and blowing his whistle.

Maybe I hadn't taken enough speed. Maybe, I forced myself to admit, I was just getting a bit too old for this kind of caper. I gazed listlessly at the bobbing crowd of T-shirted disco-groovers and asked myself what the hell I thought I was doing there. I was at least ten years older than the mean age of the Palladium's celebrants. I felt like I had been cast in an early Cliff Richard film, as the benevolent vicar condemned to remain in the background, self-consciously snapping his fingers to the swinging beat while the young things squeal to The Shadows' impromptu church-hall gig. I glanced at yet another lingerie model plunging into the pool. I bet myself good money that I was in my last year at high school when she was born.

Paul looked subdued as well, but he has always been a great one for making the best of things (a necessary virtue for someone with such a silly haircut), so he dragged me on to the dance-floor where we went through the motions.

These were the usual ones for dancing to house music.

Paul stuck to jogging up and down and jerking his head about as though umpiring Borg versus Connors. I myself favoured a more ethereal performance, with oriental hand movements and some rather seductive hip shimmying. That's the great thing about house; by spotting that the boom–BOOM boom–BOOM syncopation of normal pop can be twice as effective by simply having a constant BOOM–BOOM–BOOM–BOOM beat, and overlaying that with a dance track or hippy synthesizer stuff, house is, uniquely, both exciting to listen to and comparatively easy to dance to. After years of suffering the drawback of being white and born after 1930 (and therefore unable to dance), I think house is to be welcomed with both arms, held aloft and moving sinuously from side to side.

Dancing of any kind, even of so user-friendly a kind as house, is still a source of inhibited embarrassment, however – and quite right too. Like most members of my generation I need to be completely out of my skull before essaying even the most demure hand-jive. And it would have required a lot more class-A substance abuse to make me feel at ease that night as I tried to regress on the dance-floor to Miss Muir's gym class and pretend to be a tree swaying in the breeze.

An opportune moment, I feel, to switch locations temporarily, from a disco in Torremolinos to a comfy watering-hole in, let's say, Wentworth. Here you are, opposite me as I sit at my favourite bar stool in The Clotted Artery, tankard of the usual in one hand, panatella in the other, labrador dying at my feet. Maintain a polite smile as I take this opportunity to outline, at some length I hope, and using the cigar hand to poke you frequently on the collar-bone, my opinions on dancing.

The thing about all this disco music, all this rock and roll whathaveyou, is that no one can dance to it. Why not? I'll tell you why not. Because there are no proper steps, no *rules*. And name me one area of life where

things have been improved by dispensing with the rules
. . . You see? None. All this freedom malarkey, all this do
your own thing, express yourself rubbish, leads you nowhere but up, pardon me, Shit Creek. Look at poetry,
for instance. Free verse? Course it's free because it's
bloody worthless, all bits and pieces of whatever came
into someone's head, straggling down a page and no
capital letters. Same with tottie. I'm not saying that
there was no sowing of wild oats in the old days, but
when it came to marrying, that's what you did – find a
decent woman, marry her and stay married to her. No,
don't worry about old Faldo. On his last legs. Mind you,
I won't say I won't miss him. Been with me for, let me
see, close on two hundred words.

Back to the Palladium, where you are doubtless pictur-
ing Paul and me still shaking our funky groove thangs on
the dance-floor. Wrong. As ever, I am way ahead of you.
By this time, we have taken up position at the *side* of the
dance-floor and are busy doing some defensively supercili-
ous people-watching. On the nearby table the drunk-
turned-zippy-raver was still going berserk beside the
arsehole in the Flowerpot Men hat. They were performing in unison a manic and upright breast-stroke above
the crazed mayhem on the dance-floor. 'Fucking come
on,' shouted the DJ, as he pushed the beat up yet another
notch. 'Whaaaaaarrrggh,' replied the crazed mayhem,
pumping legs and arms even faster. A groin-tingling
blonde in front of us was running on the spot with a
speed and intensity I had thought belonged only to
cartoons. Beside her, an entranced yet acned pubescent
was devoted to miming his own wild drum-roll.

A thin two inches of speed hadn't been enough after
all. Once more I felt old, sensible and knackered. I
pointed to the exit and raised my eyebrows. Paul nodded
but we tarried awhile to appreciate, in a purely aesthetic
sense you understand, the sight of a raven-haired temptress larking in the pool with a high-breasted chum.

What, I wondered pangfully, would it take to persuade them back to the flat? We could, of course, simply go up to them, tell them they were beautiful and claim that I, for one, could guarantee that my fortunate partner would soar beyond the snow-topped heights of ecstasy. The temptress climbed out of the pool, lucky lingerie clinging to her every sweet curve, and immediately dived back in again. No. The only promise that would work would be that our flat contained all the New Kids on the Block. Or, come to think of it, a bouncing castle.

Through billowing dry ice, we dragged ourselves in a tiny-dicked, pot-bellied, hairy-eared sort of way to the exit. Outside we found three things that were very welcome. One was less noise, a second was fresh air, and a third was a youth called Davey from Newcastle who offered us a block of hash the size of a disposable lighter for two thousand. Ten quid? Back home that block would be four times the price.

Nothing cheers a chap up like a drugs bargain, so it was with a light heart that we lavishly hailed a taxi and sped back to the flat. By unspoken agreement – I think – we decided to refute the possible accusation that a quarter to four was pathetically early to have left the Palladium by proving that we could at least still smoke and drink. While Paul embarked on constructing a baguette-sized joint, I fetched some beers from the fridge. I could have defrosted it in the time he took, but the wait was worth it. For me at any rate, because after a couple of hits I discovered a fresh loquacity. That's certainly my interpretation of what happened. I was fascinating.

'You know what's wrong with the Palladium?' I asked rhetorically.

'Yes, I do,' said Paul. 'You've got grey hair and you dance like a drunk puppet.'

'Not so. What's wrong with the Palladium is that it's on the Continent.'

'Are we going to have one of those conversations where you think you're being deep?'

'Just listen,' I said. 'If the Palladium was in Edinburgh or Leeds or London, it'd be brilliant.'

'Oh, sure. There'd be no pool, no fifteen-year-old international models wearing precious little more than a smile, and it'd shut at one. Great.'

'Three years swanning around Exeter Art College with an opera scarf and a Captain Beefheart album and you think you've acquired an education. It's sad. The trouble with the Palladium is that there aren't enough Brits. Only 50 per cent, max. And there's three things the Scottish . . .'

'I knew it.'

'. . . the Scottish, the English, the Irish and . . . no. Anyway, there's three things we've given the world in living memory.'

'Hooliganism, oven chips and . . .'

'A certain style of violence is one. The other two are the long ball game and a wild and innovative youth culture.'

Paul nodded thoughtfully. 'There's a place you may just have heard of. It's called America.'

'Young Yanks are stuck somewhere between 1969 and 1972. Another decade and they'll discover platform shoes.'

'Hip-hop,' said Paul. 'Rap. Graffiti art. Everything street in the past ten years.'

'Forget about the blacks.'

'Oh, very fucking nice.'

'Black Yanks don't count. Okay, they're up there with us. But everywhere else in the world kids are too busy being poor or working twenty hours a day to pass exams or they're touring the globe in camper vans. So that leaves us and the Continentals. And Continentals just wait to see what's happening on MTV – i.e., what's happening in Britain.'

'Detroit, Chicago, New York, LA . . .'

'Then copy the new British stuff, and even if it is

originally from America, it's our lot that develop it. And when Johnny European mimics us he always has to take the precaution, mind you, to adapt it by spending a lot of money on nice clothes and avoiding anything but soft drink. I mean, things might occasionally get a bit livelier in Germanic countries, where nineteen-year-olds have been sighted nursing the odd lager but . . .'

'Have you ever been to Holland?' Paul asked.

'The Dutch, I grant you, are a magnificent exception, especially on the coffee-shop angle, but you take all the Latin bunch – places like here, Italy, France, especially France – the young are very, very boring.'

'Did I tell you about that time with Isabella in Milan?'

'Yes. Did I tell you about the time I sat in a café in Paris drinking calvados?'

'And in came a really cool dude . . .'

'And in came a really cool dude, with rockabilly hair and a bad boy's approach to gum-chewing . . .'

'And he went up to the bar . . .'

'And he went up to the bar, where he did some crucial posing, checking out the place to make sure we were all impressed, then he snapped his fingers at the barkeep. "*Un chocolat*," he said. "*Chaud*."'

'Yes,' said Paul. 'You have told me about that. Almost as often as when you're out of it and you cover your head with a white towel, then wear your specs over the towel and say that that's your impersonation of the Invisible Man.'

'You look at all the innovative things that've come out of Britain in the last thirty years. Well, only The Beatles, The Who, the Stones, Led Zeppelin, Bowie, Roxy Music, the whole Scottish scene . . .'

'Oh, no, mustn't forget Jockrock.'

'. . . mods, rockers, glam rockers, skinheads, punks, goths, new romantics, ravers, to name but a few. And what has the Continent contributed? Demis Roussos, Abba, Plastic fucking Bertrand and the Smurfs.'

'Forgetting for the moment that you've still skated over black Americans. Or that, for example, house came from Chicago. And Ibiza.'

'Ibiza only because there were British tourists and DJs there.'

'Forgetting the fact that you are wrong, what have the Smurfs got to do with the bastarding Palladium?'

'Everything. Plastic Bertrand copied punk and made it sweet and the Palladium has copied a good old British rave and turned it into a high-school dance.'

'Have you ever been to a rave?'

'That's got nothing to do with it.'

At this point Paul was overwhelmed by a huge yawn. 'Yes it has,' he said eventually.

'Hasn't.'

'Has.'

'Hasn't. Anyway, what I'm saying is that, because the Palladium is a typically twee European travesty of the real thing, that's why you get garbage like everyone dancing the same, everyone doing what they think is the right thing, waving their arms around when the dry ice comes on, and then, worst of all, every time the music slows, holding the little flames from their lighters in the air like they always do at their rubbishy pop concerts. Wankers. Okay, Britain might be a shite place to live, with a third-world economy and early closing in England, but at least we don't all dress in the same smart-but-casual way, at least we're cool, at least we show some fucking gumption . . . Paul? . . . Paul?'

So bright and early was our start the next day, we'd actually made it down the road, though not to 'Monroe's', for breakfast by just after one. This was definitely going to be a day of achievement, of tasks ticked off my list, of dedication to the travel writer's craft. There was research to be done by the seaside for a start, so I punched my clock-in card bang on twelve-thirty. I dismissed impatiently the advice of my brain's indolent fop, who was suggesting that I go back to bed because the sky really was terribly cloudy, and set to work packing a carrier-bag with beach accessories.

Stumbling as I pulled on my trunks, I was forced to admit, however, that I felt wretched, suffering a grim headache and a collywobbly yet entirely empty stomach, as well as the dry-lumped throat that is said to be a hazard of the coast in the summer. I was, in addition, finding it as difficult to focus as it was to ignore a residual chemically induced depression. Apart from that, things were looking up. We had, the Lord be praised, almost finished the speed the night before, so all I had to do was keep going, resist any temptation to cry, maybe eat something, and all would be, in time, okay.

We gambled on a pub that advertised home-made food and a weekly pool competition. God alone knows how it held the latter, with a pool-table hemmed in by a pillar, a jukebox and a one-armed bandit. The home-made food, though, was a triumph. Paul appeared to be very keen on his omelette by the way he consumed it in three shoe-sized chews. I managed one of my two fried eggs on toast, which I considered no small success since my usual Billy Bunter-style appetite had declined to that of an anorexic sparrow.

Deeming coffee the breakfast drink of big cissies, we decided to wash down our meal with a couple of San Miguels, a choice that spurred the landlord to engage us in chat.

'Off to the beach, then?' he asked, pointing to our carrier-bags crammed with towels, beach-mats, paper-backs, bottles of water and juice, and tubes of sun-tan lotion.

'No,' I felt like replying. 'We're about to start our afternoon shift as fucking traffic wardens.'

'That's right,' I said.

'A pity,' remarked Paul, in his best nice-boy-talking-to-distant-auntie voice, 'that we seem to have missed the best of the day.'

The landlord looked a bit perplexed.

'Still,' Paul continued chirpily, 'let's hope all this cloud-cover will just disappear sometime soon.'

The landlord nodded to himself. 'Just arrived last night?' he asked, switching, I assumed, to a more fruitful conversational topic.

'No, no,' Paul assured him. 'We've been here – what? – three or four days now.'

The landlord frowned. When he spoke, it was after an uncomfortable pause and in the hesitant monotone of a brainwashed agent in a sixties thriller, one who, prompted by a phrase or tune, recites a litany of top secrets. 'It has been cloudy every morning all week. And all last week. In the afternoons the clouds go away. It's the weather. It's always cloudy in the mornings. Then they go.'

He was right too. Five minutes later, when we colonized a patch of beige sand with our mats and towels, it was under a hot, blue sky. After an hour's work tanning my back, I embarked on some research with regard to alfresco afternoon naps. As a result, I can reveal that a little sleep on the beach does help a speed hangover but is not to be undertaken next to a professional numbskull who wakes you up with a prod in the kidneys and the information that a real babe has just walked by.

'You should have seen her, though. She was wearing only this thong thing and had the most amazing breasts.'

'Well, that is splendid news. You must wake me more often to keep me up to date on the babe front.'

'You're a real human dynamo, aren't you? Remind me to come on holiday with you more often.'

'This isn't a holiday. It's work.'

'Forgive me. I can't imagine why I thought otherwise.'

Insert here, if you will, a sulky pause.

'Right,' Paul announced. 'I'm off for a swim. Ooyah.'

'Be careful with your bare feet there on the sand,' I advised. 'It's very hot.'

I marvelled at his bony back and unfeasibly thin legs as he skedaddled on painful tiptoe through the crowds to crash into the sea. He swam out for ten yards or so, stopped to tread water and abruptly swam back at Olympic pace to the shore where he scrambled on to the sand and sprinted furiously back to his beach-mat.

'Something wrong?' I asked.

'Jesus Christ. Jesus. Jesus Christ Almighty.'

Paul stood on his mat, eyes screwed shut and with a mouth like a cat's bum, as he fervently towelled himself.

'Were you attacked by a creature of the deep?'

'I wish. Jesus Christ. It was when I stopped to look around. Agh. Jesus. And I saw what the water was like.'

'Yes?'

'It's only got a thin yellow scum on the top, hasn't it? And it's full of little bits, like if you only flush the toilet once when you have a really terrible case of the runs.'

'Come on, that's probably just sand or something.'

'That wasn't sand. Agh. Look at that. You see? That's just come off my leg!'

'It's only a bit of paper.'

'It's bastarding bog roll.'

'Nonsense.'

That night in Smudgers Bar we heard a report on Coastline Radio that there was a temporary health hazard on some parts of the shore, caused by raw sewage. Fortunately, we were both partially anaesthetized by then, having spent the best part of the evening in various bars in and near Combat Alley. Seeing as how we left the centre of town at midnight, the place had been relatively quiet, with the noise only reaching flight-path levels. For the first time, I was able to notice features of Combat Alley other than its pubs. I spotted a street sign, for example, that informed me that the Spanish for Combat Alley does exist and that it's 'Calle Antonio Girón'. (Here's hoping Sẽnor Girón was a pillar of the community.) I also noticed that the alley was home to several hairdressers and, even more bafflingly, people. There were flats above us, flats with lights on. There were balconies with clothes hanging on washing-lines. People actually lived there.

Perhaps the flats were occupied only by the deaf. Or perhaps the inhabitants weren't at all hard of hearing but didn't mind the noise too much. Given the racket prevailing in the rest of Spain, perhaps they thought the din of Combat Alley was bearable, even normal. I thought of the English tourists you see picnicking in A-road laybys in Scotland, regarding these as nice, tranquil, scenic spots.

'Gentlemen, gentlemen, gentlemen, what is occurring?'

'Oliver, yo,' I exclaimed, in an unconvincing effort at dude-speak.

'Sgood to see you guys. You need trips, speed, yeah? Word is that there's some E come in as well.'

'Later,' Paul alleged. 'We're cool with some hash we scored.'

Talking hip really can be a very embarrassing business. Likewise the hip handshake. My gesture of farewell to Oliver went badly wrong when he tried to grasp my elbow to start that complicated soul-brother routine and I was ungroovy enough to go for an orthodox clasp. My peripheral vision afforded me the sight of Paul rolling his eyes in disbelief.

After a slightly bamboozled Oliver returned to his propping duties, we headed off to a café in the Plaza de la Nogalera. This turned out to be an expensive move, despite our ingratiating attempts to order drink in Spanish. No amount of *por favors* and *graciases* could stop our waiter turning a request for *dos cañas* – small glasses of draught – into an order for two bulging forty-centilitre jugs of imported lager. Six hundred pesetas. At least the young Britt Ekland chatted us up a bit for that price. She was nowhere to be seen, alas, and since we had, unaccountably, not been seduced by the two German girls at the adjacent table, there seemed nothing for it but to return, celibate and poor, to Smudgers for a game of pool and a listen to the human body-waste report.

We sauntered back under a hot, starlit sky, admiring the way cockroaches would scurry off at our approach, and puffing at a pair of joints. By the time we learned of the public-health warning beachwise, Paul had won our pool match four–one (he went in off the black during the second game, probably deliberately), so we settled down to savour a last beer and chat about the kind of things you chat about when you succumb to being thoroughly stoned: how odd it is that planes aren't as noisy as they should be when you're in them, what it's like being stoned, who should play, in our Pet Hates First Eleven, in the midfield alongside Swaggart and Monkhouse.

We carried each other back to the flat where, I dimly remember, I had a brainwave for a surprise that would crack Paul up. While he was reading his recipe pages, I sneaked through to the bathroom. It was the work of a moment to prepare this wonderful new trick. I made my way back along the hall and flung open the living-room door.

'Tah-rah!' I announced.

Between my face and my specs I had draped a large, white towel.

It was a terrible, terrible, terrible, terrible hangover. God, it was terrible. I mean, really *terrible*.

Seven hours after waking to vow that I would never smoke again and acknowledge that drink was the urine of Satan, I lit my twentieth Royal Crown of the day and told Paul that, what with it being nine in the evening and all, it was high time for a beer.

'Smudgers, maybe?' I suggested.

'No need,' he said. 'There's San Miguel in the fridge.'

'Really? How?'

'I went to the supermarket.'

'Really? When?'

'This afternoon. While you were being sick.'

'Ah. You didn't, by any chance, get any, as it were, food?'

'No. I only got essentials.'

'What are the essentials, Paul?'

'Rizlas, Andrex and San Miguel. Eight litres. Plus a litre of that nice Spanish brandy.'

'Lord have mercy.'

It can't be all work, work, work, can it? Other travel writers must take it easy sometimes. Peter Mayle takes time out, now and again, from all the research he has to do, surely? Even Paul Theroux must alight at the occasional Station Hotel for a day off.

Mind you, I'm not saying it was an unproductive evening. I finally remembered the name of that newsreader I really fancy. Nanette Lithgow. And Paul came up with the third member of our Pet Hates midfield. I hope Michael Jackson wears the shirt with pride.

This can't go on, I thought, when showering the following morning. Well, afternoon. I examined my reflection in the mirror. I'd lost my tan and for the first time in seventeen years I could see my rib-cage. We'd been on a liquid diet for over five days now. The food we'd eaten wouldn't reach the calorie count of an American's elevenses. Inspired by fear, I had my second brainwave, one that didn't involve a large white towel and amusing use of spectacles.

'Paul?' I shouted into the hall.

'What?'

'It's Sunday, right?'

'Well done.'

'So let's do what people do on Sunday.'

'If you think I'm going to bastarding church, you can whistle out of your arse.'

'No. Lunch. A proper Sunday lunch. Lots of places advertise them.'

So it was that we sat in a pub, forty miles from the coast of Africa, on a day when the electronic-display thermometers read thirty-seven degrees, tackling two bowls of tomato soup followed by two large oval plates of roast beef, gravy, Yorkshire pudding, roast potatoes, mashed potatoes, green beans and peas. We passed on the apple crumble with custard and lurched back to the flat for a nap.

I awoke, moist with sweat and puzzled by a curious noise. It sounded as though someone was pissing on the balcony. Even Paul wouldn't . . . I went through to the living-room and looked out. I couldn't understand it. I registered that the bright, blue sky of our afternoon binge had become overcast. And that, down below, something was wrong with the pool. It was rippling all on its own. Someone dashed by with an umbrella. Ah, it was *raining*.

It cleared up, alas, so there was no excuse to avoid another night on the town. Variety being our watchword, we set off down the road for a promenade along the, umm, seaside esplanade. To our right was a long line of pubs and restaurants (including Onkel Willi's, home this evening to many Germanic songsters) and then an even longer line of large hotels and apartment blocks. Some were dishearteningly unattractive and unspacious, some others were just unremarkable, but several of the newer complexes were noticeably well-designed. To our left was the beach where, in its now empty state, we could appreciate one of the attractions of Torremolinos that summer – the building sites that were evenly spaced along the sand. The local council had ordered the demolition of the old, often illegally constructed, beachside bars, which were to be replaced by officially sanctioned ones. Very fine they looked too. Lots of quality timber work there. Unfortunately, they were still being built – at the height of the season, so work was going slowly because of the heat and would be completed just in time for the low-season lull. Well done, everybody.

The ineptly scheduled bar-building programme was the one ill-starred part of a general refurbishment scheme. Since Torremolinos had gained financial independence from Malaga two years before, the town had invested a good deal of money in doing itself up. It showed, too, in places like the knackering flight of stairs at La Roca that we'd walked up on our first day, stairs that, we noted on our climb up them tonight, were well lit by attractive new street-lamps. And the whole town – late at night in the Combat Alley zone excepted – was clean. Torremolinos was never going to be Cannes, but, equally, it was not the shitty place of myth. And if it really had once been as ghastly as the myth suggests, then I can only say that the two-year refurbishment scheme was costing as much as the GDP of Switzerland.

The truth is that Torremolinos does not look good from a distance, where, through the long-focus lens of fear and loathing, its detractors see only high-rise beastliness and a beach apparently holding a population bigger than that of Sheffield, lying buttock to buttock for miles. Here's a quote from a recently published book by one of those writers who go in search of the 'real Spain'. Actually, it's called *In Search of the Flamenco*. 'I personally have spent very little time on the Costa del Sol. My one trip to Torremolinos included a midnight visit to the deserted beach, where the row upon row of deckchairs stretching for kilometres in two directions called to mind nothing so much as a concentration-camp barracks.' Do what? Remind me. Concentration camps are where people are

incarcerated in huge numbers, usually before being tor-
tured and killed, isn't that right?

At least that writer looked at the place, even if only for
a moment and through binoculars and with *The Snooty
Author's Handbook of Awful Analogies* by his side. Here's
another quote about Torremolinos, this time from a sort
of guide-book. I love this one: 'The less said about this
high-rise haven of package tourists the better.'

Yip, a quick dusting of the hands and that's Torremolinos dealt with. Off to Ronda now, or the Alhambra or
a rather sweet *venta* near Bunty's *finca* way up in the hills.
Quite amazing. You can get a seven-course meal, wine
(rough but more than serviceable) and a blow-job off the
owner's daughter, all for 150 pesetas. (No, it's not amazing. It's because they're *poor*.)

That lots of people write off Torremolinos isn't really
because it's inundated by so many other people. Nice, St
Tropez, parts of the Algarve, they're also inundated by
millions of holidaymakers. But they aren't the same kind
of holidaymakers. They're, well, middle-class. As the
best-known destination of the cheap package tour, Torremolinos became 'Torremolinos', a byword, a code
word, a myth. 'Torremolinos' stands for everything that
everyone is supposed to hate about tourist resorts. It's
so . . .

So dirty, so crowded, so tawdry, so full of fish and chips
and lager louts. So vulgar. So *common*. So forget Torremolinos and pay attention only to the town with the inverted
commas around it. The place with all the high-rise
hutches and ghastly pubs and hooligans screwing on
pavements pock-marked by sick. Who goes there? 'They'
do. The masses. The vast majority which never seems to
include us. I mean, one doesn't actually have to go to a
place like this to know what it must be like. One has seen
those postcards of the seafront – just a huge line of massive
concrete blocks. My dear, a vision of hell. And have you
read the papers? All those lager louts and gang fights . . .

Well, there can be smoke without fire, especially when it's the press that's huffing and puffing. On the other hand, I don't think Combat Alley earned its nickname by being popular with outings organized by the C of E. Local opinion was a bit divided on the tendentious lager-lout issue. The posher expats usually assumed that Torremolinos was awash with thuggery. Local publicans usually dismissed the lager-lout phenomenon as the fiction of newspapers founded and funded with the sole aim of creating such adverse publicity as to put those local publicans out of business. My own – needless to say, expert – opinion is that there probably was a bit of violence here, or at least the normal hooligans' mimicking of violence, in the late seventies and early eighties, when that was something some British blokes did, or were supposed to do, or came to think that that was what they were supposed to do. And any time there was a fight, the press would be on hand to report it. Fairly and responsibly and accurately, of course, without a hint of any exaggeration or desperate desire to please the desk back home.

In the summer of 1992, though, it was said that the ten-pints-then-kick-the-shit-out-of-anyone brigade was way down on membership and had, in any case, bogged off to the cheaper destinations of Gran Canaria or Corfu. How true that is I'm not sure. All I know is that they weren't there. In the fortnight I spent in Torremolinos, I saw one instance of unpleasant behaviour. (Two if you count the sight of a group of lads wearing Spurs tops, marching down a street and singing, 'There's only one Justin Edinburgh.') A boy of about eighteen, previously noteworthy only for his comedic pudding-bowl haircut, kicked over a chair belonging to the café next to the pub where he was spending most of his pocket-money that night. Perhaps the chair had provoked him, but I tend to the view that he showed it who was boss for no reason other than that he'd had seventeen *cervezas*, had no *affaire de cœur* and no prospect of one. (This was about half past midnight, when everyone else was just getting started; the boy was many things, but cool was not one of them.) A large and handsome waiter from the café went across to right the chair and the pudding-bowl-haired youth gave him a look. 'I've been here a fooking week and I'll fooking well sit here,' he shouted. The waiter shook his head to suggest that he didn't under-stand any of this, at which gesture the pudding-bowl boy took further offence. 'Okay,' he said. 'Outside, mate.' They were outside. The waiter walked off. The pudding-bowl boy slumped against the wall, exhausted by drama and alcohol. The score in the Torremolinos I knew was Lager Louts one, Euro-Ravers untold thousands.

For the time being, Paul and I were all raved out, so the aim of that night's expedition was to follow up Tony's advice and seek out The Old Bailey, of terrific karaoke and quality minge fame.

We were given directions by a balding bloke in an Arsenal strip to a lane which I think leads up to one of the original towers that gave Torremolinos its name. Something like that. Much more pertinently, the alley was only 100 yards across the road from Combat Alley. However, The Old Bailey turned out to be far closer in spirit to a Basildon fun pub than the pan-European shambles of our favourite street. A long series of hoard-ings outside announced that inside there was Tartan bitter, Red Stripe, and Guinness from Dublin on draught, jukeboxes with over 300 CDs, two pool-tables, the chance to put your name down for The Old Bailey's beach parties, and an opportunity once a week to 'Jour-ney Into The Human Mind With Dave Kirby'.

Tragically, we were three days too early for a psychic voyage with Dave Kirby. We were bang on time, though, for a karaoke nite. The place was packed out. I secured a space at the bar by elbowing aside a young lad who was much smaller than me and didn't seem to be with any friends, and ordered two pints of Red Stripe.

The clientele of The Old Bailey was in a celebratory mood. Two boys, stripped to the waist, bodies shiny with perspiration, were conducting a singalong chorus from the podium of one of the two pool-tables. The other pool-table was supporting three girls in identical yellow T-shirts who were performing an abbreviated Mexican wave. Below them, a fat boy was drinking from a bottle of San Miguel. The bottle was held by a companion two feet above the fat boy's throat and foam was dripping down the fat boy's hair, face and neck. As he concentrated on not drowning, another mate shoulder-charged him and he went tumbling to the floor, to the detriment of several of his neighbours and not a few beer glasses. There was a constant rammy of shouting and singing and swaying but only a *Sun* reporter desperate for copy would describe it as loutish or even rowdy. Rather, the atmosphere was of late-teenage revelry: it could have been an end-of-term party at a student union.

Fuelled by drink and bonhomie, people were clamouring to perform on the stage at the back of the pub. Oddly, the performers seemed to be those least equipped to perform. Only the benevolent chorusing of the heaving crowd carried most of the attempts to provide the vocals to the greatest hits of Elvis, Madonna and the Beatles. One singer – Richard from Hemel Hempstead – had potential but he was scuppered by a glitch in the karaoke machine, which would have us believe that McCartney wrote 'Yesterday, all mu griunkes weened so fit aqat'. Simon from Bristol was undone by 'Country Roads': like every other customer of The Old Bailey, he knew the chorus and, like every other customer, couldn't for the life of him remember any other melody-line in the whole benighted song.

Their efforts were brave ones, sabotaged by circumstances beyond their control. Not so the performance of a chap from Ealing, which must have won him outright, hands-down, no messing, the award for the worst display of the evening. He looked supremely confident during the long introduction to Hall and Oates's 'Maneater'. He danced around the stage, resplendently kitted out only in football shorts, throwing the mike coolly from one hand to the other, beaming at his audience who, following his latest move, raised their hands high and began to clap joyously along to the beat.

Everything was going tremendously well. Then he began to sing. He produced a sound I hadn't heard since school assembly. It was a sound akin to, but even more appalling than, that produced by a bad poet reciting intensely, or a guru groaning a mantra. It was an approximately rhythmical rumble stuck on one note well below middle C, the rumble of someone so defiantly tone-deaf that he thinks singing involves no more than projecting the voice a bit and producing a satisfying vibration in the pharynx.

The clapping along quickly subsided but I'll never know what happened after that because by the time he was chanting the third line we were ten yards down the road. We left half a pint of Red Stripe each at the bar. He really was that bad.

Good behaviour that night – a small pub crawl, nothing special – left us equipped the following afternoon to have a go at sunbathing down by Benyamina's pool. A pair of *cervezas* from Smudgers' poolside annexe dispelled the hangovers which had been exacerbated by, a legacy of our roast-beef binge, tummy trouble. The Mediterranean was only 500 yards down the road but that was really too far, and, in any case, Paul was adamant that he wasn't going near the sea again. The drawback of our own swimming-pool was that it was the venue of various dramatic and noisy competitions. One of the more sedate was the kids' underwater handstand championship, but that was regularly postponed by the water-volleyball match of four bulky teenagers and occasional rounds of the fetching-a-five-peseta-coin-from-the-bottom-of-the-pool contest. One little boy was dedicated to the solitary task of turning his lilo into a speedboat. He'd rest his tiny torso on a fraction of the lilo and propel himself, hands flapping at either side, feet kicking furiously, around the pool at commendable speed. Luckily, his powers of acceleration were matched by his manoeuverability, for he often had to take swift evasive action during bouts of the most popular sport of all – pushing unsuspecting strollers in. This could be hilarious, as when a father, having thrown his screaming son in a high and long parabola which ended with a glorious smash on the water's surface, was so busy laughing that he didn't see the posse of his mates creeping up behind to heave him, clothed legs and arms flailing, with concerted force towards a drenching.

The pushing-in game teetered on the edge of disaster only once. This was when two fabulously pot-bellied men left their posts at the counter of Smudgers' annexe to experiment with exercise and ambush their equally pot-bellied pal. After some unseemly grappling, all three tumbled cringingly into the water, knees and mighty stomachs scraping the pool's sides. That looked really sore, but at least it didn't end, as it could so easily have done, with a visit to casualty in Malaga.

It wasn't fear that drove us indoors but the heat. All that stuff about the noonday sun is nonsense, isn't it? The hottest time in hot countries is mid to late afternoon, when the air has heated up and whatnot. I might be completely mistaken in this but it's what I think, so there. In any case, it was obviously true of Torremolinos, with its micro-climate of cloudy mornings. As evidence to back up my theory, I can cite the fact that the pool-side temperature at four-thirty was thirty-eight and my skin was beginning to itch. (The coolest temperature of

my fortnight in Torremolinos was one night when it plum-
meted to twenty-six; there were rumours of it reaching
forty in the second week, and one discussion in Smudgers
revolved around the story that a thermometer placed in
full afternoon sunshine a few years back raced past the
forty-seven-degree limit and threatened to ejaculate.)

Back in the thirty-two-degree cool of the flat, I
showered, dried myself to no effect and settled down
to browse through the owner's collection of guide-books
and, those most useless of objects, phrase-books. Extraordinary. The most antiquated was a Collins' *Spanish
Phrase-Book* dated 1953. Preliminary advice for explorers
to this untamed land dictated that they needed passport,
visa, currency declaration form, on which all transactions
were to be recorded and ultimately checked by Customs,
and traveller's cheques worth no more than £25 per
explorer and to be applied for in advance. Oh yes, and
you had to register with the local police. Remember that
men wearing shorts will be hounded out of any church,
where women must cover heads, arms and legs. Shorts
are only acceptable (for both sexes) on the beach, and
women whoreish enough to wear two-piece bathing costumes will be fined by the beach-guard. Then shot.

Crucial phrases for these explorers, lugging around
forms in triplicate for their spending money and three-
piece suits for sunbathing, included the following: 'Have
my baggage fetched from the station' and 'Can I hire
opera glasses?' The section helping out explorers suffering
toothache gave one harrowing side of the inevitable
dialogue: 'I want this tooth filled. Please be gentle. It is
very painful. That hurts. Am I to come again?' The
'Motoring' page was even worse: 'I am a stranger here. I
forgot to keep to the right. I did not see the traffic lights.
The lorry overtook me on the bend. I have had an
accident. Here is my driving licence.' I mean, apart from
the fact that 0.001 per cent of the population could
afford to lavish £25 apiece on opera glasses and shawls

and bribes to Spanish dentists in 1953, is it any wonder that 99.999 per cent of Britons stuck with a summer fortnight in Morecambe? Dearie me.

The second most antiquated book on the shelves was a McGraw Hill *Pocket Guide to Spain*, published in 1955, a year when, I can now tell you, 46 per cent of the native population worked in agriculture, i.e., were peasants. You may think this anti-Hispanic prejudice, but just listen – according to this McGraw Hill *Pocket Guide*, there was one telephone for every thirty-four Spaniards in 1955, one wireless for every eight people, and absolutely no television whatsoever. For every 133 forelock-tugging workers, there was one *hidalgo* with a car. And guess how many bicycles there were? No. Way off. One for every twenty-five people. Well, come to think of it, bikes, they're pretty flash, aren't they?

I don't know how reliable this next bit of information is, since it is gleaned from my own guide-book (the Torremolinos issue in the *Everything Under the Sun* series, a hoot), the very guide-book which told me that youngsters gathered in the Plaza de la Nogalera at night to share a bottle of wine and maybe launch into a chorus of 'We're riding along on the crest of a wave'. (While I'm on the subject of this guide-book, I'd like to pay tribute to its unique style and use of the bold typeface. The first sentence, for instance, reads: 'Torremolinos is a year-round party for the **young-young** and for **young at heart**.') This source says that, by the time of the heady year when up to 4 per cent of Spaniards could afford to invest in a bike, Torremolinos was still a little fishing village, still the 'pretty country place' described by Rose Macaulay in 1949, but with a handful of hotels. By the late fifties, according to my guide, it had become a rather chic resort. However, according to Frederic Raphael who lived down the road in Fuengirola in 1959, Torremolinos even then was considered 'a bit fast'.

As Torremolinos grew in the sixties, so did that fast

reputation. By the middle of the decade, it had become known as 'T-Town', a nickname that rightly evokes all that is groovy and fab, as well as shite, about the sixties. I came across several expats who'd come to Torremolinos in the mid-sixties and, for one reason or another, had never got it together to leave. They recalled a time when limbo bands from Jamaica played at The Blue Note, when the hippest place on the planet was The Fat Black Pussy Cat bar, and when Torremolinos had its very own acid lab. (Tripping tourists used to go to beach parties which the police would visit to laugh at the strange antics of the foreigners.)

One of Benyamina's senior citizens, who had bought her flat when the block was completed in 1964, showed me photographs of her view at that time. The town was missing. All the hotels, the Playamar complex, the other developments, they'd all been airbrushed out. There were a few tiny white cottages scattered about marshland and fields and then there was the sea. Benyamina must have looked ridiculous, a six-storey block of flats in the middle of the countryside. Aviemore-on-sea. It had also started life as a rather posh development; the charming lady with the airbrushed photos was a survivor of an age when the ancestor of Smudgers had been a bar smart enough, as another photograph disclosed, for the owner's wife to deck herself out in cocktail dresses of an evening.

Within a few years of Benyamina's construction, the cocktail-dress crowd would be fleeing for the Greek islands or Dordogne as T-Town became 'Torremolinos', the reputed capital of Crudland, the obvious place for Eric Idle to rail against in his *Monty Python* diatribe against people who go abroad to drink Watneys Red Barrel, etcetera, etcetera, etcetera.

It was midnight. I was pacing the living-room, nibbling on my fingernails. Paul was in the shower, singing, 'I'm in the mood for love.' I tried to ignore it, but couldn't ignore the spectacle of his sassaying out of the bathroom, dripping wet and wearing only a fig-leaf of a hand-towel. He danced up to me.

'Simply because you're *near* me,' he crooned into my ear.

'Don't.'

'Darling, tah tah tah *tah* tah.'

'Cut it out.'

'But it's our special night.'

'Just be fucking sensible, okay?'

He ran his fingers along my shoulder, over the nape of my neck.

'*You* know . . .' he murmured. 'When two men love each other specially much.'

'Look. You're supposed to be here to help me. Tonight of all nights. A bit of moral support would be welcome instead of winding me up.'

'Oooh, get her.' He minced into the kitchen, wiggling his scrawny bottom. When he returned, he was tongue-flicking the top of a bottle of beer. This he was holding, fortunately, in the hand that wasn't keeping the towel over his no doubt insignificant little fireman.

'What's the matter?' he asked minxily. 'Insecure in our sexuality, are we? A teensy weensy bit homophobic?'

'I am very secure in my sexuality, thank you very much. I am an extremely straight, roister-doistering heterosexual.'

'And you hate the prospect of spending tonight cruising gay bars.'

'Not at all.'

'So it's not the bars but just the gays that you hate.'

'You *know* I don't.'

'So why the touchiness?'

'I'm not being touchy.'

'You're acting like you've accidentally poured petrol over yourself and I'm about to light a fag. Oops!'

'You're the one that's being homophobic with all this John Inman act.'

'So John Inman's homophobic, is he? Homo. Phobia. Fear. Of gays. That's you.'

'Paul, I am not afraid of gays. But yes, if you must know, I am a bit bothered about tonight.'

'Aha!'

'As most straight men would be. I bet you are as well, though you'd never admit to being so un-right-on. And I'm bothered because I'll be there under false pretences. An impostor.'

'Come on, it's more than that.'

'I don't know . . . Say someone chats me up?'

'You think that's likely? Anyway, you're not to worry about that – just carry a brown hankie in your left back-pocket like I told you.'

'I know what that means, you're not getting me like that. Now. Remember our story. You and me have been together for four years, we live in my flat, we're non-scene, we're definitely not into any coloured-hankie funny stuff and we're strictly monogamous. All right?'

'So firm. So dominant.'

My packet of Royal Crown caught Paul on the hand-towel. He yelped and scampered bonily out of the living-room. 'The chasing game! The chasing game!' he shrieked.

Tonight was not going to be easy.

Our venture into gay night-life was not, I plead, a gratuitous exercise in prejudice, because one of the lasting effects of the bohemian beginnings of Torremolinos is its thriving gay community. The free-and-easy, swinging T-Town of the sixties was something of a haven for homo-sexuals who discovered they had licence here to do all manner of outrageous things – sunbathe with partners, walk along public streets openly chatting to friends, wear well-cut clothes without fear of ridicule.

Of course, ever since those heady, shameless days, young straights have increasingly outnumbered gays, but the latter – tourists and residents – continue to give the town part of its identity. (This may come as a surprise to all those people who think Torremolinos is irremediably shitty, but there you go.) One of the more memorable sights we witnessed in Combat Alley was the parade down it of three very large drag queens who acknowledged the cheers and wolf-whistles with haughty scorn. And you only have to look up Torremolinos in the gay *Spartacus* guide and see the size of (phrase in honour of Paul imminent) the town's entry to realize that it's still a resort to rival Mykonos or Sitges. As well as disclosing that the cruising area is the *estación de autobuses*, the *Spartacus* guide lists three discos and seventeen clubs and bars, many of them in the La Nogalera complex just down from Combat Alley.

So it was to La Nogalera that Paul and I headed on our special evening together. We considered that, with our best white T-shirts and button-fly 501s, we were looking the part. That delusion lasted until five minutes into our ten-minute walk to the centre of town when we were overtaken by a trio of gay men. Although two of the three were wearing white T-shirts and button-fly 501s, Paul and I realized we were going to blend in like Tory backbenchers at a fashion shoot. Sure, we were wearing the right clothes, but we weren't wearing the right haircuts, faces or bodies. Where were our perfectly handsome features? Where were our neat crops? Where were our pecs and triceps? They were couth, gainly and kempt. We were maculate.

It must be galling for heterosexual women to know that beautiful men, with the exception of Richard Gere and Jason Donovan, are interested only in other beautiful men. This is wonderful news for straight blokes – it's like knowing that all the brainy kids are going to be sent to a private school, leaving you to go for a clean sweep on the class prizes – but this was the one night of my life when I had to lament the sorry fact that I was just too damned ugly to be gay.

We plodded on unattractively towards La Nogalera, a complex of apartments and bars that isn't too difficult to spot because there's a big neon sign at the top that says 'LA NOGALERA'. We fell in behind two other men, both gorgeous, one decked out in a superb cream linen suit, the other in leather hot-pants. They turned right in the direction of an arrow with the words 'Men's Bar' below. It seemed a good idea to follow them.

Next door to the Men's Bar is a pub called The Rambler's Rest. Now that definitely is *not* a gay haunt, I said to myself, noting that the customers were exclusively families – of the sort in which the parents take it for granted that premarital snogging is a crime against nature. They were enjoying a nightcap, amazingly oblivious to the throng of young men who had spilled out in search of oxygen and conversation.

I took a deep breath and sensed that Paul was doing the same.

'Okay,' he whispered. 'Let's do it.'

I felt his hand on the small of my back to guide me into the bar, but I stepped back and around him. 'No, really, Paul. You first.'

The music was already deafening so I didn't catch what he muttered in reply as he strode in, but it didn't sound at all nice.

The bar at the Men's Bar was covered in bars. Thick metal bars that reached from the counter to the ceiling and imprisoned the staff who had to hand out drinks like Victorian convicts melodramatically begging for release. The staff were also, to a man, sporting only jeans and cowboy hats, thus displaying torsos of a uniformly mahogany, muscly excellence. I tried not to gawp and Paul tried to fight his way through the crowd to buy a couple of beers.

As Paul returned, bottle of *cerveza* in each hand, he was staring at me with the sort of frozen expression that says either, 'I am being held at gunpoint' or 'Whatever you do, don't turn round.' What the hell was going on? It occurred to me that I didn't know because I hadn't dared pan my focus away from Paul buying beers. Very slowly I eased my head round ninety degrees.

What I saw reminded me of an erection, but only in the way that a 125 Inter-City Express would have reminded me of the Fuengirola choo-choo. It was on a video-screen and it was hammering in and out of the anus of a blond bodybuilder lying flat on his back with his feet clutching the neck of the owner of the 125. I flinched at a particularly extensive thrust and told myself that, unimaginable though it was to me, the bodybuilder was enjoying this. As, judging by the vigour with which he wanked himself, he was. Since the 125 was regularly hidden from view, the camera concentrated more and more on the bodybuilder's own lance of manhood, which soon ejected huge spurts of come that decorated his chest. One cleared his shoulder.

The video-screen, itself the size of an aristocrat's dining-table, as was only appropriate for displaying such a Brobdignagian seeing-to, went blank. Paul and I sipped our beers absent-mindedly and gazed at the grey screen. After a moment, I reminded myself that we should be looking at home here rather than like Shetlanders on their first visit to Harrods, and glanced casually round the bar. I needn't have worried. Everybody was staring at the screen. It was reminiscent – but only in this one respect – of a pub in Manchester showing United live.

Suddenly, and to the accompaniment of even louder music from the jukebox, the screen showed a new image, of a chap on a lilo in a pool. Soon he was joined in the pool by another chap. They exchanged a few mute words, then, without so much as a candlelit dinner or a bunch of flowers, the second chap tugged at the first chap's busy trunks to unleash another vast, thick, veinous cock. This was somehow – don't ask: frankly I was astonished – accommodated in the second chap's mouth.

Thinking I could guess the rest, I turned away to exchange a few bogus sentences with Paul. Picture my surprise, then, when I swung my stare back to the film, to see that the first chap was now out beside the pool and on his knees, fucking the second chap in the mouth while being fucked by a third chap.

I knew it. I should have gone before I left the flat. I beckoned Paul close so that I could shout into his ear, 'Where do you think the loos are?'

He raised his eyebrows in a well-if-that's-what-you're-into-each-to-his-own sort of way. 'Search me,' he yelled back.

'If I'm not back in two minutes, come and look for me.'

'No.'

I made my way through the crowd of hunky men to the back of the bar. No sign of a bog. I selected a particularly lush guy blond enough to be English or English-speaking and asked him for directions. Surprisingly, he raised his eyebrows as Paul had done and pointed to a spiral staircase leading to a basement. Uh oh . . .

The descent was a gloomy one in two senses. I sidled down past a gauntlet of boys standing on the stairs which led, I discovered, to a sepulchral corridor. The corridor was much smaller than the video-screen but managed to contain a lot of men who would have been milling around had there been room to mill. I non-milled around too, under the impression – no, rather in the forlorn hope – that this was the queue. It wasn't. A ray of light slanted through the deep murk as someone clattered out of the Wild West saloon swing-doors of what had to be the, er, men's room. No one was taking his place. I moved forward to do just that but when I reached the doors and tried to push them open, someone pushed forcefully back. Suddenly, my bladder felt fine, really quite all right, only achingly full. As I turned to ascend back to the light, I noticed an opening opposite me. It led into an even darker room, a room so dark I could make out only the movement of shadows and the dull glint of what I guessed to be a cage. I caught a chlorine whiff of amyl nitrate and eased my way back up the stairs.

The fruitless expedition could only have taken a minute but, by the time I regained my position at Paul's side, the video had moved on apace. Lost by the plot, I watched a young man pout at the camera, kneel on all fours, then stroke his perineum with a licked finger. I didn't find him at all good-looking. His pinched eyes and nose, his plastic blow-wave and his mouth distended by teeth showed him to be American and, like all young, white Americans, he bore a distinct resemblance to a character in *Thunderbirds*. And he had a hairy bottom.

It seemed an opportune moment to go. Stiff-legged with the agony of my bladder, I led our way outside where I headed, as phlegmatically as I could, next door to The Rambler's Rest, rambling straight to the *servicios* and a violent slash.

Refreshed, I told Paul that we couldn't give up this easily. We made a reconnaissance tour of the block and picked out another bar, Contacto. Two boys were standing outside it, fidgeting their fingers in sign language. It was my turn to go first. It was a confident entrance but one that terminated as soon as I saw that there were only four customers at the bar and that all of them had turned to inspect me. I stumbled into Paul as I went into reverse.

'Nah,' I claimed as we left. 'Not enough action.'

The two deaf-and-dumb boys started fidgeting with great speed as we left. Perhaps they were saying that we were really cool, really handsome ... Then I saw that the flurry of their hands had stopped because they were holding their ribs, rocking back and forth in silent hysteria. One of them pointed at us, then wiped away a tear of hilarity. Hmm.

We would try one more place. A few yards away there was a poster for a floor-show at the 801 Club. It showed a man grinning and holding the crotch of his packed leather trousers. 'Hi! I'm Randy,' said the poster. 'You've seen the rest. Now FEEL the best.' And there indeed was the 801 Club opposite.

'There's the 801 Club opposite,' I observed.

'Yes, there it is,' said Paul.

'There's another place next to it, mind.'

'The Pourquoi Pas? Yes, it looks very nice.'

'We could pop in there . . .' I suggested.

'After you.'

'It's your turn to go first.'

'Oh, good grief, man.'

Over Paul's shoulder, I assessed the Pourquoi Pas as a much friendlier place. It was very compact, a narrow room with a short bar that occupied most of one side and space enough in front of it for a couple of tables and a three-sided sofa. It looked, in fact, like the kind of select, intimate, sophisticated joint that I had assumed existed only in episodes of *Jason King* or adverts for Martini Bianco.

We perched atop two high stools at the bar and noted that the gantry featured a black dildo the size of its neighbouring whisky bottle, and a comedy willie with elephant's ears. Paul ordered a couple of gin and tonics from the barwoman, a sequinny beauty flirting with her prime.

'Hello,' said the man next to us. 'Brian,' he said, as we shook hands. 'Haven't seen you in here before.'

'No,' I replied. 'It's our first time. In Torremolinos.'

'Nut?' he said, sliding over a bowl of them.

'Why, thank you,' I said. This was all right, wasn't it?

Brian caught the barwoman's eye. 'Another J and B on the rocks, please, mighty,' he said.

The proprietress, Maithe – for such, we learned, was her status, her name and the spelling of it – prepared

Brian's drink, then asked us with a smile if we were going on to the 801 later. We said we weren't sure, she said the best time was after two when the dancing was out of this world, we registered interest and she said that of course, even with good new places like the 801, Torremolinos had lost its chic long ago. Not a point, I thought, that would need stating, but it transpired that Maithe was a wistful veteran of the good old days of T-Town. She'd come here for a holiday, she told us, in 1969 and had been putting off her return to Bordeaux ever since. Why had she stayed? Because back in the sixties Torremolinos was a real gay town and 'piss elegant'. 'When I first set up the bar, I was packed every night and it was fun every night.' Brian nodded nostalgically and Maithe reminded him that he was a whippersnapper of only eight years' experience of the place. 'By the time you were coming here,' she said, 'it had already changed, hadn't it? All those families. All those nice mummies and daddies.'

'I've seen it change too,' Brian asserted. 'And for the worse. All the smart gays you used to get here, they've all moved on. To the Canaries, California ... Most of the British gays here, they live here, don't they? And the younger, designer lot, they wouldn't touch this place with your barge-pole.'

'I suppose we can't be designer, then,' I remarked.

'Nor,' said Brian, 'are you gay.'

'Well, not ...'

'I mean, *look* at you.'

Once we'd confirmed that Paul and I were straight, I asked Brian about the Men's Bar.

'Not my kind of place,' he said. 'A bit heavy, isn't it? But that's what the scene here is getting like. Cottaging is coming back. And where's the safe sex? You're talking about two men full of gin and poppers. It's like some of the scenes in New York. Kids are all Aidsed out, so they just think, to hell with it. You used to get a lot of lovely queens here, but now it's all hustlers and rent boys.'

I risked telling Brian that I had been perturbed by the Men's Bar basement. To my relief, he wasn't offended. 'That room with the cage? Yes, I had a drink there once, although I stayed put upstairs, I can tell you. Apparently, one guy was down in the cage with the whole SM bit, you know, hood and manacles, and there was a rush to get down there. Well,' he reflected ruefully, 'you know what men are like.'

Shallow, voyeuristic, temporarily voracious, with a yen for casual sex without any snuggly-wuggly stuff afterwards. Yes, we did know.

Before we left, I arranged to meet Brian again for a night out, at the end of the week, after Paul had flown home. 'We could go to the 801,' Brian said, and Paul agreed. On our way home, by the bus station, we passed the Bronx, a gay disco Brian had recommended strongly.

'We could check it out if you want,' offered Paul.

'I don't know, I'm feeling a bit pooped.'

'Yeah, it's getting on a bit.'

'Gone one.'

'Smudgers?'

'Smudgers.'

Over brunch of San Miguel and toasties the following day Paul reminded me again that he had only two days left here.

'So what do you want? A present? A round of applause?'

'Yes to both. Plus I think we should do something different.'

'We could spend the evening in, playing Scrabble, that'd be different.'

'I have something else in mind. I have a plan.'

'My heart it soars like an eagle.'

'Just you wait.'

With no superhuman effort, I controlled my sense of anticipation throughout a day in which I accompanied

Paul on a less-than-spellbinding souvenir hunt. For those keen on souvenirs, I can recommend a passageway – I forgot to find out its name – that twists down from the Calle Casablanca to the seaside. The stairs are very steep, unlike (ahem) the prices. Yes, if it's leather goods or sombreros you're after, that's the place for you. It's also the place where I saw for sale the most extraordinary T-shirt of all the extraordinary T-shirts available on the Costa. This number showed a cartoon of a little baby boy and a little baby girl. Three loopy lines above his head indicated that the little baby boy was swivelling his head to stare at his partner in astonishment. Small wonder, because the little baby girl had her dummy stuffed, not in her mouth like the little baby boy, but up her vagina. 'Because I like it,' was the slogan beneath. Say what you like about the Spanish, but they really have a great sense of humour, no?

Burdened with several postcards, two small fans that cost about 80p each and a genuine Spanish pencil (lucky friends and relations of Paul, I say), we made it back to the flat where he started to pack.

'But you're going tomorrow night. Late tomorrow night,' I pointed out.

'That's as maybe.'

It was a vital clue and I ignored it.

We set off after midnight on Paul's great mystery tour. In no time at all, he'd led me to – hey, great surprise – Combat Alley. Following his instructions, I sat meekly at a bar while he went off on an enigmatic errand.

'What a great guy that Oliver is,' he announced on his return.

'I can't take any more speed, Paul. I can't, I just can't.'

'Don't fret, my precious. It's not speed.'

'What, then?'

'Ecstasy.'

'Oh, no.'

'Oh, yes. Party time.'

He discreetly opened his palm to show me two red and yellow capsules. Rhubarb and custard. We washed them down with mineral water and I waited a little nervously, for what I did not know.

'How long before they take effect?' I asked.

'Depends. Three-quarters of an hour, something like that.'

Forty-five minutes later I found myself smiling as Paul recalled the glory-days of Bristol City. He seemed to be rambling, but it was good that he was enjoying himself. Meanwhile, I was itching my scalp with sweating hands. Very slowly, I turned my head to look into the mirror beside me. My eyes were black with only a speckled rim around the dilated pupils. Wait a minute, though . . .

'Is it okay to feel a bit odd, a bit dodgy?'

'That'll pass soon,' Paul said through a smile. 'Relax into it. Wow, feel my T-shirt.'

'I need some fresh air.'

'That's fine. Oh, and the tips of my fingers.'

With the speed of convalescents, we walked out into Combat Alley. 'Taxi,' I said. 'Home.'

'Lovely idea.'

Have you ever noticed how wonderful it is to stare out of the back of a speeding car? And to stroke upholstery? Paul guided me to the flat. The feel of his hand on my spine was luxurious. Sitting on the sofa was even better.

'Do you want to listen to some music?' Paul asked.

'No,' I whispered. 'Let's be gentle and silent.'

'Lovely idea.'

I thought E was supposed to make you dance like a maniac, but the only thing we wanted in the world was to sit there in the wondrous quiet. Occasionally, I would think for a moment about my only worry – that the drug would slip away from me and that this full and empty bliss would end. Paul managed a slow expedition to the balcony at one point. I was glad when he came back because I wanted to continue massaging his bony neck and running my fingers through his furry scalp. I had contented myself in his absence by kneading a cushion. It was really, um, you know . . . yes.

We seemed to be coming down when we went to sleep around six, but, waking the following afternoon, we were still possessed by slow contentment. Now I realized why Paul had packed so prematurely. We idled the rest of the day and evening away in Smudgers, playing uncompetitive pool and appreciating the texture of various soft drinks. Shit. I'd turned into a hippy.

Somehow Paul organized a taxi to take him to the airport. I gave his back a last stroke goodbye and meandered back to the flat where I sat on the balcony, wondering which of the planes jetting out over the sea was his. I selected one and monitored its long U-turn until it went out of sight. Bye bye, Paul.

How was I to know that when I woke next morning at the civilized time of ten, Paul would just have reached Madrid? A delay of nine hours had consigned him to a long, sleepless night watching some passengers playing in an impromptu tennis tournament in the non-Departures Lounge. What a shame. He could have been giving me another massage.

I celebrated my hard-won freedom from Paul by conducting some research on poolside sunbathing. I read a book. I had a coffee – a coffee! – in Smudgers. I went to the supermarket. It was great.

Since I was now unencumbered by Paul, I aimed to venture further afield. Tonight would be the night for a journey down the road to Benalmadena. Check out a disco or two, I thought. Maybe pick up a chick if I saw one I fancied.

My knowledge of Benalmadena to date amounted to what I'd seen from the two coach trips presided over by the verbose Thomson guide. So far, then, the place meant only a series of pubs and hotels divided by the race-track of the N340. I had a notion that there was the village of Benalmadena inland and, down by the sea, the resort of Benalmadena Costa, where, according to another notion, there was a new marina. After a night out on the town, I can clarify that Benalmadena, or at least my version of it, is, in fact, a series of pubs and hotels divided by the race-track of the N340.

The hotels seemed to be concentrated beachside of the main road. This seemed not only sensible but, as far as I was concerned, fortunate. The explanation for that good luck will, I am sexistically convinced, strike most men as obvious and baffle and bore most women. I had treated myself to a taxi, you see, and since Torremolinos is east of Benalmadena, the taxi was heading west, and, this being Abroad, the car was on the right, so, to get to the pubs, I didn't have to cross the road, whereas I would have had to if coming in from the west or if the pubs and not the hotels were to the south. Anyway, the thing is, I didn't have to risk crossing the bloody road, okay?

Having paid the taxi – risible tip, natch – I wandered along the N340 (northside) and admired the array of hostelries. The Bees' Knees, claiming to offer The Roast of the Coast. Bogey's. Buzby's Fun Pub. The Tavern. The Good Companions. Lillie Langtry's. Molly Malone's. Tom's Manhattan Bar. Chubby's. The Doghouse. (Spain? I love it.)

It's not that these places weren't inviting. Apart from The Doghouse, which was shut. They just looked a bit too full of families or groups of people, or a bit too couply-douply. I was after a bit of action, me. And after a short walk back in the direction of Torremolinos (that's to say, *east*), action is what I found in the shape of Twenty-Four-Hour Square, so called because it is open twenty-four hours a day and is, in addition, a square. I hung around, appraising the glory of neon and waiting for one of the many proppers to give me tickets for free entrance. But which of the many discos to go to first? Should it be the Borsalino Palace? Or the Mango Disco? Then again, the Sol Y Mar Music Pub looked like a happening place . . .

I hung around a little longer. Long enough to be disconcertingly reminded of not being propped in Fuengirola. Of course, it was much easier to be propped if you weren't on your own. By dint of some smart manoeuvering, I attached myself to a bunch of blokes wearing the uniform of the Irish football strip. In the five yards that I managed to march covertly by their side they all collected sheaves of leaflets and I amassed one flyer for a car-rental firm.

I knew it had been the right decision to go solo again when an outrageously mini-skirted brunette approached me. I smiled in readiness.

She smiled back. 'Are you waiting for Anastasia?' she asked.

Dumbfounded, I gestured that I wasn't but wouldn't mind giving it a shot.

'You're not Mr Chambers, then?'

'No, I'm not. I'm sorry.'

She looked peeved. 'Well, he said he'd be here by now.'

'Who's Mr Chambers?'

I might have asked her what year it was.

'He's coming to *collect* us. Anastasia's *dad*.'

What? This one must have been at least seventeen, so how . . .? Well, that's ridiculous. I didn't even give Anastasia's pal the courtesy of a goodbye and stomped up the road. There was always the Jive Bunny British Fun Pub, I suggested to myself, but thought the better of it. The Silver Pub across the road looked more promising, especially the two girls at a table near the front. I took up position by the bar, where I was to spend the next hour chain-drinking and plucking up the courage to chat to them.

I'm really sorry about this but there's no story here, no anecdote, no punch-line. I just didn't have enough courage to pluck up. It was an hour fraught with nerves and one that ended when they departed for the Mango Disco and I sloped back to the taxi-rank. Something else happened in the queue there but I don't want to talk about it. Women, eh? Tcch.

Now, *tonight* was going to be different. It had been a good day. I'd bought my own souvenirs – those little fans really were very reasonably priced – and tidied up the flat, so I owed it to myself to have a good old Friday night out. And where better to start than Combat Alley?

Almost any other street in the world, is a possible answer, and one I came up with after a solitary mooch up and down its length. But the outlook brightened on my second sortie; I bumped into Nidge again and we exchanged a few words, after I reminded him who I was and where we'd met. And there was, as ever, Oliver.

'My man, my man, my man, what's up?'

'Oliver, great to see you.'

'Where's the other one?'

'Oh, he split couple of nights ago.'

'Drag. You need any more E?'

More Ecstasy! More bliss. And after that, more. And more. A life of endless, drifting contentment. 'No, thanks, Oliver . . . How are you doing?'

'Cool. See you around, yeah?'

I walked up to the main street where, after only a little while, I was – way hay! – propped. For, what is more, the Palladium. This leaflet was different from the others, with a relatively complex rubric in Spanish and English. Well, I say English . . . 'Friday 31th,' it read, 'we invite you to our 3th Birthday. Will be a lot of *cava* and cake and a magnific lotery of a nice regard. Don't loose it.'

Too right I wouldn't loose it. I hurried along to the

Palladium, where, already by one, there was a promising queue. Inside, the noise was deafening, the strobes were manic, dry ice was billowing around me, and the guy with the Flowerpot Men hat was dancing on a table and blowing his whistle. I found a tiny space where, thrilled by the hammering bass, I started to dance myself, and by myself, though right next to an awesomely sexy blonde and with an excellent view of a lingerie model swallow-diving in the pool.

Some seductive hip shimmying and oriental hand movements later, I took five. Time for some *cava* and cake, which was being handed out on a podium overlooking the pool. I joined the mêlée and finally secured my freebees. The cake wasn't too bad, not too much aerated gunge, and the *cava* (that's Spanish for champagne-style sparkling wine, by the way) not *too* warm. I spectated indulgingly as two lads cleared a space around them to give an exhibition of break-dancing. This entire scene changed when the DJ switched the music to a very familiar thudding intro, an intro that was greeted by screams of approval and a universal move to the dance-floor. Almost universal. I stood on the poolside podium on my own, munching cake and sipping warm *cava* to the tune of 'Please Don't Go'.

Everyone seemed to be having a brilliant time, whooping and running on the spot and blowing whistles and pretending to be trees swaying in the breeze. I'd been like that once. Happy. Not a care in the world. Before Paul left me.

'BABE. AH LIRVE YOU SOH. AN AH WAN-CHOO TWO NOH. THAT AHM. GONNA MISS YIH LIRVE. THE MINUTE YEW WALK OUT THAT DOH. PLEASE DOHN GOH.'

I went. I just walked out that door, I can tell you. The magnific lotery and its nice regard? I haven't a clue. Give me a break, will you?

*

'Do you come here often?'

'No, not really, I can't say I do. Not really.'

'Lucky for me you came here tonight then, isn't it?'

Thank you, Jesus. Finally, after four weeks on a coastline famous for summery romance – or, at the very least,
summery creaking bed-springs – I was being chatted up.

'Kim.'

'Harry.'

'So where do you come from, Harry?'

'London. But I come from Scotland.'

'Scotland!'

'And you?'

'Denmark. Copenhagen. A beautiful city. What is it
you do, Harry?'

'I'm a sort of journalist.'

'How interesting!'

'What about you?'

'I'm a policeman. A detective.'

'Now, that's much more interesting than mine.'

'Some days are good. It's like any other job, I think.'

Kim and I covered a range of topics – the necessity of
holidays, the footballing success of Denmark's national
side, why Scotland should be independent – while I
awaited the tardy arrival of my other new best friend,
Brian. He and I had arranged to meet in this café in the
Pueblo Blanco, a side-street off the Calle Casablanca, at
eleven. It was now twenty to midnight. Well, I didn't
mind at all . . .

According to both Brian and the *Spartacus* guide, the
Pueblo Blanco was a key gay meeting-point, but my
initial impression of it made me think that both Brian
and the *Spartacus* guide were either barking or very out of
touch. What I had seen at first was an alley containing
an unlikely number of cafés, pubs and disco-bars, and an
impossible number of people. I had begun to shuffle
forward in a crowd of a density I've known only at the
exits of big football grounds. The crowd was exclusively

comprised of effervescent, prosperous, straight Spanish teenagers elaborately and deafeningly courting each other. Ten minutes on, and three-quarters of the way along its thirty yards, I could only conclude that the Pueblo Blanco was the biggest Scout disco in the world. A few minutes and yards later, my heel-to-toe progress had brought me to a firebreak in this jungle of yelling, yelping pubescents, and I had glimpsed civilization – a fetching courtyard of restaurants and bars. The court-yard was packed with men but, by comparison with the crowd I'd just left, it had seemed welcomely underpopu-lated.

Eventually Brian turned up and, quite a few drinks and topics later, he and I bade Kim farewell. He looked gallingly consolable at my leaving. It was a business getting out of that place, but a policy of tactful and constant elbowing, shoving and kneeing cleared our path eventually. Thence to Pourquoi Pas, which wasn't as quiet as we'd hoped, owing to the booming presence of two pukka-voiced Englishmen anxious to display the fact that they were very much in love. The one with the even louder pukka voice was in his very well-preserved mid-fifties, beautifully dressed and with the classiest bald-patch-concealing haircut I have ever seen. The slightly less ear-shattering one was some twenty years younger and could afford the luxury of cropped hair as well as a work-out vest that revealed a splendidly exercised body.

They really irked me, that pair, not just because of the decibel-level of their endearments and avowals but also because I'd seen them somewhere before. Brian came up with the answer. They were actors. Not famous, but successful enough to be familiar. They were of the calibre who get bumped off before the first ad break in *The Sweeney*, or run the antique shop where Kate O'Mara is taken aback in mid-browse by the arrival of an old flame who whisks her off for coffee and the confession that his stud farm is in big trouble. The way those guys were creating, you'd think they'd come hot-foot from starring in all twenty-six episodes of the latest Alan Bleasdale. It was a huge bonus when, after some ostentatious debate, they decided they would take themselves and their mutual love elsewhere. At last we could plan the evening ahead.

'It's your final night,' said Brian, 'so you decide.'

'Disco?'

'Fine. Let's see. Far too early for the Bronx or Bavaria . . . The obvious place is next door at the 801.'

I remembered what Maithe had said about the dancing there being good, especially around two. It was just after one now. 'Perfect,' I said. 'A drink for the road?'

'What a good idea.'

'. . . Brian, I hope you won't think this offensive, but I am slightly nervous about going to the 801. The floor-show aspect of things. That slogan on the poster about feeling the best . . .'

'Nothing to worry about. Audience participation isn't compulsory, you know. And it's a disco, for God's sake. There won't be a floor-show tonight.'

'Another thing. I don't want to . . . cramp your style.'

'Nor I yours.'

Maithe had been right about the dancing. You could just about squeeze two tennis courts into the 801 but the place made the Palladium look as joyfully uninhibited as a Wee Free wedding. The music was so loud there was no question of using speech to order our drinks so I mimed two gin and tonics at a stupendously attractive barman and just watched those guys dance. Were they all professional, or what? Brian had real difficulty persuading me on to the floor. I did it for him and I really did my best but have never felt such a klutz to music since not learning the Dashing White Sergeant in the school gym. I lasted five minutes and retired gracelessly to the bar, leaving Brian gyrating and grooving with the best of them.

There was a tiny consolation to be had in the fact that two other people stood out in this carefree crowd – the transvestite at the other end of the bar and the elder of the two ack-tors. His partner was expertly striking a lot of muscled attitudes (hands behind head, lots of hip-flexing and groin-rotating), but every movement the elder of the pair made shouted that he was not happy and here under severe duress. He was even worse than me. Hah!

Even so, the dancing of all the others was too good to watch for long, so I switched my attention to the video high behind the bar. And I realized afresh that there's a distinguishing feature of porn other than that it portrays people having some kind of sexual experience. It's silly. With the clarity of disinterest, I followed most of a short film – American, to judge by the yellow block-lettering of the credits, the Dougs and Dirks of the cast, and the plasticky, toothy, Thunderbirdsy look of same.

Doug and Dirk were replaced in mid-sesh by a new video, one that had been shot on a pretty ropey Cam-corder. It showed a disco-floor whereon disported a massive black guy with a shy-makingly long cock. Egged on by his cheering fans, he selected one of their number and stripped him, played with his member, waggled his own about and mimicked putting that in the guy's mouth while he sat on his face. It was all tremendously good-humoured, but it worried me. Half-way through watching this videoed performance, I had recognized the venue. It was here. So *that* was the floor-show.

There was a floor-show of sorts that night, but not of the kind I had just witnessed on video. It was signalled by a dramatic change in the music, from the Village People to some kind of Spanish guitar voluntary. At that all the non-Spaniards left the dance-floor. Even the younger ack-tor. Brian hurried towards me.

'Watch this,' he instructed, redundantly.

There were several dozen men left on the floor. At the

sound of the first chord they had all immediately struck the haughty pose you always associate with flamenco, so I bawled at Brian to ask if that was what they were going to dance.

'This is a bit different. It's the sevillana.'

Given a couple of years, I might just come up with a paragraph that accurately described that dance. Probably not. I don't even know how long it lasted. Fifteen minutes? Thirty? I can only say that it was like flamenco but a little statelier and far more joyous, involving a lot of turns and stamping and grace, to music that swooped and swirled.

That dance was one of the most magnificent things I have ever seen and it has depressed me ever since. The insight took a while to occur to me but finally it did – like every other Northern European male, I am woefully incapable of creating even a travesty of such a beautiful, proud, sexy display. Those guys can dance the sevillana. I can pretend to be a tree.

In due course, I said goodbye to Brian and left the 801 to walk back to the flat for the last time. Back in Benyamina, getting on for four, I repaired to the balcony to watch the planes. I was armed with a hefty brandy, a thick spliff and my Walkman. It was a matter of real regret to me that I didn't have any sevillana-type music, but this tape would do. I clicked it in, adjusted the headphones and thumbed the volume up to ten.

I gazed contentedly down at a fair chunk of Torremolinos and up at the planes whizzing into the night sky. Inside my head there was a disco. 'PLEASE DOHN GOH. DOHN GOH OH OH OH OH. DOHN GOH AWAY.'

3
Marbella

It *was* him. He was window-shopping, oddly enough, outside the Boutique Esmerelda, intrigued by its selection of hats and beachwear. He himself was sporting, somewhat uncharacteristically, a migrainous shirt and purple patterned shorts.

I couldn't pass up the chance to talk to him. I *had* to do this.

'Mr Connery,' I said as I approached. 'Can I just say what a very great pleasure it is to meet you?'

There was, I swear, more than a hint of a demure smile below his quizzical frown. (He really was astonishingly handsome.) Encouraged, I persevered.

'Perhaps I could offer you a drink? Actually, I'm writing something about Marbella and I'd be hugely grateful if I could ask you a few questions.'

He still said nothing in reply, but there was still that hint of a smile.

'But if you don't want to be pestered, I'd quite understand. Please, though, let me buy you a drink. You've always been, well, one hesitates to say role model, but certainly a hero of mine.'

For a moment, Sean looked utterly baffled. What would he say? 'Come over to my housh for a drink' would be ideal. But a 'shplendid to meet you' would be more than enough. What Sean actually did was shrug and point towards a sign for the Oficina de Turismo.

'*Paracaracarosamente,*' he said, before smiling helpfully and walking away.

It was an understandable mistake, honestly. For a kick-off, if there had been a Sean Connery Lookalike Contest, the great man himself would have been pipped for first place by that guy. And anyway, I continued to reason, as I put my head in my hands and tried not to curl up into the embryo position, Marbella is supposed to be the haunt of the rich and famous, and, famously, of Sean Connery. Cilla Black had been spotted the week before at a restaurant just up the road. Bruce Forsyth, alas, has a place just outside town. And Jimmy Tarbuck. And Shirley Bassey, who was said to have been sighted recently near one of the prom's amusement arcades. I'd met people who'd known people who'd definitely seen Sean Connery walking around the town, just like a person.

But I should have guessed he wasn't really him. It was too much like good luck, on my second day here, bumping into the one man I would have killed to bump into. The shirt was a bit of a giveaway, I suppose. And, on reflection, it had to be admitted that Sean Connery has never been the sort to wear purple patterned shorts.

'Marbella: the showpiece resort of the Costa del Sol,' trumpets the Marbella issue of the *Everything Under the Sun* guide-books. 'Tourism in Marbella is a state of the art,' it goes on to explain. Here I would find 'the international **jet set**,' 'the truly grand, the mere poseurs and the ordinary mortals,' for this was a 'celebrity playground'. At last. Fuengirola had felt more like a PTA meeting and Torremolinos like a school dance organized by Keith Richard, so a playground was just what I needed.

In a rare bout of research I'd read that Marbella has the highest per capita income in Europe and that only London has more Rolls-Royces. Well, I thought, when I arrived here, it all just goes to show that appearances can be deceptive, doesn't it? I'd led myself to expect a modern equivalent of Nice, all boulevards and swish hotels, and everything bespoke and exclusive. Yet the outskirts, save for a brief rash of car showrooms, looked mundane. Even, in some places, poor. When I had arrived in the centre, things had seemed a bit better, but not significantly. Fair enough, this impression was gained from the vantage-point of the bus station, but my initial trek down the main street to the tourist office yielded no sights of glittering wondrousness.

Four weeks on the Costa had bequeathed me the confidence not to worry about amateurish nonsense of booking accommodation beforehand. I'd just turn up at the tourist office, check into a hotel for a day if need be, then rent myself an apartment. I could do what I liked because I wasn't going to be encumbered by any companion for this fortnight. No, I would be muscling in on the international **jet set** on my own. I'd duck and dive, play it by ear, be cool at all times, and, before I knew it, I'd be toasting the good health of Cilla Black. With money provided by some sobbingly grateful sugar mummy. Okay, so the place didn't look up to much so far, but I'd suss out the in places soon enough.

It was at the tourist office that my attitude changed a little. From confidence to fear. My guide-book had assured me that there were over fifty hotels in Marbella, and enough rooms and apartments to accommodate 400,000 people, five times the resident population. Yes, but the difficulty I faced was that, this being August, there were already 400,001 people in the town. And, never having been a great one for learning from my mistakes, I'd overlooked the prevailing discrimination against the one-person family.

So what was available? Apartments? None. Maybe something next week but the boy at the tourist office was doubtful. The Marbella Club Hotel had a single room: 24,000 pesetas plus 6 per cent tax, not for a week but for one night. What about the Andalucia Plaza? Only 14,000 pesetas a night there. No? Perhaps I should try another town, the boy said, while appraising my clothes to estimate my spending-power. Had I thought of Torremolinos?

I ended up lugging my luggage into Marbella's old quarter, a warren of squares and hilly lanes quite unlike the concrete ordinariness of the main street. So now I knew why one of the brochures declared that Marbella was a city of contrasts. The one contrast bugging me was that of the spruce elegance of the people strolling around compared to my own sweat-soaked dishevelment as I sought the *hostal* (that's Spanish for cheap hotel) recommended by the tourist office boy. It did have a single room. It was a sultry box but it wasn't 24,000 pesetas a night. This, then, would be the headquarters for my raids on the haunts of the slick and sleek.

Marbella is thirty-eight years old. Some might argue that the town is really two thousand years old, seeing that there was a settlement here for the Romans to take over and then an earthquake to destroy it in 365, and that it had become a walled Arab city called Marbil-la by the tenth century. The same pedants would also point out that there was such a thing as the Peace of Marbella, ending internecine Moslem conflict in 1285, that Marbella had become a busy lead-mining town by the eighteenth century, and that for centuries it had also prospered intermittently from iron-works, vineyards and sugar mills. They might add that not many thirty-eight-year-old towns have a higgledy-piggledy old quarter with a sixteenth-century church.

Details, details. The Marbella that is a celebrity playground and holiday home of international jet-setters was invented in 1954 when Prince Alfonso Hohenlohe of Lichtenstein kidnapped the beautiful Princess Maria, heiress to Andorra's throne, to be thwarted by Errol Flynn, whose swashbuckling rescue earned him Maria's fair hand.

Sorry. Start again. The Marbella that is a celebrity etcetera was invented in 1954 by Prince Alfonso Hohenlohe of Lichtenstein. I know, I know, and my one answer to all the obvious questions is, beats me. I don't even know how to pronounce the man's name; my best guess sounds like a greeting pronounced by Bluebottle. Be that as it may. This unlikely character had the ridiculous idea of setting up an exclusive establishment in Marbella, a town that by 1954 had so benefited under Franco that it had developed into a small, scummy fishing village notable for its spectacular unemployment figures. The establishment would be a twelve-room hotel-cum-club, and it would be called the Marbella Club Hotel. Guests, attracted no doubt by its imaginative title, included Gina Lollobrigida, Frank Sinatra and the Duke and Duchess of Windsor. In 1957 the four-star El Fuerte hotel opened in the town. Then the Melia Don Pepe hotel sprang up. Then the Don Carlos, the Puente Romano, the casino, the golf-courses, the villas, and, before you knew it, Marbella was the centre of a coastline that desperately wanted to be called the Spanish Riviera.

Sheikhs and the like have nurtured a particular fondness for the place. King Fahd of Saudi Arabia has a place opposite the Marbella Club Hotel on the Golden Mile west of the town. It's the usual holiday home, an imitation White House with its own mosque and heliport. Adnan Kashoggi, prince of peace and all-round great guy, has been a regular here, in his modest £34 million estate, enjoying the fruits of his labour and vision.

Even with such regular visitors as Kashoggi, and Forsyth and Tarbuck, Marbella has somehow never achieved its ambition to rival Monaco. It has attracted cash rather than cachet. And, sad to tell, it suffered something of a decline in the late eighties. Addicts were seen on the streets. Litter was sighted. Thank goodness that a saviour was at hand.

Marbella's can-do new mayor, Jesus Gil y Gil, has been a celebrity in Spain for several decades. His face alone would mark him out as someone special, since he is the only Spaniard to possess no regular features. He looks like a cartoon of himself. Or a potato. Not that I would say that to him in person because he is also very large and very short-tempered. Gil first sprang to fame in 1969 when a property he developed proved not to have been developed enough. A small matter of a restaurant collapsing. Fifty-eight people dead. The inquiry discovered that, to cut costs, Gil had built the restaurant without the services of an architect, or, indeed, an engineer. Showing a flagrant disrespect for the entrepreneurial spirit, the court found Gil guilty of criminal negligence. The poor man was fined two million quid and sentenced to five years in prison. Fortunately, he was eventually pardoned by Franco.

One of the many controversial episodes surrounding Gil started in the late eighties, when he became president of Atletico Madrid football club. Always one for speaking his mind, Gil announced that unappreciative supporters were ne'er-do-wells from families of junkies and whores. Gil appointed as manager Ron Atkinson, who hauled Atletico from the threat of relegation up to third place in ninety-four days. So Gil sacked him. He sacked the team's captain for smoking. He sacked another player for being single. It may come as no shock to learn that at one time Gil had twenty-one law suits pending against him.

Gil was prompted to stand as mayor for Marbella because its falling reputation meant he couldn't sell two expensive apartment blocks that were part of his sizeable property portfolio in the town. The place had to be sorted out, and he reckoned he was the man to do the sorting. He established his own political party – the Grupo Indipendiente Liberal (great acronym) – and won the 1991 election in a landslide. He immediately set about cleaning the place up. On one occasion this involved Gil, plus many policemen, confronting some locals who were drinking outside at three in the morning. Gil told them they were 'scum' and 'drug addicts'. In the ensuing debate thirty people were injured and a police car was burned.

A year into his reign, the results of other Gil initiatives were everywhere to be seen. Palm trees. Flowers. Lots of police. Lots of posters proclaiming the initiatives of the GIL party. All the pavements edged in blue and white, not the traditional colours of the town but of the GIL party. You can tell where Marbella's town limits are on the N340 because the central reservation suddenly stops being coloured blue and white. Even the triumphal arch Gil has built at the town's easterly entrance is decorated in blue and white (not, sadly, in the gold leaf he really wanted). Compared to Marbella's new mayor, Robert Maxwell was self-effacing.

Marbella thinks it's found a messiah in Jesus Gil, but it hasn't. He's promised that Marbella will soon outclass Monaco, but it won't. Not unless it transforms itself into a city-state with its own monarchy and Grand Prix and the world's most famous casino. Still, Marbella is attracting back many of the wealth-creators I wanted to mingle with, so on my first evening here I set about entering its high society. I would have a shower and everything, and leave my *hostal* in search of . . . I was never sure, but it was my unswerving aim to go somewhere dead posh. Somewhere where I might bump into Sean.

The price of a room there, and the fact that it had a casino, made the Andalucia Plaza hotel seem a promising place to start. Less promising was that it was a fairly long taxi-ride out of town, and I had to stump up an entrance fee to the casino and hand in my passport. Puts you in a really good mood, that. I walked into a room the size of a postal district. Every one of the many, many tables was crowded. At each blackjack table the croupier seemed to be reliably starting with a face card and finishing with a face card. I saw a couple of punters amass four cards worth fourteen or so, but every time – whoops! – there was a ten. (No one – curiously – seemed surprised by this, so it must have been coincidence, mustn't it?) The blackjack games looked predictable but they were at least quick. The rounds, or whatever you call them, of roulette were predictable and slow. In the outside world, frontiers had shifted, ice-floes had melted, the unborn had turned senile, and here in the exciting casino the croupier was still placing counters on the table with his glass scoop. One quick spin of the wheel and them he'd be raking all the counters back in. Goodness, what fun gambling looked.

There weren't even any rich or famous people here. I'd hoped for a glimpse of, at the bare minimum, Cilla. No cigar. Chilled by the air-conditioning and bored witless, I retrieved my passport and hailed a taxi back to my sultry box. Almost 3000 pesetas that evening rushed me, and I hadn't had anything to eat or – help, help! – drink.

The next day I went back along the Golden Mile to try my luck at finding Sean, or at least some Second Division celebs, by hanging round the Marbella Club Hotel. What a place. Past the limo-spattered car park I found a vast sub-tropical garden dotted with villas and bungalows. This wasn't a hotel. It was a village. Let me bore you awhile with some information from leaflets I snaffled there. The Marbella Club Hotel has expanded from Prince Hehehello's twelve rooms to comprise the following: seventy rooms, twenty-three suites, cottages with private gardens and pools, three restaurants, three bars, two swimming-pools (one heated in winter), eleven-court tennis club, fitness centre, beauty spa, branch of Harrods, beach club, paddle tennis courts and gymnasium. (By the way, one of these is made up.) Village? There are *cities* with less.

One of the leaflets advertised a five-day, five-hour, beauty-care programme for male guests: two facial treatments, one facial lymph drainage, three complete body massages, three bath sessions (relaxing and ozone), two body lymph drainages, two foot-reflex massages, one medical pedicure, and a supervised tan. Whatever all that meant, it was surely a snip at 46,000 pesetas. Christ, a coffee was 600 pesetas. A single room for one night was a bargain at 24,000 pesetas – I could have paid 140,000 for one night in a bungalow. Eight hundred quid? You could buy Partick Thistle a goalkeeper for less.

Having banned myself from the bar, I toured the grounds. Like everyone else, I was dressed for tennis, but there was no way I could pass muster as a guest. I didn't have a big gold watch. My face hadn't been drained of lymphs. I tried to look like I'd come to repair a jacuzzi.

The sub-tropical garden was endless and beautiful. Dinky paths meandered through olive trees, orange blossom, bougainvillaea, waterfalls, pools. The guests were beautiful as well, nurtured and tended by cheques. Unfortunately, none of the guests was Sean. None of them had even performed at a Royal Variety gala or hosted a game-show. No sign either of the two home-grown celebs of the Marbella Club Hotel – lovable, eccentric Don Jaime de Mora y Aragon, erstwhile piano-player at the hotel, and working-class heroine Gunilla von Bismarck. (I'd never heard of the pair before I came here, but local papers and guide-books always mention them, so I thought I had better too.)

Maybe I'd have better luck at the sister hotel, the Puente Romano, a short but sweaty walk down the road. Its sub-tropical garden seemed even larger but it contained no visible glitterati. Actually, I thought the place was a bit downmarket. Nearly two hundred suites and rooms and only three swimming-pools? Come on. However, it did have Olivia Valere, allegedly one of Marbella's in discos, so I returned that night to shmooze with the chic.

Most of my schmoozing was with the bouncer. He didn't like the look of me or my dusty espadrilles, but my legendary charm, plus the distraction of a nymphet asking him about taxis, secured my entry into a disco constructed of glass and leather. At one in the morning, the dance-floor had yet to warm up. One man, who may have been paid to do so, was dancing superbly and alone amidst an excitable light display. There was much more action at the bar where handsome men were being debonair with women who looked like the women in backing groups or hairdressers' photographs. I wormed my way to the counter, through an assault course of teeth and hair and cleavage. Now came the wonderful boon of that night – the barman was busy, so I had time to look at the drinks list.

Fine. I now know that there are creatures on this planet who will pay for a cocktail what I would pay for a three-course meal with wine. The cover charge dictated that even a glass of juice or a beer would be £15. Or I could buy myself a bottle of Johnnie Walker Red Label for 23,000 pesetas, the price of a return flight from Gatwick to Malaga. Perhaps Olivia Valere was a theme pub evoking the last days of Weimar.

No one else was perturbed by these preposterous noughts. What do you have to earn to bat no eyelids at handing over the equivalent of thirteen tenners for a bottle of blended whisky? Who *were* these people? Not only were they incomparably wealthier *and* far better-looking than me, they were younger. Jesus.

Armed with no drink but a ferociously bad mood, I sulked off in my dusty espadrilles (three quid the pair) to the neighbouring cabaret-bar. Well, not to the bar, naturally, but to a small space by the nearest wall, where I was surrounded by many more suave men and much more teeth, hair and cleavage. This convention of juvenile millionaires was being energetically entertained by a salsa-ing trio, one of whom I thought might be Cuban and was certainly the most beautiful woman with whom I have ever shared oxygen space. (If you read this, whoever you are, write to me. We are destined to be together.) I stayed there for as long as a raging thirst allowed me, then went to the loo for a free drink of water. Sean wasn't there either.

Nor was he to be seen the following night at the El Fuerte, a peach building where the drinks were cheaper than at Olivia Valere. No surprise in that, since the prices almost anywhere else in the world would have to have fewer zeros in them, even if they were given in lire. The drawback was that there were no coiffured million-aires at the El Fuerte. What would have been the attrac-tion for them in spending a normal amount of money of an evening?

The hotel had abandoned itself to the giddy debauch that is a dinner-dance. A handful of women aged between four and seventy were waltzing to a medley of golden oldies which were being expertly mauled by some local combo. 'And send all my laughing too yoo,' they sang. 'All my laughing. Lie lie lie lie lie. . .'

There was only one thing to do. Run away.

I had a problem. After four nights I'd come no nearer to meeting Sean. Or Brucie. Or Cilla. Or, far more perti-nently, a sugar mummy whom I'd pleasure in many and various ways in return for hard currency. And money was something I needed desperately. I was being cleaned out by taxis, a daily burger and occasional glasses of water. Even sultry boxes do not come cheap in Marbella in August, and the boy in the tourist office had just informed me that the cheapest apartments had definitely all been taken. Homeless penury loomed. I was in the soup.

There was a faint ray of hope. It came from the phone number of the one person I knew who lived here. If I played my cards right . . .

Nigel Bowden was promisingly friendly, ribbing me about my alleged singing the previous time we'd met, in Fuengirola. And something about my trying to talk to the waiter in Spanish. I had to put him right on that because I can hardly speak a word of the language. Then I'd fallen asleep in a basket of bread. Well, there was an element of truth in that, but still . . . Anyway, did he, by any chance, know of any cheap places to rent? No? Ah, that was a pity because in that case I'd be forced to sleep rough for ten days. He would? Oh, that was too kind. No, I didn't mind at all that he and his family were leaving on holiday tomorrow. No, his daughter's bedroom sounded ideal. If he could just give me his address . . .

Thus it was that I found myself staying in a house in Marbella's northern outskirts, in a room full of gonks. Not quite what the juvenile millionaires would be used to but it was a hell of a lot better than a sultry box. Or a cardboard one.

This was rather agreeable. A house to myself, an end to luggage-laden quests for hotel rooms, fewer feverish bouts of mental arithmetic to assess how near I was to my Visa limit. Close, was now the answer to that one, so I took to spending time rather than money, by pursuing the cut-price hobby of people-watching. I'd make my way into the centre, sprinting in terror across the ring-road, then assuming a nonchalant air stroll for the rest of the journey down through a modern high-rise scheme to the old quarter and Marbella's main drag.

Here I'd join in the local sport of window-shopping. This is not a terribly well-informed opinion, but I thought the shops were crap. Marbella conjures up, does it not, an image of expensive boutiques? There were a few of those but far more ironmongers and kitchen-mop franchises. There was even a branch of Dorothy Perkins. I rest my case.

It was outside Dorothy Perkins, where I was admiring an artistic display of high-thigh swimwear, that I saw my favourite window-shoppers of the fortnight. They were typical swanners-about-Marbella, a wealthy, well-preserved couple in their late thirties. He was wearing a Donald Duck T-shirt, track-suit bottoms, and Ray-Bans balanced on his coiffure. She had on a grey leotard, short pink shorts, and pink sockettes above sparkly trainers. The kind of sports kit that you're not supposed to play sport in. She was also glancing covertly at the Dorothy Perkins window. Not covertly. Almost shiftily. It's only high-thigh swimwear, I thought. They're not selling handcuffs or rubber frocks. The couple moved on and both gave a wine shop a furtive once-over. Same stealthy inspection of a chemist's. What was it with these guys?

I think it was in fact an ironmonger's where the woman gave the game away. She couldn't stand the tension any longer. She just stopped, full-frontalled the shop window and hand-combed her mane of dyed, tinted, highlighted, crimped and waved blonde-ish hair. Bastards weren't window-shopping at all. They'd been maintaining a constant check on their reflections.

They were strong contenders in my Wealthy Well-Preserved Arsehole of the Fortnight championship, but they were pipped by the male member of a wealthy, well-preserved couple in their late forties who took the table next to mine at a café on the promenade. Both of them were a little out of sorts after a hard day on the beach. After they'd flopped themselves and their various bags of essential seaside cosmetics down, the male member ordered their drinks.

'Yuh, I want a beer. And a shandy for my wife.'

The young, evidently non-Anglophone, barman squinted diffidently.

'A beer and a shandy,' repeated the male member.

'Beer, *si*. And . . .?'

Well, we all know there's only one way to deal with a

Spic when he's being stupid. Shout at the bugger. Slowly.

'A BEER. AND A SHANDY. *COMPRENDAY*?'

'Señor . . .' The young barman, anxious, and unable, to please, gave a little shrug of dismay.

'LOOK HERE. A BEER, OKAY? GOOD. AND. A. BLOODY. SHANDY.'

'Ah, bloody Mary. *Si*.'

'OY. COME BACK, YOU FOOL. All right, all right. A BEER, YES? AND, um, ORANGE JUICE. JUICE DO ORANGE.'

'Si, señor. *Zumo de naranje*.'

'NO, YOU CRETIN. *ORANGE JUICE*. Oh, for fuck's sake, this is hopeless. Come on, Erica, we're going somewhere else. YOU'RE AN IDIOT, YES? EEH DEE OH. Christ, we never had this trouble even in Martinique.'

Sunbathing was cheap as well. My tan was coming along splendidly. I now looked like I had jaundice. Interestingly and disappointingly, there was much less topless sun-worship here than in the other resorts. The beaches were different as well. Not only were they quieter, they contained mock oases with palm trees and showers camouflaged as the trunks of sculpted elephants. Sweet.

Having stood under some Babar to be hosed down, I'd usually take a little air along the promenade, where, by day, there'd be many people walking nowhere at one mile an hour, and, by night, a lot of noise from youths hanging out in the beachside bars below. Plus, of course, even more people walking nowhere at one mile an hour.

There weren't more youths hanging out below the promenade because some of the young at heart and the young-young favoured Banana Beach. Crazy name, crazy place. You could go bungee-jumping there in the daytime. (Had it not been for a long-standing knee problem I'd have done it like a shot. Honestly, I was really jealous of those privileged enough to leap from a cage hundreds of feet in the air with only a rubber band to stop them from leaping head-first into the sand.) In the evenings Banana Beach provided a network of bars dotted about an oversized, open-air, concrete disco which blared out the latest Eurobop (i.e., 'Rhythm is a Dancer' and 'Please Don't Go') to a high-voiced, barely menstruating clientele. Banana Beach was a new, purpose-built initiative designed to replace the old, ramshackle beach bars with a proper, organized place. It was the disco equivalent of Milton Keynes.

I went there once with a crowd from Nottingham I fell in with one splendid night. (There were normal tourists to be found in Marbella if you looked hard enough.) We did not linger in Banana Beach but walked straight through it and down to the last remaining beach bar, where a live group was bashing out competent cover versions and the *cerveza* flowed freely. So much so that we had to make frequent visits to the unusual alfresco lavatory facility. Which leads me to offer this advice: if you ever visit Banana Beach, don't go swimming.

I came across the Nottingham crowd in a little place in the old quarter called The English Tavern. I have to confess, though, that I also began to frequent Spanish places. Don't get me wrong, it was only because some of them were really cheap. Especially the locals in the high-rise scheme south of the colon-irrigating ring-road. I found one place where a beer was sixty pesetas, half the price of English bars and forty times less expensive than Olivia Valere. The barman was very pleasant, which might have been remarkable because on leaving I spotted a notice that makes me suspect I'd been drinking in a private club for the disabled.

The bar-club contained three customers/members and a very large television showing a bullfight. Now, bullfight-

ing has been described many times before, often by
Ernest Hemingway, so there's no way I'm going to have
a shot at capturing the passion/disgrace/glory/spectacle
of the event. However, I did think I had gained a new
insight into Andalusia's pet sport, one that even Hemingway had missed. It was at the moment when the man on
the armour-plated horse was sticking little spears into
the bull's back that an old chap in the bar shouted
'Bull!' He did it again when the bull was charging one of
the matador's back-up team: 'Bull!' And during what I
thought was a lull after the animal had been killed:
'Bull!'

While I wondered what I'd missed, the programme
took a break for adverts. It struck me as incongruous,
somehow, looking at images of fruit juice and cars speeding around in quarries, after watching the ceremonial
killing of a beast. Now it was a yuppie eating some cereal.
'Bull!' shouted the old chap. Back to the studio and some
gabbling presenter. 'Bull!' So that was the explanation.
He was insane. (There's a moral for all of us in that tale,
especially for those of us who write about things in
foreign countries, but I'd much prefer to ignore it.)

In one Spanish bar-restaurant I even went native to
the extent of eating some *tapas*. Very nice, too. Almost
worth the embarrassment of asking for it. I must have
seemed as socially challenged as the 'Bull!'-heckler. I
mean, I don't usually order in a British bar by just
pointing at something and saying 'Pliz.'

I did strike up a conversation there with my neighbour
at the counter, in the monoglot style of the furious man
in Fuengirola, me in pidgin English, my neighbour
mainly in sign language. But it's amazing how you get
by, and I was able to appreciate the fellow's earthy
common sense and his deep, intuitive knowledge of the
seasons. To be more precise, the football season, for we
were watching a televised friendly featuring Atletico
Madrid. Gil's team was advertising Gil's town, with

strips carrying the slogan, 'Marbella'. With many gestures, my neighbour told me that Marbella's own team is magnificent, and, by playing an open, attacking game, has risen for the first time to the eminence of the Second Division. Possibly. He also conveyed that Malaga's football team is forever in decline. That he worked for Marbella town council, morning, noon and night, either driving a lorry or laundering shirts. And that Jesus Gil was a man as deserved to have his throat cut.

This was going to be a great moment in my life. I hurried over to meet him at the glass-topped bar.

'I hope I'm not late,' I said.

'Not at all. I'm early.'

'First of all, I want to say thanks so much for agreeing to meet me. You must be very busy and I appreciate this hugely.'

'No problem. I've only got a game-show to record tomorrow. And I live nearby . . .'

'I assume you like it here.'

'Good golfing, wonderful climate, great people. Itsh a shpeshul plaish.'

'It must be. Now, can I get you a drink?'

'A whishky would be very welcome.'

'A whisky for Mr Connery, please, and a glass of mineral water for me.'

'Coming up, sir. That'll be five thousand four hundred pesetas.'

'But that's exactly thirty pounds!'

'There is naturally a cover charge, *señor*.'

'Ish it too eckshpenshive for you?'

'No, no, really, meeting you, it'd be worth three hundred pounds.'

'If theresh one thing I hate itsh shickofanshy. I'm shorry, I can't shtand it.'

'Mr Connery! Come back, please, I didn't mean any offence.'

'Then how do you alsho eckshplain the fact that you're cuddling a couple of gonksh? You sheem like a very shilly boy. The kind of shilly boy who wetsh the bed.'

'No. No. No.'

My shouts woke me up. I lay staring at a shelf of trolls until a nasty thought occurred to me. I skimmed my hands frantically over the sheets. Phew.

There were many odd things about Marbella. The blue and white pavement edgings, for a start. The elephants on the beach. But the most puzzling was that the images I'd seen of Marbella in postcards and brochures bore no resemblance to anything I'd seen in the town. Where was that sun-drenched marina, those dinky boutiques, all those very undinky ocean-going yachts? Photographers can concoct an azure sky or two, but surely not a parallel universe?

In fact, Marbella as it likes to be thought of is not in Marbella but in its new annexe of Puerto Banus, a 1200-peseta taxi-ride west along the N340. From the road you see a line of what in any other context you would call tenements – tall, whitewashed blocks with red-tiled roofs. You know you can't call them tenements when you walk down the swish boulevard from the motorway and quickly arrive at the 'centre' of the 'town'. This is the marina of the postcards, packed with the yachts of the brochures. And, what do you know, the marina is surrounded by dinky boutiques.

Most of Puerto Banus is less than ten years old but my first impression was of an old quarter of some medieval city which had been spruced up and transported here, stone by stone, tile by tile. Or that it was a lavish film set for a Mediterranean remake of *The Prisoner*. There was one particularly baroque development of flats boasting sparkling domes and a riot of marble and greenery. I peered at it from a distance of twenty yards, the nearest vantage-point allowed by the security system. It looked like a condo from paradise and the only inhabitants I could see were security guards.

Puerto Banus's main attraction, though, is the marina. On two sides are pathways with their own special litter bins that say 'Keep Clean The Port', and kept clean the port and everywhere else certainly is. Were it not for the people who had come, like me, to gawp, the place would be immaculate, the perfect setting for the obscenely grandiose boats moored here. Shame we spoil the view, really. But we did play an essential part in the grand scheme of things – as an audience, for the only reason anyone would moor a boat in Puerto Banus is to have it gawped at. And it's difficult not to gawp at a boat like the *New Horizon*, that is actually a floating palace. It had fairy lights all over the rigging, presumably to warn off low-flying aircraft. Or the *Maridome*, a floating three-storey block with a speedboat nestling insignificantly in a corner.

On a couple of the dozen largest craft the owners were occupying themselves by looking at us poor people looking at them. One owner was making sure he had an audience by swearing loudly at an abashed oriental employee. For not polishing the fronds of the palm tree in the ship's atrium, maybe? Failing to dust the poop's leisure complex? I'll never know because the owner was letting off steam in Arabic.

I moved away from that unedifying spectacle and approached a couple of nautical types standing at ease beside the gangplank for the astounding *Shahzaz*. They were friendly enough but asked me not to take notes, because we were being recorded by one of the ship's many security cameras. My memory tells me that they were two of a crew of twenty-one and that the *Shahzaz* cost a billion dollars. More or less. Working on it might look glamorous, they said, but it was dead boring because the unnamable owner only used it to go on little day trips. An even more circumspect interviewee was a

Yorkshire lad who'd been recruited from a London hotel to work on the unfeasibly grand *Il Vagabondo*. After much gentle persuasion he decided to inform me that the craft had nine bedrooms, all with en suite bog, and that the R2/D2 device on the very top deck wasn't a satellite, as I had thought, but part of a disco system. Now, why had *Il Vagabondo*'s owner, a bored patriarch who was occupying a fair fraction of the eighty-five-piece suite at the ship's stern, bought that? There were two explanations. One was that he was a keen raver. Unlikely. The second was that he bought it in the same spirit as I bought my 80p fans in Torremolinos.

The latter reflection reminded me that I really ought to take part again in the local pursuit of window-shopping. The first place I ogled was a kind of yacht showroom. There was a cracking speedboat for sale, so I started to divide by 180 to convert the price from pesetas to sterling. Ah. The price *was* in sterling. Weimar prices had also been adopted by the boutiques. The consolation was that they were shops selling things only rich people apparently want. You'd struggle to buy milk in Puerto Banus but you were spoilt for choice if you wanted to buy luggage, bulky cigarette-lighters, leopardskin dresses, leopardskin beachwear, or, for particularly exorbitant sums, the sort of trinkets you win for hitting the dartboard three times at a fairground stall. Undoubtedly the best place for trinkets and *objets* was an antique shop that answered all one's most arcane consumer needs. Want a portrait of a fat bastard in a wig? That shop is for you. Be the envy of your friends by acquiring a statue of a bowler-hatted sambo proffering a box of matches. Stumped by lack-of-novelty-table misery? Simply buy a French-polished construction of two coolies facing each other and holding poles that support a charming sheet of glass. Oh, and that gold-plated Egyptian handmaiden striking an attitude of deep obeisance and holding up an electric lamp was just *too* lovely for words.

There were thousands of us gawping at these preposterous boutiques – Poco Loco, Roger & Fredy, Elite, Spirit, Princesse. Not forgetting Naf Naf. So these were the kind of emporia where we would have to spend our pools' windfall? Maybe Puerto Banus was the creation of hardline reactionaries averting the egalitarian threat by showing that the rich folks' goods are not worth hitting a dartboard three times for, far less a revolution.

As evening fell, I sloped into Sinatra's bar-café, where I discovered how surprisingly well you can eke out a small glass of lager when it costs 275 pesetas. The disco-grooving owner of *Il Vagabondo* wouldn't raise an eyebrow at that price, but I wondered for a moment if I was expected to haggle.

Gradually, we gawpers were joined by the resident gawpees. As midnight approached, Sinatra's changed from a quiet bar-café to a loud polo-club dinner-dance. Tall, after-shavey, cigary, trousery, short-sleeved-shirty men eyed up tall, spangly, hair-doey, tight-skirty women, objects of desire by design. Even glossier than the clientele at Olivia Valere, they were the first people I'd seen in my life who actually wore the kind of gold lamé, leopardskin outfits on sale in the neighbouring boutiques. I'm afraid I was excluded from the flirting games because I wasn't wearing Ray-Bans on top of my head. So I watched. I like watching.

The person who intrigued me most was a pretend-desperado of some fifty years who was unwisely costumed in tight denim. He made a great business of smoking his Dunhill cigarettes, fag hand moving as if carrying a large glass of ale to his mouth, and looking at his watch, a Rolex or Cartier number so large he'd have been better off hanging it in his hallway. The reason he intrigued me wasn't just because he was a screaming prat, it was the grim fact that such a screaming prat as he should be accompanied by such a disgracefully beautiful woman. And she was kissing his ear. Damn.

It was more fun to look at the passing parade of

tourists and residents who now filled the road that ran alongside the marina. What I thought had been a pedestrianized street evidently wasn't. There was a regular procession of Cadillacs and Rolls-Royces and BMWs, with number-plates from Gibraltar, Andorra, Saudi Arabia, Kuwait, the USA – all the world's dodgy places – squeezing the crowds to either side of them. The old and frail struggled to keep their balance. Toddlers barely escaped being hurled into the harbour. That cars were being driven there was a nonsense, but banning them would have inconvenienced some yacht-owning big-shot, and that'd never do. So what's a drowned kid?

It wasn't difficult to distinguish the tourist gawpers like me from the resident gawpees. The latter had a series of identifying characteristics, like the Ray-Ban plumage and the stonking big gold watch. An all-over tan – even on the underarms – was a must, together with a sense of casual chic. The older men tended to enjoy grizzled tans and the company of women much too pretty to be their nieces. The women, no matter their year of birth, wore clothes that managed to be at once very informal and ostentatiously expensive – ripped jeans decorated by gems, bodices and leather hot-pants with Chanel chains, or – a favourite, this – very little. Why did they reveal so much of their flesh? Because they were young, or because they were more mature but wished to flaunt bodies honed by diets and liposuction, or because they were more mature and had wrinkles and cellulite but could afford not to give one single shit.

Especially at night, Puerto Banus was dedicated to fanciness and glitter and sparkle, an all-singing, all-dancing attempt to evoke the spirit of flash cash. The mainly British visitors of the daytime were either slightly flummoxed or cowed by the place, but the nocturnal tourists were enthusiasts who belonged to the two categories of people attracted by all that glitters and sparkles – children and Italians. As a result, it was also very noisy.

Unfortunately, there was no drowning out the muzak of Sinatra's and neighbouring bars. Once you notice muzak, try as you might, you can't ignore it, as I assume you're supposed to. They can't expect you to *listen* to something like a tinkling piano solo of 'We Are the World', can they? I tried another café, where the only sounds were the yells and howls of Spaniards having a quiet conversation. No sooner had I ordered than the muzak started. The first number was a love-duet with regulation tinkling piano, a bit of guitar, then regulation orchestral crescendo to the sudden melodrama of the regulation drum/bass intro. And then the regulation singers − huskily emotional male, tweeting female. Bad enough, but I was in such a muzak fury I had to notice the words as well. 'Out of the blue. Stormclouds came. Out of the blue. Let it rain. Ooooooh, musta bin careless love. Careless love. Careless love. Didn' we.' Who the fuck is responsible for that? Eh? Eh? Someone actually sat down and wrote that. *And was paid for doing so.*

Being a slow number, the song also trapped me into the task of guessing the next rhyme. 'Ooooh, had it good didn' we.' Right, something something can't you see? Or maybe, careless love real free? No. They just repeated that 'good didn' we' line again. Bastards.

I hadn't paid up by the time the next ditty started. 'You and me were walking down the line. You and me babe we had the time.' Agh. Jeez. I was stranded there, transfixed by a spot-the-rhyme addiction. Love, that usually rhymes with stars above, since the other candidates are dove and shove, though hand in glove has an outside chance. Time, as we have seen, can rhyme with line, or mine, or fine, or, easily the worst, something about looking for a rhyme. Sky? That'll be fly or high. And there's night. Light, fight, bright, though, sadly, not shite. You may argue that there are other words in the language to end lines with, but not in muzak lyrics there aren't. Unfortunately, I know this now.

Having paid the bill, I evaded the tannoy from hell and joined the Cadillac-dodging throng on the roadway. Anything was better than cultivating a nervous break-down while sipping molecules of comically over-priced lager. The efforts of a Mercedes to cull the tourist popula-tion forced me up a side-street, where I found myself, by chance I must stress, walking past the International Sex Shop.

Well, why not? Being seen coming out of there by boss/aged relative/old girlfriend/Miss Muir, was one reason why not. However, after giving myself a stern, muttered talking-to, I managed to entice myself into an establishment which proved itself to be truly inter-national, in so far as undressed women of many nations were featured on the cassettes for sale. 'Fick mich in die hölle' was the title of one of these cassettes; German speakers among you will have the advantage of me. Another cassette cover, displaying a mouth encircling a stallion's erection, soon enticed me out into the street again. Then I turned right. Where it was still bright. Although it was night. Because of the neon light. Didn' I.

Up another side-street and I was on the perimeter of Puerto Banus. No, it doesn't have much depth to it. Opposite me now, I saw with a whoop of joy, was a house made briefly famous by an Alan Whicker documen-tary – the less-than-des res of two relics of Marbella's society heydays, Sir Ian and Lady 'Tinker' Abercromby. It must have been absolutely charming when it was first built, a secluded villa with a fine, uninterrupted view of the sea. These days it is secluded only in that it is surrounded by high jagged-glass-topped walls and as many tall trees as the garden can handle. And even if Ian or 'Tinker' scaled their tallest pines, their view would still be of the seven-storey non-tenements of Puerto Banus which have sprung up ten yards away. How completely ghastly for them.

The villa was bordered on the other three sides by rubbled wasteland which looked like it was awaiting development into an amusing multi-storey car-park. Circling the house, I found several chinks in the Abercrombys' besieged defences but couldn't spot any signs of life within. Dunviewin, or whatever Ian and 'Tinker's' benighted house is called, was something of a disappointment. It was a sprawling, single-storey building with barred windows and blended in rather successfully with its wasteland backdrop. Actually, it was exactly the kind of ramshackle homestead you see in programmes about reclusive sibling smallholders in Rotherham who threaten social workers with shotguns and defiantly share a bed.

I wandered over to the taxi-rank and mulled over the thought that I may just have been looking at a house once visited by Sean. So struck was I by this notion that it took me a moment to register that the black velvet of the night had been rent in twain by laughter and squeals. They were coming from a flat – or rather, deluxe apartment – three storeys above. Stepping back, the better to appreciate the merry scene, I saw that the deluxe apartment was heaving with yelping youths, one of whom now swaggered out on to the balcony. He was a git. I say this for two reasons: he was wearing a cream jacket and he had rolled up its sleeves. He looked to be of an age when normal chaps are obsessed by penis size and Clearasil, but he was already possessed of a marvellously self-assured bellow. And it delivered the mid-Atlantic accent adopted either by deejays or Home Counties cool cats.

'Cihmon, babes,' he shouted, and a stunning girl who might well have forgotten to put on her skirt joined him on the balcony. The git wrapped a meaty, unsleeved forearm round her improbable waist.

'Eowkay!' he bellowed to someone inside. 'Led's ged on with this fuckin' phodograph!'

There were more of his ilk in a square of clubs and

bars up a flight of stairs from the street running parallel
to the marina. Even a Spaniard would find the decibel
count a bit much in that square. It was mobbed by the
kind of seventeen-year-olds called Josh or Emm or Steph
or Tobes whose wrinklies give them soft-topped run-
abouts and let them smoke joints in the kitchen. A lot of
hair-flicking going on in that square. Quite a bit of
desultory groping, but they'd probably grown bored
with sex long ago. Been there. Done it. Got it. Hey!
Heard the ladest? Steph's splid up from Roops so she's
havin' a pardy on her boat. Led's geouw there afder we
snord some of Emm's ceouwk.

Struggling to think of nice things to write about Puerto
Banus, I can come up with the fact that it hasn't been
taken over by the Joshes and Jakes. The place really
belongs to their parents who've bought into Europe's
most glam new town. Puerto Banus is a Camberwick
Green for the moneyed middle-aged. And, like Camberwick Green, there aren't many taxis about at half past
one in the morning.

I joined the appallingly long queue of fellow-gawpers
at the sign that said 'Taxi', but after five minutes a cab
had yet to appear. I reckoned that even if one were to
arrive now, and every five minutes thereafter, I'd still
have to wait two and a half hours to get a ride back to
Marbella. The buses had stopped running long ago.
Hitching was not a possibility, since the traffic was
composed of Porsches and swanky jeeps, so all I'd get
from them would be a windblown thumb. It was a
feasible four miles to walk home, but yomping along the
N340 in the dark was not on. I might as well save myself
the bother and jump in front of a speeding Merc here
and now.

I was facing the prospect of becoming the first person
to sleep rough in Puerto Banus's brief history. I was also
facing a poster advertising a Rio spectacular at some
night-club; the drawing was of a mulatto woman dressed

in glitter alone and sticking out her high bottom. More consumer goods were featured in the boutique window alongside the poster. Items of trinketry here included a silver champagne bucket filled with glass dried flowers, and a big gold writing lamp held up by a gold-plated wave. Super. It was the wave that inspired me. No way was I spending a minimum of a hundred and fifty minutes looking at that. I'd trudge along to the Andalucia Plaza hotel up the road and get a taxi there. It was a plan of great daring and frightening simplicity. (It worked, too, although I still arrived back in my room of gonks at four, having spent two hours of my life in a multi-kilometre tailback of tone-deaf sentimentalists returning to Marbella from a Julio Iglesias concert.)

Before I set off for the hotel with the casino, I stopped to take one last look at Puerto Banus. All its Andalusian tiling and baroque architectural whims and sub-tropical foliage couldn't disguise its shopping-mall blandness. But that's what the filthy rich want, isn't it? What they're used to. They have the opportunity to enjoy all manner of exotic experiences but they spurn it. They live in a world of their own the world over, where the shops all stock luggage and leopardskin bikinis, where yachts have palm trees, where everyone rolls up the sleeves of cream jackets to show what will always be a Cartier or a Rolex, where everyone has year-round mahogany tans, even on their underarms, where muzak is always tinkling in bars built for posing, where every interior decoration is gold or embossed with gold, where the drinks cabinet is always mounted on a statue of an onyx shepherd boy wrestling with an onyx duck, where all there is to do is waste money and time, where there's always a Korean to curse, a Brazilian to bugger.

I pinched a jaundiced arm. This was definitely not a dream.

Enough 100-peseta coins were lined up on top of the

phone to fund a desultory call to Melbourne. Beside them was a slip of paper with the number I had acquired. Don't ask how – I can't reveal my sources. Fingers slippery with nerves, I dialled.

'Hello?'

'Hello. Can I speak to Mr Connery, please?'

'Who is this?' (Was that a Filipino accent?)

'My name's Harry Ritchie. I'd like to speak to Mr Connery, please.'

'Why?'

'With regard to a book I am writing about Marbella. I would like to ask him about his life here.'

'Oh . . . '

'It needn't take very long. Mr Forsyth, Miss Black and Mr Tarbuck, they have all agreed to talk to me. And Miss Bassey.'

White lies, we scoop-hounds sometimes have to use them. I was pretty impressed by my quick thinking. She seemed taken with my spiel as well.

'Just a moment, please.'

Silence. I listened to the white noise, remembering, as I pressed the phone to my ear, what it had been like as a child wanting, and failing, to hear a seashell's waves. All I could hear now was that faint high buzz that you also get, disturbingly, near electricity pylons.

'Hello?' I said, in that forlorn way one has when speaking to white noise.

Still nothing.

'Meester Reech?' It was another woman, with an accent I guessed might be Portuguese.

'Yes, hello, I'm still here.'

'I am sorry you cannot speak to Meester Connery. But een answer to your question, he likes eet here very mush.'

'That's wonderful. Can I speak to him myself, please?'

'Um . . . no.'

'Why not? Ten seconds of his time will be enough.'

'He cannot.'

'Why?'

'He ees not ear. He ees een, um, Los Angeles.'

'Please, it really won't take very long. Mr Tarbuck and Miss Bassey . . .'

'Los Angeles.'

'You expect me to believe that? Jesus Christ, woman, come on, ten seconds, that's all I ask.'

'Los Angeles.'

'Well, thank you for your help. And fuck off back to Lisbon. Goodbye.'

'Goodbye, Meester Reech.'

Dame Rumour had it that one of the hang-outs of Marbella's celebs was a restaurant on the Golden Mile called Toni Dalli's. Cilla, inevitably, had been seen there recently. Much more important was that it was said to be Sean's favourite haunt. Toni Dalli's was obviously my kind of place. Fearing that, if I went there for dinner, I wouldn't be in a position to pay for anything more than a piping hot bowl of steam, I decided to wander in one afternoon and try to waylay Signor Dalli himself.

Which is, remarkably enough, just what happened. I walked into the restaurant, which turned out to be fairly grand in a Moorish-ish way and which had a swimming-pool and lots of framed pictures, of Tarby, Princess Margaret, Rod Stewart, Diana Dors, Tony Jacklin . . . and Sean. The mid-afternoon lull allowed me the chance to approach a stocky man with slick-backed greying hair and the face of the friend of Sean, Tarby, Rod and Co. in the framed pictures. Toni Dalli – for it was he – said he would be delighted to talk to me and guided me over to a table surrounded by more pictures of Toni Dalli and posters of same heading the bill at various Empires and Palladia in the fifties and sixties. I wondered if it was bad form and/or ludicrous that I'd never heard of this man before. And when he spoke I also wondered why he did so in an ice-a-da-creama/Yorkshire accent. 'Ah've been-a 'ere eleven years four-a moonths now,' he said, in answer to my opening pleasantry. 'It was Tarbuck convinced me. Took me 'ere to play-a golf and ah saw this restaurant. Now it's-a woon of the best-a-known places arahnd.'

And off the conversation went. I thought I'd ask him a few questions about himself before moving on to quiz him remorselessly about Sean. However, my polite tactic backfired because after a minute or two all I wanted was to find out more about Toni Dalli's own life-story.

The explanation for his accent was that he'd emigrated from dire poverty in Italy in 1952 when he was sixteen. To a new land of opportunity – 'England! It was like paradise to me.' Well, that was what he'd thought in Pescara, but he'd been enticed into exile by the NCB to Mexborough, to work in a mine that still had pit ponies. He stumbled on a way of supplementing the magnificent fiver a week he earned as a miner when he went for a drink one Sunday to the local Station Hotel. Everyone was singing, so he sang too. He was so good he was hoiked up on to a table and told in no uncertain terms to sing some more. After twenty minutes he'd run out of songs, so he had to belt out any nonsense that came into his head. No one noticed or minded, and at closing time he was given a hatful of money. The next week he won a talent contest in Swinton, which set him up on the local circuit of working men's clubs.

Things looked up further when he moved to work in a steel mill in Sheffield, a city full of working men's clubs ('Ah'm a-talking about oondreds'), where he could earn five quid a night but where no one could pronounce his name, so he shortened Antonio D'Alessandro to Toni Dalli. When his tale reached 1957 it developed into a hectic blur of big breaks. Holiday in Scarborough ('I thought it was fooking Florida'), persuaded by girlfriend to audition for performance at town's biggest hall, taken on for five weeks, packed every night, spotted by Twenti-eth Century Fox, coached by them in London (together with Harry Secombe), hired by posh Mayfair club, spotted by Max Bygraves, signed by Bygraves's agent, topped bill everywhere, cartoon story of his life in *Romeo* magazine, screaming fans, acclaim as the new Mario Lanza . . .

And then it went wrong. He was contracted to play Lanza in a film of his life, kicked his heels for four years, but the film was never made. There were highlights after that – his own TV show in America, playing the Carnegie Hall, touring the world – but the fact that I'd never heard of him strengthened my impression that his was a stardom of the kind experienced by winners of the Euro-vision Song Contest.

That's a bit harsh. Toni Dalli is no one's idea of a failure. His albums of cuttings may be mostly thirty years old, but he still makes records, and he still sings every night at his restaurant. (His is a powerful tenor, as I know to my cost. He burst into song a couple of times in mid-conversation and blasted me back in my seat.) More to the point, the man is supremely enviable. He's so happy. He's found the perfect life for himself, playing golf every day, singing in his restaurant every night, mucking about with his mates.

Which reminded me of my original purpose in coming here. Did he, I asked in a desperately offhand manner, see much of Sean Connery these days?

'What can I say? Sean and I are very close.'

Here I was, not three feet away from a man who was very close to Sean. 'What's he, you know, like?' I asked.

'What can I say? Sean, he's one of the nicest human beings. Sincere. One oondred per cent a man's man.'

My God. 'Do you think it might be possible for me to, as it were, meet him? He comes here quite a lot, doesn't he?'

'Sure, sure. He does come here a lot. I see him or speak to him every day. But not just now.'

'Why's that, then?'

'Because he is in Los Angeles.'
Oh.

I returned to the restaurant, at Toni's invitation, that evening to watch him sing to his customers and to drink as many complimentary beers as I could. He boomed out 'O Sole Mio' and several songs about someone being his heart's delight, holding a completely unnecessary mike at, thank goodness, stretched-arm's length. I was mightily impressed but when he joined me at the bar he lamented an off-colour performance. A middle-aged couple who obviously didn't think that was the case either interrupted us to tell him that he'd lost none of the magic that had made them cry when he did the Palladium in the sixties. Toni was so chuffed he celebrated by telling me his Des O'Connor story.

'Des and me were at the Glasgow Empire. Toughest audience in the world. Des was the act before me so I watched from the wings. Nothing went right for him. He was a-dying. And what the audience used to do there, if they didn't like you, they threw pennies at you. So they were chucking all these pennies at Des. You know what he did? It got so bad for him out there, he pretended to faint and was carried off. Hah!'

'So how did you go down?'

'I was prepared. I went on next, sang a coupla songs, then did a number I'd been practising specially for the Glasgow Empire.'

And with that Toni re-created the performance that had won over the Glasgow Empire, launching into a vast rendition of 'My Ain Folk'. Now, Italian just-one-cornetto tenors are not my scene, but it wasn't the many complimentary beers that had me dabbing my eyes. The man had me in a mess. Okay, so I'd drawn another blank with Sean. But I had been personally serenaded by the one, the only Toni Dalli.

*

I had two days left in Marbella. Two days in which to meet someone famous. Anyone would do, now that I knew I'd never bump into Sean. My last-ditch effort in the celebrity hunt started with my phoning a man whose name always seemed to be cropping up in conversations, on the local radio, in the local newspapers. If anyone was going to introduce me to a celeb, people said, it would be Maurice Boland.

We arranged to meet in a café at midday. He was only five minutes late, which I regretted because I'd been listening in to two English businessmen discussing the perils of a weak dollar and of having one's patio paved in marble. Maurice Boland arrived in a flurry and immediately made up for lost time by telling me that he was the man who'd discovered Mandy Smith. He gabbled on about the beauty of the sometime Mrs Bill Wyman, but I was much more interested in him. He looked to be in his mid-forties, a bit jowly, not at his best in T-shirt and shorts. His middle-parting could be carbon-dated to 1974, but his zippy, fingers-in-many-pies, the-world-is-my-lobster style placed him spiritually in 1987. I'd found out about Toni Dalli's life through tact and then choice. I learned about the career of Maurice Boland because his was a rapid-fire chit-chat that contained information about nothing else.

'Yeah, Mandy, she was a friend of my young cousin, I saw her at a disco down here and I knew she'd be a great star. I had to drop this book I was writing, *The Posers' Manual* it was called, to go back to the UK with her. Pete Waterman, he was nobody at the time, he asked for a deal, Christ, we were charging seven grand a day for a photocall for her. I was worried about the London press, but I've sold the same story to the same newspaper twice. I've got two filmscripts in Hollywood at the moment, a bit like Spielberg's stuff, great hopes of those. Oh, the real bombshell with Mandy was finding out her mother was suspected of having an affair with

Wyman's son. Word is, they might marry. If Mandy and
Bill had stayed married, Mandy's mum would have
become Mandy's step-daughter-in-law. I wanted to move
to LA originally, but my wife preferred here. She'd seen
the Costa del Sol with James Hunt's wife. Yeah, James
had a disco here, and I bought that from him. Do you
know I'm the highest-paid entertainer on the coast?
Most get 20,000 pesetas a night. You know what I get?
I'll tell you: 150,000 pesetas. Do you know I played
drums in Hamburg in 1965? All my life I've loved to
perform. I had a club in Dublin in 1969, that's when I
was nineteen. Eire's first disco-restaurant. I come from a
middle-class medical family, Jewish. You know what I
wanted to do? A remake of "Je t'aime" with this
fourteen-year-old girl, beautiful she was. But then I
thought of this line, "I'm too yuh-ung. To cuh-um",
went like that. My wife, she said, "Maurice, you're
sick", but I could see the video, the girl's in school
uniform looking through the bars of the playground at a
guy on a motorbike, and she's singing, "I'm too yuh-
ung. To cuh-um". It was one in the morning here, I
phoned Martin Rushent, produced the Human League,
sang that down the phone, he said, "Get your ass on a
plane." So the next day I'm in Berkshire, some studios
there, Rushent had everything set up, and all I had was
five words. Twenty-four hours later, we had a song.
Now, the girl I had lined up to do it was gorgeous, photo
in the *News of the World*, but that didn't work out, so I
got another, we did it in one take when she was nervous.
Knock-out song. Hasn't been released. But something
else happened, I bumped into Shirley Bassey, she has a
place down here, carried her shopping home, and I
asked her, "How come Tom Jones has a new hit and not
you?" Four days later we're on a plane to London. You
know something? I once sued RTE and Channel 4 for
slander, 250 grand plus costs, highest awards ever given
in Dublin. But I'll tell you, the disco I have along the

road, you wouldn't believe it. And I've got my own show, The Maurice Boland Celebrity Show, you won't believe it, I mean I can't sing, but Glen Tipton, you know, the guy in that group Judas Priest, he said to me, "Maurice, you're the best singer that can't sing." He's right, God, I love to get up on stage, do the star bit. I *love* stars, all the attention with Mandy, that was a large, year-long orgasm for me. The trouble with this place is it's too small. And too full of people who should have BS after their name. Bull Shitter. But I'm different, I know I'm a product, like a packet of cornflakes, and I've begun to hype that product so I can make it big back in Britain. I'm *talented*. You know what I want to do? Replace Wogan.'

Words I had said to Maurice Boland so far: 'really', 'blimey', 'did' and 'you'. I said three more words, and in sequence, after he'd told me about his mobile Jewish deli and his column in a local newspaper, when he'd moved on to tell me about his love of television, television game-shows and an idea he'd come up with during our meeting for a game-show for posers. Now, what could it be called? 'The Pose Show,' I said, less than brilliantly.

Those were my three words. He thanked me for the suggestion, then got up to leave. Shit. What about my intro to the stars? Somehow, I think by shouting, I managed to interrupt his parting appraisal of a fantastic jazz show he compèred, to ask him if he could introduce me to any stars.

'Sure, sure. Tell you what, your best bet is to come to The Maurice Boland Celebrity Show, you'll love it. I get stars there all the time, discreetly though, they just like to hang out at the back of the audience, have a good time. Come along. Tonight at Rudi's, the details are in the papers. Okay? Look, I've got to run. See you tonight, you'll be knocked out.'

Eardrums a-tingle, I recuperated with a coffee and a look through the local paper. There was Maurice Boland's column right enough, this week about some beauty contest he'd judged in Gibraltar with Frank Bruno. And an advert for The Maurice Boland Celebrity Show. I had a strange feeling that tonight was going to be the night.

The taxi cost me ten quid, but at least it got me to Rudi's in time to see the start of Maurice Boland's act. He was wearing baggy black trousers, a white shirt with a stiff upturned collar and diamanté buttons. He was coming to the climax of his opening bout of patter. 'Irish girl says, "Mammy, I'm pregnant." Mammy turns to her and says, "Are you sure it's yours?" And now for my first number, which I'm sure all of you know, so don't be afraid to sing along and let it all hang out.'

Glen Tipton, you're wrong. The man has the musical sense of a crow. Boland's first number was 'Swing Low, Sweet Chariot'. He recited it. Nor was that a difficult task because he was performing with a karaoke machine which showed him when and what to sing. Or, rather, say.

I took my first good look at the audience. A lot of people here, but I had as much chance of spotting Cilla or Brucie among them as among a bus queue. Not soon enough, Maurice Boland finished his song and introduced his two dancing girls. Off he went as they pranced about, then on he came again, to introduce the first of the night's karaoke singers. I hung around for over an instructively painful hour, on the off-chance that some star of stage or screen would come in here by some dreadful mistake. But no. The Maurice Boland Celebrity Show was called that because Maurice Boland thought he was a celebrity. My penultimate night and all I had to show for it were taxi receipts for a total of 3,600 pesetas. My last chance to meet someone I'd seen on the telly flushed down the pan.

Thanks, Maurice.

Maurice Boland. Friend of the famous.

*

What had I gained from my fortnight here? An overdraft.
And the insight that if I ever make a mint I'll have to
wear Ray-Bans on top of my hair. I'd come looking for
Sean and hadn't set eyes even on Tarby. I'd gone glitzy
night-clubbing and ended up drinking tap-water in the
cludgie. My adoration of Marbella was as strong as Des
O'Connor's love of the Glasgow Empire.

But today my heart was filled with joy. I only had to
last out one more night, then I'd be shot of here for ever.
It was with a spring in my step that I sprinted for my life
across the ring-road and headed down to the old quarter
of the town. Having given up on spotting any stars or
mingling with the chic, I thought I'd celebrate my
imminent release by visiting one of the town's normal
pubs, where normal people would be. Maybe The English Tavern where I'd met the Nottingham crowd. That
that particular part of the plan was never fulfilled was
the result of my taking a farewell detour of the old
quarter and being waylaid by the sound of familiar
accents billowing out from a very un-English tavern.

The snug interior of Jimmy Tramps bar was busy with
floral-covered banquettes, an extensive collection of film
posters and a bar whose gantry contained Saltire ashtrays and plaques with clan emblems. Tartan Special
was on draught. With one step I had travelled from a
small square in the old quarter of Marbella to a pub in
the middle of Tillicoutry.

It was immediately obvious that the place was domi-
nated by one man, a tall and formidably handsome
bloke with a pop star's bone-structure and immaculately
layered white hair. I guessed he was the owner from the
'Jimmy' monogram on his pristine polo shirt. Besides,
everyone called him by name. 'Jimmy, another big vodka
here, please.' 'How's it going, Jimmy?' 'Pint of special,
Jimmy.' 'Hey, Jimmy!' 'Jimmy!' 'Jimmy!' 'Jimmy!'

That there wasn't even more Jimmying going on was
simply because it was quite difficult for any of the

customers to get a word in edgeways. Jimmy's own
patter was, like divine love, constant and all-embracing.
If he wasn't cracking jokes or anticipating orders with
uncanny prescience, he was singing along to his tapes –
snatches of tunes, a word or two of lyrics, anything to fill
a silence, keep the bonhomie going.

'All right there, pal? Nutbush *siddy* limits. Another
large vodka, eh, hen? That's the game. Nutbush *siddy*.
Enjoy that? Want the dessert menu? Oh, *nut*bush.'

There was a very brief break in his monologue as he
sprinted out from the bar and up to two old dears who
were tottering out. 'Stop!' he said. 'I'm not letting you
out yet.'

'But Jimmy, we want to . . .'

'No, I forbid it.'

'. . . have an early night.'

'*Dar*lings. Youse cannot go yet – without a kiss.'

Leaning far down, he held each of their faces tenderly
and kissed them. 'God, youse are gorgeous.'

Flushed and giggling, the two old dears were then
allowed to leave. As they reached the door, Jimmy
shouted after them. 'Take care now, eh? Oh, and mind –
good luck with the manhunt.'

Acknowledging with a royal wave the half-ironic applause of a family seated near the bar, he swaggered
back to the counter to serve me.

'So what's it to be, pal? A menu there if you want it.
Treat yourself to a steak – it's good Scottish beef. Pint of
lager, is it? 'Course it is. There we go. So where you
from, young man?'

'Fife,' I said. 'What about you? Glasgow?'

'*Oh*, no. Tillicoutry, my friend. Sunny Tillicoutry.'

He pulled my pint, changed the tape to Queen, puffed
at a cigarette, told someone else at the bar that Airdrie
were terrible, marched through the swing-doors to the
kitchen, returned laden with two gigantic melon cocktails
fizzing with sparklers, came back to the bar, sang along

with Freddie Mercury for a second and attended to a newly arrived couple who ordered 'two very, very, very, very, very small rum and cokes'. What they received was two tall glasses full to the brim and containing as much coke as would have filled a tablespoon.

'I hate coke,' said Jimmy, as he handed over these octuple Bacardis. '*All* we hear is radio ga ga. Ready for another pint of special there? Okaydokey. Raydeeoh ga ga . . .'

Since I belong to the one ethnic minority in London with no area or pubs of its own, I'd never been to a Scottish bar outside Scotland. Pat and Adrian's in Fuengirola didn't quite count because perhaps half the customers were English. Here, though, almost everyone knew what happened in 1314. And it was not difficult to make new friends. Or get drunk. So I did both. I teamed up with a foursome from Wishaw, old hands at Jimmy Tramps, who knew not to bother about asking for small measures. The two men had been working up a great thirst on the golf-course, where both had acquired tans the colour of their Marlboro packets. They had also acquired an easy intimacy with Jimmy's photograph albums which were propped on the bar counter. The albums were full of snaps of Jimmy plus various revellers. Many of the photographs wouldn't have been out of place on the gossip pages of the *Daily Record*. Jimmy with the Rangers team. Jimmy being hugged by Denis Law. Jimmy seen sharing a joke with a couple of Scotland internationals. 'There's Coisty,' one of the Wishaw men pointed out. 'Best centre-forward in Europe. And Supermo, look. Great player, but what a tube. And that left-back, whatsisname . . .'

When the Wishaw foursome left, coping as well as could be expected with Jimmy's measures, I fell in with a couple of guys from Aberdeen. More or less silly with drink, they still managed to do their party tricks, contributing in no small way to the growing hubbub, roaring with glee every time I couldn't work out how they knew which five-figure number I had thought of, or how the two coins were now under my hand.

Impressive though they were, the Aberdeen pair were only a sideshow for the star attraction who was still performing with unfailing energy. Someone's birthday? On with the complimentary champagne and the chocolate gâteau decked with sparklers. A child in a hooped T-shirt? Cue the Dennis the Menace jokes. The arrival of a family with a fourteen-year-old daughter? A serenade to the girl and a proposal of marriage. His judgement of what to say and how and when to say it was unfailing, especially as the party atmosphere grew and with it the chance of someone turning sour at his banter. Someone never did.

I tried to remain as sober as I could so that I could use consonants if I ever managed to talk to Jimmy by himself. The opportunity came at one-thirty when he cleared the pub. He was jovially pissed but not too far gone to be quizzed. So I thought, but when he sussed out that I was a reporter of some unspecifiable sort, he switched to a wholly business-like manner. He'd been increasingly merry with the rest of us and he hadn't touched a drop all night.

It seemed a sensible move to let Jimmy do all the talking. He told me that he was forty-two, had worked in Saudi as an engineer, and had taken over the pub seven years ago, to discover that he was born to be a landlord. He was more or less teetotal, spent all his time working and got his kicks performing. The way he saw it, his job was to make sure people who came to his bar had a great time, because he liked people to have a great time – and besides, they'd come back for more. Now, didn't that make sense?

I'm glad I took notes because I really wouldn't have remembered any of that. Thank God also that Jimmy gave me a lift home because walking was a bit of a trial.

I stumbled back into Nigel's house and up the stairs to sleep off the drink among the gonks. As I pulled the single sheet over me, I mulled over some of the conundrums Marbella presented: why it was, for instance, that capitalism and altruism rarely combine as they did with Jimmy, and why being rich meant being bored and boring. I have a feeling that I came up with some convincing analysis of these and other issues, but I am buggered if I can recall what. But I have retained a very clear memory of my solution to rid the world of the Costa del Sol's blackspot. Unfortunately, I don't think Puerto Banus is on a major fault-line.

4
Calahonda

'What time did you say your friend was arriving?'

'Seven. On the nose of it.'

'His plane's probably been delayed, that's all.'

'You're true.'

'Do you want to phone the airport?'

'No need for troubling.'

'Well,' said George as he cleared away my umpteenth *cerveza*, 'can I treat you to a coffee?'

'Many kind,' I said. 'Thanks of you.'

I was, you may have already gathered, a touch squiffy.

One of the many boons of always being unpunctual is that I rarely have to wait for other people. One of the drawbacks, besides a steadily dwindling social life, is that when someone does manage to turn up even later than me, I have no practice in coping with the situation. Thus, on that first evening in Calahonda, awaiting the arrival of my pal Phil Smith, sitting in our arranged meeting-point of Bogart's ('The Legend Lives On') bar-restaurant, contributing in no small way to the evening's profit-margin, talking increasingly incoherent nonsense to George behind the bar, I had spent five hours succumbing to first boredom, then fear. Had I Reaganed the arrangement? Had Phil stood me up? The shit. Had something gone wrong? But what could have gone wrong? He was flying down from Barcelona, so there was no question of any passport kerfuffle, he'd lived in Spain for four years, so he knew how to work the country, he was driving a hire car from Malaga airport and the directions I'd given him to Calahonda were faultless . . .

The plane had crashed. He was being extricated from a flaming pile-up on the N340. He'd decided not to bother coming because he'd never really wanted to be my friend.

A catastrophe was long overdue because everything had gone according to plan for my stay in Calahonda. Phil had readily agreed to come down for four days' holiday as my chauffeur and translator, and I'd hoodwinked my sister and her family into joining me for the second week here, when they'd provide a share of the expenses and be perfect victims for the local time-share touts. The bank had been understanding about extending my overdraft. And, by some fluke, the house I'd rented for two weeks had turned out to be marvellous. A real home from home it was.

Or would have been, had I been used to marble-floored homes with veranda, garden and swimming-pool. The exterior was Wimpey Moorish, with the standard-issue whitewashed walls and red-tiled roof, and the standard-issue accessory of grilles covering every entrance and window, to guard against the coast's bogeymen – gypsies. If you weren't careful, these thieving scum would creep into your house while you had a shower, remove all your furniture, kidnap your spouse, enslave your children, and, as they crept out carrying their booty in bags marked Swag, paint your walls with their diarrhoea and set fire to your garden. (So it was said, but for some reason – I suspected ethnic cleansing – I laid eyes on one gypsy in my two months here, and that was a poor soul who toured Fuengirola's bars selling roses.)

This gypsy-proof house was in an ideal spot – a tran-quil enclave and but a couple of minutes' drive from Calahonda's shopping centre, El Zoco, so called because it was a mock souk. El Zoco was an unabashedly pink construction with all the amenities you'd expect to find in a traditional Muslim marketplace – newsagents, amusement arcade, pubs, restaurants, supermarket, and a video store. Plus a handsome selection of hostelries – Options, the Stratford, the Jolly Good Chinese restaurant, the Trafalgar pub, the Dickens Bar, Alan's Plaice (a fish 'n' chip shop that must be the only eatery in Spain to close at eleven), and the Cactus Room (which must be the only eatery in Spain to include baked potatoes in its *tapas* menu). There were even more hostelries a short stumble up the hill along Calahonda's main street, the Avenida España. Something of a misnomer that, considering that its row of pubs contained the Red Lion, the Welcome In, the Raj Indian restaurant and the Yellow Lady, as well as Bogart's. And, should good old British fayre prove a little too starchy, a twenty-four-hour medical centre promising the imminent arrival of a crucial heart-monitoring device.

I'd conducted my own thorough consumer research into many of these places in my first three days here. My conclusions were these – the food at Bogart's was particularly fine, and it wasn't very advisable to alternate between San Miguel and Guinness for any length of time. In the Yellow Lady I bumped into the father of the family who lived next door. In keeping with the suburban restraint of Calahonda (whose by-laws forbade, for example, the hanging-out of washing), the family seemed always to be on best behaviour; the first evening I was here they had held a barbecue, in a silence that was complete save for the regular chinking of cutlery. On his own in the Yellow Lady, though, the father became increasingly effusive as he recalled the riotous holidays of his youth and persuaded me to follow his regime of alternating San Miguels and Guinness.

Badly hungover though I had been, I'd kept an appointment the following morning with Calahonda's elected officials. The president of the community, Tony

Meredith, had been something in insurance in Southend before he came out to Calahonda for his retirement, which appeared to be entirely taken up with the business of running Calahonda. There were about 4,000 permanent residents here, he thought, and a peak population of around 25,000. Seventy to eighty per cent of the residents and holidaymakers were Brits, which helped to explain by-laws forbidding you to hang out your washing, something of a national sport for the Spanish. Mr Meredith was a man with many worries. How was he going to get people to pay their community fees? Would the water main burst again? How could he protest to the BBC about *Eldorado*, a series he'd heard was based on Calahonda, but not that he could see, this was a respectable community, people didn't jump into bed with each other all the time, did they?

Even that hangover hadn't prevented me from enjoying a pleasant talk with Mr Meredith, which only went to show that I'd been on something of a roll. But now, waiting and waiting and waiting for Phil, the paranoia, which had been so easy to fend off at nine o'clock, three hours before, at a stage when I was still looking up hopefully at every car that slowed down or parked nearby, was being horribly vindicated. (By unhappy chance George had told me much earlier in the evening that in his five years here he'd witnessed five fatal accidents at the N340's turn-off to Calahonda. A nurse I know had spent a week on holiday along the road and twice had to interrupt a meal to tend to dying crash victims.) Even the outlook on the bright side was growing dimmer by the minute. Say Phil's plane had been delayed. Disaster still loomed because Bogart's would be shutting soon, and Phil didn't know the address of the house I'd rented, and even if I did put a note and a map on the door, it'd be a miracle if he found it because I couldn't remember the address either. I was sunk in drunken gloom, wondering if the switchboard operators at Malaga's airport and hospital spoke English, when Phil walked in.

'So *there* you are,' he said, as if it was me or Bogart's or Calahonda that had gone missing for nigh-on five hours. Which, in a way, was what had happened.

Phil gulped down some San Miguel and explained. Everything had gone swimmingly – plane on time, car in perfect working order waiting at the airport, not much traffic on the motorway. A quick consultation with his map and off Phil had set along the N340. The drive took longer than I'd said it would, but eventually he'd arrived safe and sound at Calahonda. The other Calahonda. The fishing village called Calahonda a hundred kilometres east of Malaga. He'd asked for directions to Bogart's bar from stunned locals, and milled around for a while, wondering why my description of the place had turned out to be so comprehensively inaccurate. Then some gnarled pensioner mentioned that he might be looking for the other place, the big holiday town near Marbella . . .

There was a reason, apart from the fact that his brain enjoyed the neural activity of a shrub, for Phil's error. It was his map. A fine map, a detailed and up-to-date Michelin job, but one produced in Spain, so it acknowledged the existence of Calahonda the Spanish fishing village though not its namesake, a much larger town but as Spanish as Eastbourne.

Having celebrated Phil's arrival long into the night, we woke the following day just in time for lunch. At my suggestion, we opted to eat at the Red Lion, where I – no other verb will do – plumped for the breaded hake, and Phil for a Spanish omelette which contained, to his incredulous disgust, tomatoes.

'I have a suggestion,' he said, amid burps of indigestion. 'This evening, let's find a Spanish restaurant for you to research.'

'Was your omelette that bad?'

'Worse. And don't tell me you enjoyed that fish.'

My breaded hake had not, it was true, been an out-right triumph. In fact, it had been disgusting. 'It was all right,' I said, taking a patriotic stand on the argument which I knew would now follow.

It was rather a one-sided argument, for Phil was eloquent to a fault. In sum, the honour of our national cuisine was besmirched. British pride had to be defended. How could I take these insults from some quisling, turn-coat, expatriate traitor?

'Fair enough,' I said. (Come on, the guy had a car.)

The following day we ate in a *venta* (Spanish for dirt-cheap restaurant) patronized by local workmen. It was, I'm afraid, neat and clean, and the food – pint glass of gazpacho, grilled fish, salad, bread, coffee and a litre of wine, all for under four quid each – delicious. In return for my letting Phil take me for a wonderful meal, he agreed to drive me around on a tour of Calahonda. The car was indispensable, not because Calahonda was amaz-ingly large but because it was built on a series of steep hills that run up from the motorway.

The higher we climbed, the newer and emptier the developments became. Finally, past a half-finished Finn-ish complex of flats, the developments stopped, and then the road did too. The dead end was embellished with a shrine to one Don José de Orbaneja y Aragon, 'founder and developer of the Sitio de Calahonda *urbanización*', and commemorating the twenty-fifth birthday of Cala-honda in 1988. The shrine itself was embellished by hundreds of small-calibre bullet-holes, and the empty Rizla packets and torn cigarettes which suggested that Don José's plaque was a popular target for gun-toting dope-smokers.

We had reached an altitude Bob Beamon would have appreciated so the view was spectacular. The Costa's ribbon of development between the sea and the sierras was spread below us. This was the coastline where Laurie Lee found villagers fending off starvation, children eating the small fry of the day's sorry catch raw on the beach. That was forty years ago. Brigands were said to be still roaming the hillsides then. And before us now was a vista of gleaming white buildings and vivid, lush greenery. Behind us, however, were reminders of what much of this coast had recently been like – hillocks of beige scrub dotted with tumbledown shacks and occasional tinkling herds of goats. We were standing on a border between Miami and Morocco.

The price of the tourism from which most Western Europeans have benefited in the past thirty years has often been very high. From Tenerife to Turkey to Tunisia the holiday industry has created cultural, economic, ecological and aesthetic problems, but one of the places where you'd struggle to find convincing drawbacks is the Costa del Sol, unless you can't stand the idea of a previously unprized coast of impoverished fisherfolk and oppressed peasants discovering prosperity by a microclimate, which had for centuries only helped to harshen life on the land, being turned into a sellable commodity. (A symptom of the Spaniards' enthusiasm for development was their use of the word *urbanización*, a term that doesn't exactly indicate any guilt about reclaiming scrub with bricks and mortar. In Britain Calahonda would be disguised as part of a pastoral heritage by being described as a 'holiday village' or 'executive hamlet'.) Try to find an Andalusian nostalgic for the good old days before the tourists came. Try to find an Andalusian resentful of the foreigners. I did try. I couldn't find one.

Looking down from that hilltop on the area of Spain's Florida where we were staying, I was struck by the impression that there was no real reason for this place to exist, other than because Don José de Whodoyaflip had decided to convert this particular section of dreadful farmland into holiday-home real estate. (Before his initiative, Calahonda consisted of a beach, a watch-tower, a hotel, and a camping site.) And not only was there no natural incentive for Calahonda's existence – no crossroads or river and little easily developable land – there was no man-made focus. Normal towns have things like high streets and main squares; Calahonda was a series of developments with a supermarket placed not in the centre but at the extremity of the motorway.

Actually, that takes into account only the *urbanización* of the Sitio de Calahonda, for 'Calahonda', as I could now appreciate from that hillside view, is an umbrella term for a succession of time-share complexes and other *urbanizacións* bordering the N340 between Fuengirola and Marbella. And because each development is separate, there's no linking infrastructure other than the N340. This sprawl is the nearest I hope I'll ever come to experiencing the American phenomenon of 'edge cities', white-collar commuter-belt towns built in the eighties, towns with populations running into the hundreds of thousands but no name other than the numbers of the nearest intersecting highways.

Like an edge city, Calahonda is unworkable and senseless if you don't have access to a car. (There had been a bus service of sorts here, a twice-daily service round the Avenida de España, but even that had recently been abandoned.) The place was an insult to pedestrians, pavements were a rarity, street-lights often didn't work; and dog-shit was rife; security men hadn't stopped me as I'd strolled about on my evenings alone here but I'd half expected them to. It was clear that I'd have to make the most of my chauffeur while he was here, so I persuaded Phil to drive down the hill again to tour assorted developments.

Picture the scene. The easterly edge of Calahonda (as I'll persist in calling the Sitio de Calahonda for the sake of convenience). More hillocky scrub in the background. And in the foreground an enormous sports complex – the Club del Sol Sports and Country Club, which advertised at its entrance facilities for the following: badminton, horse-riding, archery, bowls, roller-skating, volleyball, basketball, mini-golf, tennis (twelve floodlit, all-weather courts), paddle tennis (four courts), squash, snooker, fencing, table tennis and aerobic classes, in addition to a water-slide, gymnasium, games room, bar, restaurant, boutique, jacuzzi, children's playground and conference room.

How come no one had mentioned this amazing place before? Because it was closed down. We drove in to marvel at the drained swimming-pool, the shattered streetlamps, the peach clubhouse adorned with graffiti. So this was what a sports complex would look like after being walloped by a neutron bomb . . .

Further on, we stopped at a club that hadn't gone bankrupt – Calahonda's very own golf-course. Now many, many golf-courses have been created on the coast. Some of them, like the handful of courses around Marbella's outskirts and the fiendish Torrequebrada, are world-class. Calahonda's course is not. Since I come from the golfing mecca that is Fife, and learned the game as a boy on courses that I assumed were ordinary because they charged a shilling a round, but if transported to Japan would have businessmen killing each other to play on, I had no choice but to sneer knowingly at the scene before me. A couple of chaps were hauling their trolleys up a one-in-two gradient to the last green. The rest of the course stretched, not to the horizon as any self-respecting course should, but to its limit the length of a chartered-flight queue away. There was no level ground, no rough and precious little fairway. I picked up a score-card in the clubhouse to check out just what this course amounted to – nine holes, I discovered, all par threes, the longest being a testing 175 metres, the shortest being fifty-one metres. This was no golf-course. This was pitch 'n' putt. Why those chaps were bothering with trolleys defeated me – they were playing the only nine holes in the world which required two clubs, a sand-wedge and a putter.

As I pointed out to José Romero, the resident pro, whom I met in the clubhouse bar and regaled with stories about the wonderful links I'd played in my home county. No jury in the land would have convicted him of any offence other than justifiable homicide had he swung a seven-iron into my skull, but he was remarkably pleasant about my condescension. I was recalling a (fictitious) birdie at Lundin Links when Phil interrupted me with the whispered comment that he couldn't take any more of this, so I bade Señor Romero a smug farewell and suffered my chauffeur to drive me back to the house.

One of the discoveries I made that first week in Calahonda was late-night telly. Two factors encouraged the development of this hobby. The first was that the house had a television. The second was that the night life in Calahonda kept to a British schedule. Even the Spanish restaurants would be closing by one. Phil was, inevitably, aghast and sought consolation in litre bottles of San Miguel while watching football round-ups and dubbed films. Friday night TV was the most interesting, for that was the slot when Canal + broadcast porn. We didn't have a decoder, so we guessed the plot from what we could make out through the electronic haze and murk. Women gorged themselves on bananas, men performed grunting press-ups – it was like watching a French surrealist art film, only much more fun.

Forgetting, yet again, the moral of the story of the 'Bull'-heckler in Marbella, I can state from my viewing of the local television that the Spanish are a sick race. No healthy society should tolerate televised cycling, for example, or import soaps from South America. The worst symptoms of Spain's cultural disease were, by some way, the late-night cabaret programmes of the kind that have not infected Britain since the passing of the Young Generation. One that sticks in the memory, despite my best efforts to remove it, was a celebration of old-time Spanish vaudeville, which featured very old women re-creating their long-gone music-hall glory with the aid of eight coats of make-up and spangly costumes that contained, but only just, vast reaches of wobbling flesh. One old woman sang a ditty that had the studio audience incontinent with glee. According to Phil's translation, the song was about a naïve couple's use of Vaseline on their wedding night. His translation arrived long after the song was finished because he spent a good while staring at the television in horror.

Since we couldn't receive Sky or BBC World Service programmes, English-language broadcasts were restricted to Gibraltar TV. Fantastic station. Particularly good on fillers. One showed, for five entire minutes, various views of . . . Gibraltar. But Gibraltar TV really came into its own after midnight, when it broadcast a loop-tape of cheapo adverts for local businesses. Video snapshots of restaurants, shoe-repair outfits and so forth were accompanied by an unconvinced commentary which took care never to marry itself with the images. 'Bertie's Bar in Estepona offers the finest in pizza cuisine,' the voice-over would say, as we watched a still of cars parked outside Bertie's Bar. 'And a friendly family atmosphere' (shot of Bertie standing to attention and trying to outstare the camera). 'Situated in the heart of Estepona's outskirts' (shot of chef twirling pizza dough), 'you will find Bertie's Bar has marvellous car-parking facilities' (shot of Bertie's family showing us their fearful grins).

The car skidded round the corner, rally-fashion, and Phil pumped down on the accelerator so that he could overtake the lorry in front on the next hairpin bend.

Four years of olive oil and cured ham had clearly fuelled the man with an authentically Hispanic driving style. When I opened my eyes again, we had swerved violently to the right and were hurtling down what my map claimed was a real road but was in fact a dirt-track. Loose stones clicked against the car's bodywork and the windscreen and I shut my eyes again. More by luck than cunning, we were still alive when we reached the town of Coin, some twenty miles inland. I had broken my rule by leaving the coast but for a good reason – somewhere around here was a place, inspired by Calahonda, which many a BBC executive must wish had remained mythical.

'*Paracaracaros Eldorado?*' Phil asked various locals. Some of them had a notion that there were film people up the hill somewhere, others hadn't a clue what he was on about. A curious response from the good folk of Coin, if you believe the BBC's publicity sheets stating that the whole town was abuzz with the excitement and new jobs created by 'El Miraglo'.

'Nope,' Phil reported back. 'No one's heard of any miracle around here. And no one has much of an idea where it is.'

'All right. I'll phone *Eldorado*'s press office.'

That proved as futile as I'd anticipated, despite all the publicist's usual first-name mateyness. You see, Harry, it was difficult to arrange a visit, Harry, because this was a cleared film set. Besides, Harry, if you normally work for *The Sunday Times* as you say you do, you'll appreciate why that's not one of our favourite newspapers. No, I'm sorry, Harry, but I won't give you directions to see the set from outside. Harry.

Phil's renewed efforts to find anyone who knew of *Eldorado*'s whereabouts finally gleaned a nugget from an unimpressed barman. Up the hill, take the second turn on the right, not counting the small turns before, go through the forest, turn left, take the road you wouldn't think of taking, knock three times on the ceiling, twice on the pipe, and ask for Maisie.

Many wrong turns and false leads later, Phil pulled up on a forest path going nowhere, and advised a re-think. We got out to stretch our legs and keep our tempers. I clambered up over a couple of boulders in a clearing to take a discreet leak. Look on the bright side, I told myself, the view's lovely. Pines, rolling hills, white dusty roads, white dusty villages in the distance, an enormous cut-out of a bull. What? It was the bull-shaped billboard for Osborne brandy that you usually saw stuck on promontories and the like. But this one was in the middle of a pine forest and was facing away from the road. And I could now glimpse, poking out from the pines in front of the bull, part of a pink wall and a red-tiled roof.

'Phil! I think I've found *Eldorado*!'

'Where?'

'Looks as though it's about a mile along this track.' I slithered back down to the car. 'Let's go!'

'On two conditions.'

'Yes?'

'You stop this newshound impersonation. Then do up your zip.'

We bumped and bounced along the path until we reached a high wire fence. Skirting that, we arrived at a conglomeration of cars clustered around what was presumably the main gate. We could make out bits of the set beyond but, more importantly, in the fore-ground was a guardhouse and a patrol of guards accom-panied by dogs. We'd stumbled across the secret head-quarters of Doctor No or T.H.R.U.S.H. The guys in the uniforms would be the extras cross-bowed in the final reel by 007, catapulted into the air by Ilya Kuryakin's grenades.

Unfortunately, they were playing their parts for real. Phil's ingratiating Spanish and my proffered press pass had no effect other than to encourage a barking hound to strain more vehemently at its leash. I gathered that Phil then attempted a more obstreperous, now-look-here-my-good-man approach. I also gathered that this didn't go down too well. One guard grew quite shirty in his demeanour and seemed to suggest that we fuck right off. His colleague made to loosen his hound's leash. *Eldorado Schmeldorado*. I didn't want to see round their stinky set anyway.

I would like to stress that it's not sour grapes that makes me want to skip past the topic of *Eldorado*. My reluctance to deal with it is akin to that of a town-planner avoiding any contemplation of Canary Wharf. However, *Eldorado*, the set, the series, the embarrassment, did exist, and it was inspired by Calahonda, so, with nose snuggling up to a grindstone, here I go.

That set I failed to visit cost £1.5 million and a year's production of the series cost £10 million. *Eldorado* was not owned or run by the BBC because they just shelled out the cash from our licence fees to the two companies who secured the BBC's biggest-ever commission, Cinema Verity and JD&T. The former is run by the highly respected Verity Lambert. The latter is run by the highly respected film producer John Dark, and his partner, the, Australian James Todesco. Tony Holland developed the soap from an idea of Dark and Lambert, and Dark and Todesco acquired that unlikely location on a hillside in the middle of a forest in the middle of nowhere, dozens of miles from the sea where the series would also be filmed. Handy.

The least-known but most intriguing of *Eldorado*'s bosses was Todesco. His name is very familiar, though, to the 4,000 passengers and 7,000 debtors left in the lurch in 1972 when his travel firm collapsed. And to Stewart Granger who lost millions of dollars after Todesco approached him to front a real-estate project in Spain and the project went spectacularly bust.

Todesco lived in a *hacienda* with tennis courts, stables, swimming-pool and a driveway that contained a Mercedes, a Range Rover and a Seat. The car he drove, however, is rented from Avis and paid for by the BBC. Product placement is banned by the BBC, but agents for JD&T attracted various deals, one of which could explain the presence of the Osborne bull facing the wrong way into a forest. It was said that £25,000 would secure a brand-name appearance on a shop-front. NatWest were offered their own pretend branch on the set for £22,000, but the space was eventually bought by the Banco de Jerez. San Miguel kitted out Joy's Bar which, by an extraordinary coincidence, did a roaring trade in San Miguel. After Coca-Cola donated a drinks dispenser, Pepsi gifted hundreds of cans (one of which caused an uproar when a character received a Pepsi upon asking for 'a coke', Coca-Cola's licensed trademark). With real justification, one insider called *Eldorado* 'the longest commercial in history'.

It was also undoubtedly the longest televised flop in history. Never mind Todesco's eventful past, never mind about the Osborne bull facing the wrong way in the middle of a forest and the close-ups of the San Miguel tap, the greatest scandal surrounding *Eldorado* was that the BBC invested millions in a series that was jaw-droopingly awful. *Eldorado* replaced the ailing *Wogan* in the crucial seven-o'clock slot to boost the ratings. The BBC would have had greater success filling those key half-hours with Open University broadcasts by frizzy-haired, Fair-Isle-jumpered chemistry lecturers. At its nadir *Eldorado* attracted an audience of 2.8 million viewers. For an episode broadcast at seven o'clock one Friday evening. *2.8 million*. You'd have thought that would be the number of people who left their sets on BBC1 by mistake. A level-three OU programme on hydrocarbons really couldn't have fared worse.

A fine assortment of theories has been forwarded to explain *Eldorado*'s militantly abject failure. BBC types sought comfort in blaming the hostility of the press, and hostile the press indeed was. (The reason my *Sunday Times* credentials buttered no parsnips with *Eldorado*'s publicist, I learned after finally unearthing that week's copy, was that the paper had just run a story about BBC mandarins being so embarrassed by *Eldorado* that their only solution was to scrap it.) But that's like some brain-dead royals blaming newspapers for reporting the break-down of their marriage.

To appreciate the glib silliness of the nasty-newspapers theory, look up *Eldorado*'s press cuttings before the first broadcast let the shit hit the fans. It's difficult to credit now, but *Eldorado*'s publicists used to have reporters licking crumbs from their palms. 'Stand by for lots of sun, sangria and sex in the BBC's new telly soap opera,' trumpeted the *Sun* when the series was first promoted in December '91. What a brilliant idea for a soap, opined the *Daily Mail*: 'From chars to countesses, Casanovas and crooks, all human life is here. The Costa del Sol is really just one long-running soap opera.' *Eldorado* was going to knock spots off *EastEnders*, and the Rover's Return would be emptied in the rush to watch what the *Sun* christened 'Toro-nation Street'. 'I've seen the future of the BBC,' claimed the *Sun*'s Andy Coulson, 'and it works.' (At least those were Andy Coulson's own words; bits of his copy the previous day had born an uncanny resemblance to the *Eldorado* press release.)

A few scandals did break in the seven months before *Eldorado*'s first broadcast. the *Mirror* reported that locals were distraught about the destruction of the hillside's ecology; Equity threatened a boycott because the actors were being given ungenerous Spanish contracts; the *Sun* revealed that Polly Perkins was a lesbian and the *News of the World* carried nude portraits of her by her lover Sally; and Sandra Sandri was discovered to have sent in topless

photos of herself to audition as a *Sun* page-three girl. But
stories such as these just helped the publicity mechanism
to keep on ticking until the series was launched. And for
that launch *Eldorado* found an eager marketing partner
in the *Sun* which inaugurated 'Eldorado Week' with a
spot-the-difference competition. (First prize was 'a fantastic apartment in the luxury Wimpey Las Palmeras complex' and 1,000 runners-up received a packet of Vesta
paella. Mmmm.)

Then the first episode was shown. 'It's El out there',
'It's Eldora-dodo', 'Helldorado' ran the headlines. Even
the *Sun* had to admit the soap it had zealously promoted
was a partner in grime: 'Eldora-doze' they called it. The
first show had a feeble audience of 6.5 million; one
million people switched off after the first few minutes.
Within three weeks, its viewing figures were down to 4.4
million, less than *Panorama*'s lowest ever score on the
appreciation index, and just one-third of the programme's
meagre audience found it at all enjoyable – which I am
told is the lowest appreciation index ever measured.

An account of the ensuing panic makes for unpleasant
reading, so I'll make this short. A psychologist was flown
to Spain to counsel distressed actors, senior members of
the cast demanded script rewrites, the producer Julia
Smith said that if the scripts went she went, the producer
Julia Smith then went on extended leave with no date
specified for her return, Verity Lambert said she'd stay
until the show was a hit (whereupon the *Sun* wisely
advised her to take out Spanish citizenship), and some of
the cast were given acting lessons, since they were struggling to cope with their first speaking roles. Others were
just written out, among them the teenage Kai Maurer
who had been a beachbum until offered a part in *Eldorado*, and Kathy Pitkin, a 17-year-old whom the BBC promoted as a sex kitten and then dumped when they
realized that her CV as an extra on a film, *The Pied Piper*,
hadn't quite prepared her for telly stardom.

Is it just me or does this not all seem a bit ridiculous? And even if *Eldorado* had starred John Gielgud, Glenda Jackson and Al Pacino, rather than a bunch of teenagers whose collective thespian experience amounted to one *Pied Piper* extra, one walk-on part as a lantern man and one appearance on *Jim'll Fix It*, it'd still be complete bollocks because the plots and scripts were so wonderfully inept. Edith Evans would have struggled to say 'Ah loov you, Booneh' every three minutes. Laurence Olivier couldn't have enlivened an episode whose drama and tension consisted of one character asking other characters for their vote in the coming election and the other characters saying they would think about it. The writing did improve a little after the first few months – but then again, the test card got snazzier when it appeared in colour.

So there's no need for any recourse to intellectual theorizing about *Eldorado*'s failure. It's not the Zeitgeist or Europhobia or resentment at life on the Costa that explains why the series has bombed. As the first press response showed, the idea of *Eldorado* sounded great, far better than any outlines for soaps set in some grimy Lancashire back street, a square of Cockney sparrers or a precinct of idle Australians. But there was no call for waffle about there being no place for *Coronation Street* in Wilson's Britain, or *EastEnders* being an anachronism in the eighties, because those series had the scripts and acting that made for good viewing. The only plus point for *Eldorado* is that it faithfully reflected the fact that a lot of people who live on the coast don't do very much.

The day after our patchily successful trip to *Eldorado* was Phil's fourth and last in Calahonda, so I thought it would be nice to spend it on the beach. Besides, the best beach, the Cabo Pino, was too far away to walk and I wanted to exploit Phil's car to the full. My chauffeur and I zipped alarmingly but without mishap down the N340 and turned left down a road that had a new tarmac surface. I know that's not usually a point of interest except for the keenest road-spotters but it wasn't to be expected for such an uninundated place as the Cabo Pino. The explanation for the new tarmac, if I may drone on about it for a little longer, is that it was laid to cope with telly traffic, for Cabo Pino was the setting for the beach scenes in *Eldorado*.

The camera angles must have been carefully calculated because Cabo Pino is not only beautiful and quiet, but, like many such beaches, has attracted a discerning population of gay nudists. As Phil and I walked along the strand, we became aware that our progress was being monitored by a succession of men sunbathing naked in the dunes to our right. The beach itself was scattered with pairs of men, most of whom had short hair, luxuriant moustaches and irritatingly large schlongs.

While fully committed to my own *membrum virile* – our deep, loving relationship is one built to last, and I shall continue to look on its whimsies and flaws with patient and profound affection – I prefer to think of other chaps as groinless. For whatever reasons (and I don't doubt that some or most are dark and dingily shameful), I interact with other chaps on the unilateral understanding that, down there, they, unlike me, taper to a demure bottom-of-the-stomach-top-of-the-thigh absence. Like Action Men.

So even had Cabo Pino's regulars not been equipped with prize-winning appendages, I would still have been bothered. As they were, I was very bothered indeed. So no way was I going to take all my kit off. My shreddies were staying on, thank you very much. There would, on no account, be any possibility of a public appearance by Mister Wobbly. When I told Phil of my resolve that neither of us reveal our white bits, he seemed surprised, disappointed even. A bluff? I'm not sure, but his reaction pissed me off, I can tell you. For the following reasons:

(1) he was implying that I was an uptight, repressed sicko whereas he was mature and unashamed of his body; (2) he was implying he was well hung and no error. Anyway, whether as an act of solidarity or not I will never know, he too kept his trunks on for our afternoon session of sunbathing, swimming and that inexplicably compulsive activity, stone-skimming. Thence to the charmingly dilapidated beach bar, a rickety wooden number on stilts whose collapse looked imminent. It stayed upright long enough for us to have a few beers, make friends with a young Irishman and his 'puppy' (a hyperactive mongrel the size of a donkey), watch a couple of locals catch a series of fat-lipped fish, and admire the start of a glorious sunset.

Fabulous will-power had to be called on to tear ourselves away from this idyll, but somehow we managed it. As we walked back along the now deserted beach, I turned to take one last look at Cabo Pino. The anglers were still there, silhouetted in the orange glow of the falling sun. It was easier to imagine that we were in the Seychelles or a Bounty advert than on a supposedly devastated coastline. Maybe all of the Costa del Sol looked as wonderful as this once, before people like us ruined it by the sheer weight of our numbers, but I don't think so. In the 500 years since the final collapse of Moorish Al-Andalus, this coast was completely unprized, especially by the locals, until the tourists came. I am unlucky enough to own a copy of a book published in 1950 called *Spain*, by that prancing ninny Sacheverell Sitwell, who lugged his aesthete's sensibility all over the country in search of its majesties and wonders. How many entries are there in the index for the Costa del Sol or any of its towns and villages? None. The whole coastline wasn't worth even a footnote.

I rather suspect that, had Phil been compiling a guide to Spain, his attitude to the coast would be not far distant from S. Sitwell's. Not only had he acquired a

Catalan's disdain for the work-shy/primitive/untrustworthy Andalusians, he had developed a very un-Spanish anxiety about a corner of Spain that was no longer Spain as he knew it. Several clues gave away the fact that he was not happy in Calahonda – outbursts of crying, beating his head against the wall, that sort of thing. It hadn't occurred to him that the Spain I'd invited him to visit would be overwhelmed by foreigners, whose invasion the Spaniards encouraged but whom Phil resented with the passion of the convert. Alan's Plaice, the Red Lion and the Yellow Lady had no place in his adopted motherland, to which he returned the following day. I attempted to cheer him with the profound reminder that every cloud had a silver lining, which in this case was that Phil, or rather Phil's fluent Spanish and Phil's fluent car, had been very useful to me.

My chauffeur/translator left early the next morning, giving me a few hours to prepare for the arrival of my guests for my second week in Calahonda, and my last week on the coast. I decided to give the house a really good clean, and then decided to do no such thing. I had a more important task to fulfil down at El Zoco.

It was worth displaying a tidemark of untanned face on my final seven days to have my hair cut out in Spain, for one reason – the barber wouldn't be able to ask me if I was going on holiday this year. It was this rather than the discomfort of a heavy head in the heat that prompted me to visit Shapes, Ladies' and Men's Hairdressing, above El Zoco's supermarket.

An English youth – the only person in the shop – greeted me timidly and led me to a chair.

'Just a trim is it, sir?'

'Yes, a light one, not too much off.'

He scissored half an inch with his fingers. 'This much maybe?' he asked my reflection.

'Perfect,' I replied to his.

'And tidy up the loose ends?'

'Wonderful.'

'Enjoying your holidays are you?'

Ah, fuck it.

There are people in this world who always have success-ful haircuts. They pay someone to make their hair look tidier, shapelier, better. I belong to the other category of people whose friends and colleagues have to regress to primary-school taunts of Baldy and jokes about chloro-form and lawn-mowers. (There is an obvious explanation as to why haircuts, like photographs, always make me look crap – I just look crap – but I tend to think there are other many and varied reasons for both phenomena.) So when the timid youth claimed he'd finished and I hooked my glasses back on to inspect the damage, it came as no surprise whatsoever to see that the man in the mirror was not me but Buzz Aldrin.

Furry-scalped, I sloped off for a restorative beer at the neighbouring Dickens Bar, the place where, legend has it, Tony Holland sat and watched the locals and came up with an idea for a soap series based on their lives. So it was here that *Eldorado* was stillborn. Framed articles profiling the pub as *Eldorado*'s inspiration dotted the walls of the Dickens Bar, but the landlord, Colin Camp-bell, was less than keen about his role in TV history.

'Yes, that Tony Holland was supposed to have come here. Mind you, I can't remember him. To tell the truth, I'm well and truly pissed off about the *Eldorado* business. All the reporters coming in here ...' Colin Campbell shook his head. He could have been a Saxon elder recalling the arrival of horned men in long ships. 'Even the *Independent*. They came down here and did an article like a play, you know, Scene One, the Dickens Bar, and they wrote things in that I'm sure I never said and customers never said ...'

The bloke next to me, who had apparently bought a season ticket for his bar stool, announced, with the demagogic slur of the very well refreshed, that the trouble with *Eldorado* . . . you see, *Eldorado*'s trouble . . . was . . . the thing about it, you see . . . they had . . . the wrong . . . not the right . . . thingy. Characters.

'I've been out here eight years now,' he continued painfully. 'The things I've seen . . . But what that . . . *Eldorado* . . . shows about the . . . us expats . . . is totally wrong. Totally. Wrong. Totally . . .'

'So what's wrong about it?' I asked with as concerned an expression as I could manage.

'Totally.'

I did a lot of thoughtful nodding, as TV reporters do in those shots that break up interviews.

The season-ticket holder persevered. 'Oh yes. There's some *real* characters out here.'

'I bet there are!' I enthused while wondering if this was what it was like working with the massively deranged.

'Oh, yes.'

'Could you maybe give me an example?'

'Oh, now then . . .' He smiled into the middle distance. 'God, yes . . . Oh, *real* characters,' he explained.

It was maybe time to try a different angle. Having established that he was a resident, I asked the season-ticket holder what he did before he retired to his bar stool.

'Three guesses.'

'Err . . . publican?'

'Nope.'

'Something to do with sales?'

'Nope.'

'Politician?'

'Nope. Bank robber.'

I should have known. It was the wonderful quip of every witless expat on the coast.

'I imagine that must have been very exciting for you,' I said.

'Yip. No, not really.'

'Oh dear.'

'Actually I was in retail.'

'Ah.'

'Some real characters, though. Colin? I was . . . just saying . . . some real characters.'

'Oh Christ, yes. Real characters.'

'Shaky Keith, eh?'

'Oh dear God, yes, Shaky Keith.'

'Remember that time I met whatsisname coming down the road and he was only wearing his . . . thingy . . . socks? And Baz and Tony, eh, Colin?'

'Oh yes, Baz and Tony. Right enough.'

'Baz and Tony.' The season-ticket holder mulled over their names a final time before adding a tsk of indulgence, and then a completely untranscribable grunt of surprise.

'Well, talk of the Devil!' said Colin.

Two men flopped into the bar. One was tall, bearded and very drunk, the other was small, spherical and even drunker. The tall one found a resting place by the door but the small one waddled over to sit between me and the season-ticket holder. With his white and outrageously unkempt mop-top coiffure, frayed jerkin, shirt unbuttoned to the groin, and sinking jeans overshadowed by a huge all-bought-and-paid-for stomach, the small guy looked like a lager-addicted troll. He smelt like one as well.

'Baz,' he growled with a catarrhy rumble.

'Harry,' I replied.

'Tyne a piss,' said Baz, though to Colin not me and evidently about a third party not Colin. 'Tyne a fuyyin piss. Hundredfifty puzeas a beer, tyne a piss. I toll him, all the stuff I done for him, tyne a piss, hundredfifty puzeas fuyyin beer, tyne a piss.'

Baz was upset, clearly.

'We were just talking about real . . . some of the whatsit . . . characters . . . out here,' said the season-ticket holder.

'Hundredfifty puzeas?'

'Like you Baz . . . you know . . . you.'

'All things I done for him? Tyne a piss.'

'So what is it you do, Baz?' I asked gamely.

'Fuyyin cun. Woh? Me? Woh do I do?'

'Yes.'

'Naffin is woh I do.'

'A man of leisure, then?' (And, yes, I did feel a prat when I said that, but these were trying circumstances.)

'Do woh? See these espadrilles? They're fuyyin crap. Cheap. I'm skint, thas woh I do.'

'Back home then?'

'Hundredfifty puzeas? Fuyyin cun. Woh? Woh I did? Bank robber, mate.'

Give me strength. There were five of us in that bar, all laughing at this riposte, but 20 per cent of us didn't feel much like doing so.

Judging that he should make his exit after his best punchline, Baz drained his drink, slapped me chummily on the shoulder and went off with Tony to find other people to entertain.

'A real character that,' observed the season-ticket holder. 'Yes, they broke the . . . thingy . . . mould . . .'

'So what is it that Baz and Tony do out here?' I asked. 'Or did back home?'

'Hah! I thought he told you.'

'Seriously though.'

'Seriously. Bank robber. Done thingy . . . porridge.'

My first and only bank robbers on the Costa del Sol and I thought they were tyne a piss.

I trudged back up the hill to await the arrival of my sister and her family. In happy contrast to Phil, they were bang on time. Greeting them, I was painfully reminded of Billy Connolly's observation that it takes Scots two weeks' hard sunbathing to turn white, since our natural skin colour is blue. Margaret (thirty-two),

Ken (thirty-two) and Iain (one) emerged from their airport taxi with caution and blinking like newly released pit ponies. Ken told me it was hot, in the manner of an awed scientist who has just invented heat by accident.

They had left behind an Edinburgh 'summer' so consistently atrocious that when they did manage to turn off the central heating they'd done a lap of honour round the kitchen. Now they dropped their bags on the grass and simply stood there, smiling, nodding slightly, silent.

They evidently needed time to acclimatize. An orderly overseeing the inmates' outing, I led them into the relative cool of the sitting-room. Several hours would pass before they dared to brave the patio.

During that time, the house was efficiently transformed from a site of laddish hedonism into Iain's portable kindergarten. But on that afternoon no amount of gaudy balls, daddy, mummy and baby bears, squeaky men, picture-books and smiley green dinosaurs could distract Iain from his favourite game. Obsession is more like it. Crawl at great pace to item of furniture, climb up same and leap towards the oblivion assured by the welcoming marble floor. I hasten to add that he only ever completed two-thirds of this routine, but only because he was constantly surrounded by three adults who followed his every move in the pose of scrum-halves about to attempt a delicate drop-kick.

It was because my nephew was so devotedly practising for his audition as a Tom and Jerry lemming, and had also acquired an immediate and unshakeable fascination for the marble stairs, that the house was also transformed into zones that had to be partitioned, fenced off and zealously guarded. I found myself living in the domestic equivalent of Cyprus.

Outside Cyprus, on the patio and the lawn, Iain was frustratingly blasé about the things I had longed to see him entranced by – the bright light, the springy warm grass, the little conifers that edged the lawn. I had nursed a vision of the little treasure tottering around a soft-focus garden, enraptured by butterflies flitting around his sun-hat. (More worldly readers will conclude, correctly, that I am not a parent.) Instead, he tottered around, pointing at miraculous features of Abroad, such as clocks and light switches, babbling to himself (with such convincing speech patterns he'd have been a star turn at any meeting of born-again evangelists), and trying out his facial expressions – the gormlessly happy drunk, the dotard falling asleep in the Athenaeum, the resolute leader of men, and, when Ken gradually lowered him into the pool, the hammy tragedian's collapse into grief.

Iain awoke at seven and let out a long, piercing wail to let it be known that he was disoriented and miserable. So was his uncle. I suppose I must have dropped back into sleep, because by ten I had missed a vital plane flight after being chased by prefects down some suburban stretch of the Piccadilly line.

The house was suspiciously quiet. I hobbled down to the kitchen, where I found the explanation in a note that read, 'H. Have gone to supermarket. Back soon.'

It was two-thirty when the threesome reappeared, tired and slightly hysterical. They had indeed been to the supermarket but one some ten miles down the road – no small feat for a family with no car and one baby in a pushchair. They'd got as far as the Red Lion on the Avenida España, ten minutes' gentle stroll away, before they were set upon by time-share touts. Young marrieds with baby and the pallor of the newly arrived? It was surprising they'd survived unmolested for as long as ten minutes. They might as well have gone shopping with a 'Please Subject Us To A Heavy Sell' placard round their necks.

'This bubbly girl came up to us,' explained my sister. 'And she asked us if we were on holiday, so we said yes and then she asked if we were English and we said . . .'

'And you said, no, in actual fact we're Scottish . . .'

'Well, yes, and then we had to do this holiday survey, she called it, which was very short as it turned out, asking where we stayed, did we have British passports, did we like holidays, that sort of caper. And then they did this prize draw.'

'And – let me take a wild guess. You won first prize,' I said.

'No. I won sixth prize. This.' Margaret held up a bottle of alcoholic fizzy pop designated as *vino espumoso gasificado*.

'*I* won first prize though,' said Ken. 'A dream holiday.' He produced, with a great flourish, a glossy leaflet sloganed 'Dream Holiday'. 'I wasn't bothered but that girl got very excited about it. She kept jumping up and down and clapping her hands and telling me I should be thrilled. Then she called her friend over.'

'Debbie,' said Margaret.

'Yes, Debbie. They drove us down to the taxi-rank and bundled us in a taxi.' He frowned at the memory.

'Did you want to go?' I asked.

My sister pondered this one. 'No. But you know what it's like. You're on holiday . . . and saying no would have taken quite an effort. Besides, they said there was a supermarket at the place they wanted to show us, and we'd get a free ride in the taxi there and back. Anyway, when we got to this place, kind of a holiday camp it was, they kept telling us it wasn't a time-share. Except they also kept talking about time-share as well.'

'Who's they?'

'Salesmen. The first one was called Jim and there was another one right at the end, I can't remember his name.'

'That's because he never told us,' Ken reasoned. 'He was too busy trying to get us to sign on the dotted line.'

'So what happened with Jim?' I asked.

Margaret swooped down to prevent Iain connecting

himself to the mains supply. 'Oh, Jim was the one who showed us round,' she said while now failing to restrain Iain from attempting to scale her chest to reach the launch-pad of her neck. 'It was quite a fair-sized complex and, you know, all *right*, I suppose, if you like that sort of thing . . .'

'What sort of thing?'

'Awful. And the only people there seemed to be men in suits like Jim walking around with couples like us. And every time we passed a group of these people, Jim and the other bloke in the suit would make a big deal of being ultra-matey, you know, to prove what a happy, friendly atmosphere they had there.'

Margaret interrupted her account at this point with a yelp as Iain tried to pull out a sizeable clump of her hair. Ken took up the story.

'The funny thing was, I kept on asking this Jim character about the cost of the thing and how it worked, but all he told us was that the minimum cost was six grand. For what I still do not know. Whatever it was was appreciating at 20 per cent a year, according to him.'

'Mind you,' Margaret reflected, 'we learned a lot about Jim. How he loved Canada, how his daughter was doing really well at Oxford, what he thought about Ian Woosnam, how he'd stayed at some of the leading hotels in the world and they didn't compare with this place.'

'Which was ridiculous, because it was more like Butlins,' said Ken.

'Especially that poster they had with photographs of everyone who had stayed there waving at the camera. Ow. Iain, if I get alopecia, I know who to blame.'

'So what kept you so long?'

Ken shook his head. 'Jim's life story, the tour . . . And then, after he'd done, he took us through to a big room packed with punters and sales people where this other suit grilled us.'

'Thank God for Iain playing up,' said Margaret. 'The poor wee thing was needing his lunch and his bed, so that gave us a reason for escaping. Otherwise we'd probably be there yet.'

'Still, it was an experience,' said Ken. '*And* I've got my dream holiday . . .'

Ken and Margaret were to spend a significant proportion of the rest of their week in Calahonda puzzling over the leaflet that outlined the glories of Ken's premier-prize free dream cruise around the Caribbean. What was the catch? Was it for two people with only one paid for? Would they have to shell out untold thousands extra for a cabin? Was there a Caribbean in north Wales? (They discovered the catch some weeks later; the free £1,000 dream holiday cheque did not include the £700 per person airfare.)

Because I fell into one of the two categories of punter the touts were said to spurn – singles and the tattooed – I had yet to visit any time-share complex myself, so that evening I popped down the road to the Club Riviera. Calahonda has several time-shares, including an extensive and vastly billboarded Barrett development, but Club Riviera was the one resented by many of the locals such as our next-door neighbour. 'It's lowered the . . . the place,' he told me one afternoon by the pool, showing his tan and a reluctance to use the word 'tone'. 'It just doesn't fit in here. Don't get me wrong, I'm not a snob,' he assured me, 'but . . . you know . . .' (I lost a bet with myself because he didn't actually say that some of his best friends were working-class.)

As I'd been led to expect, belying its normal exterior, Club Riviera was a disgraceful site of unwashed low-life. That's if a few dozen families gathered round a pool for a karaoke evening strikes you as offensively vulgar. It so happened that the karaoke performers that evening outdid even The Old Bailey's in awfulness, but I stuck it out to strike up conversations with some of the time-sharers by the bar. My usual line was that I was dreadfully discontented about my time-share with the same firm in Tenerife, so that I'd hear any grumbles going in chats based on mutual complaints. Didn't work. Everyone was sympathetic but said I'd have been far better off owning a time-share here. Great it was. Fabulous holidays. Tremendous value when you thought about it.

I tell a lie. There was one bloke who was well pissed off with Club Riviera. 'I know just what you mean,' he exclaimed as we propped up the bar together to the sound of a caterwauling nine-year-old girl screaming out the words to Madonna's 'Like a Virgin' on the karaoke mike. 'Worst holiday I've had in years. I've been completely ripped off here.'

'Go on,' I said. 'Tell me about it, go on, yes.'

'Well, for one thing I had my pocket picked down at the supermarket. And what's more, the first day here I drove into a pothole, did two tyres in, and you know how much it cost to repair them? 20,000 pesetas. I was well choked.'

So, too, was I. What about the notorious time-share rip-offs, scams, miseries, traumas and angsts? Well, I suppose the last people who would complain about time-share, apart from the salesmen, are those who've bought one. Certainly, the only other grumbles I heard from all the time-sharers I talked to on the coast were that the mornings were a bit cloudy, taxis seemed more expensive than last year, and the pool could do with being a bit bigger. There was nothing for it but to listen to the company propaganda as delivered by one of its salesmen.

The local English-language newspapers were carrying full-page ads enticing human dynamos to join Club Riviera's sales force: 'EARN IN EXCESS OF £2,000 PER WEEK,' howled those ads. 'DRIVE A FERRARI. EAT CAVIAR. LIVE IN A CASTLE. DRINK DOM

PERIGNON'. What kind of people replied successfully to that kind of situation vacant?

People who were young, burly, go-getting men from the north of England who liked double-breasted suits and lots of after-shave, I found out when I walked into the sales office. It was like being surrounded by a coked-up, off-duty rugby-league team. I was given a guided tour by one of their number, Barry, who proved himself to be the sort of person I just don't understand, someone who exuded boundless job satisfaction and a messianic fervour about the company he happened to work for.

'So,' I said as he showed me round an empty flat in the Club Riviera complex, 'how do you like your job?'

'*Brilliant.*'

'Goodness.'

'*Love* it, mate. Working on commission? *Love* it.'

'What if you have a run of bad luck?'

'No such thing as bad luck in this game. Luck doesn't come into it. Lack of talent, yeah. But I make money because I'm *good.*'

'What, two grand a week, caviar and Dom Perignon and a mortgage on a castle?'

'Sure, an averagely good salesman can earn that. Easy.'

He could afford a lot of after-shave, that was for sure. 'What do you think about people here looking down on Club Riviera?'

'Doesn't bother me. I tell you, we've had so much bad publicity, in the press, everywhere. You know why? Because we opened up the market to the working-class. Used to be only a middle-class thing, time-share, before we came along. And because of our selling techniques.'

'With touts you mean?'

'No way. We don't use OPCs, they're old hat. Stands for outside people catchers,' he explained when I frowned. 'No, people call us sharkish, but we just get down to the nitty-gritty. No gimmicks, no shite like

warming people up. Not like Barretts, they just hoity-
toity around. The closers at Barretts couldn't sell water
to a thirsty man, I tell you. They say things like, "Go
away and think about it."' Barry shook his head in
wonder. 'But even we don't compare to our guys in the
Canaries. Hell, you should see those boys. They're not
bothering with selling the time-share any more, they just
go for the big deposits, grand a throw, take their chances
on that. I tell you.'

'But aren't you ripping people off even more, making
them pay through the nose for something they don't
need?'

'*No way, José.* You take regular holidays, you want to
be certain of the standard of accommodation, this is a
good idea, I tell you. And we're part of an exchange
scheme so you're not limited, are you? You want a
yachting holiday, horse-riding maybe, a cruise, you can
have one, no problem.'

'Really?'

'Sure. Really. You interested?'

'I told you. I'm here to see if I can write something
about time-share, not buy one.'

'Why not do both?'

'I don't want to. Anyway, you should see my overdraft.'

'No problem. You could afford it, I tell you. Come on,
one week a year you could come here, for the rest of your
life, only three thou. Plus maintenance charge, but we're
talking two figures. Ninety-nine quid. Come on, do yourself a favour.'

'Honestly, no thanks.'

'You won't regret it.'

'Sorry.'

'Let yourself go.'

'I can't.'

'Why not? Just do it. Enjoy yourself for once in your
life.'

'Oh God . . . do you think I should?'

Somehow, I escaped without signing on any dotted line. A close shave, though. But impressive though Barry's sudden pitch had been, I'd yet to experience a proper time-share hard sell. Kidology, self-delusion and indolence couldn't prevent me from acknowledging that I still had to go through with Plan B.

'Right,' said Margaret, 'let me run through this again. My husband is my brother, my brother is my husband, and your nephew is your son.'

I nodded my head. 'Which means, come to think of it, that our parents are also our parents-in-law.'

'Let's stick to the basics, okay? And if anyone asks, you're doing Ken's job because that always shuts people up.'

'Correct. Just pretend I'm Ken. But remember that you've gone back to your maiden name.'

'I don't see why we have to pretend to be married anyway. I'm beginning to think it's some sick fantasy of yours.'

'Margaret, even if you weren't my sister, I would rather tear my own head off my shoulders than be shackled to you.'

'Charming.'

'But we have to be married for the next few hours to be propped by time-share touts. They only go for families. They'll be swarming all over us. Iain is the perfect accessory.'

'Did you hear that, wee man? What a nasty uncle . . .'

'Daddy.'

'What a nasty daddy your uncle is. God, I hope this doesn't give him a complex. Okay, you push the buggy. And remember, I want to go to the Four Seasons time-share place because the leaflets say you get 5,000 pesetas just for being shown around.'

Coping with voluntary misery is not one of my strong points, as various dentists, inoculators and shop assistants will attest. So it was with a heavy heart and many a heavy sigh that I set off with Margaret and Iain to experience the plight of the time-share victim.

As I had hoped, our incestuously rejigged family proved as tempting a prey to Calahonda's touts as a plump baby seal to a hungry polar bear. Our first prop came when a Renault 5 squealed to a halt and two salivating youths got out to tell us the news that if we answered their holiday survey and took part in their prize draw, we could win a dream cruise in the Caribbean. That approach happened after we had walked a full twenty yards. We spurned a series of other pesterings until a Four Seasons rep at last stopped us outside the El Zoco supermarket, and Margaret at last received a leaflet offering her 5,000 pesetas if she completed a tour.

A taxi was summoned and the three of us were bundled in for a trip down the road towards Marbella where, at the Four Seasons Country Club, we were bundled into a reception room full of cavorting children and parents being talked to by besuited men. It looked like an open day at a branch of Relate.

The besuited man assigned to us – I'll call him Terry, shall I? – began by making a fuss over Iain, then asking what jobs we did.

'Nurse,' Margaret said.

'Civil service,' I said.

Terry turned to me. 'Oh yes?' he said. 'Which branch?'

'Inland Revenue.'

'I see.'

Having filled in our obligatory holiday survey (which asked us not about our holiday but our income bracket), we were subjected to Terry's pitch. This started gently enough with him telling us details of varying intimacy about himself, but once we'd seen the photos of his children and got over his divorce, he swung into action with a prolonged advert for the benefits of a small time-share flat.

'That sounds okay,' I said, 'but we were thinking of something a bit more expensive.' Out of the corner of my eye I could see Margaret frowning at me. 'With the legacy we've got, dear,' I explained, 'from old Uncle Bertrand.'

'. . . yes. But we don't want to spend it all in one go, do we, dear?'

'Quite right, dear, but there's enough of it to go round . . .'

'Whatever you say, dear. Put that down, Iain love. Yes, give it to your unc . . . uncompromising daddy.'

'Well, then,' said Terry, 'perhaps you would be interested in a more upmarket flat. Would you excuse me for a moment? I'll just fetch the details.'

'So what's all this rubbish about Uncle Bertrand?' Margaret whispered when Terry had sprinted off.

'It's to get him really keen.'

'Well, that's a shame, egging him on like that. And what about your son here? It'll be even harder to shake that Terry off now. We'll be here all day and Iain'll be needing fed in a couple of hours and I've only got a wee pot of strawberry yoghurt to keep him going.'

'Calm down. If Iain gets unhappy that'll be our excuse to get out. Just remember your lines and nothing will go wrong.'

What indeed could go wrong? The one person who could blow the whistle on us was too young to talk. And Terry hadn't commented on the giveaway in our appearances – for Margaret's skin was still the colour of Alpine snow whereas I was by now brown. A wonderfully deep, smooth, glistening, gorgeous brown. Apart, that is, from my underarms.

Terry returned with a couple of brochures to show us the wonders of the Four Seasons' exchange scheme. Yes, as affiliates of Interval International we could swap our Four Seasons time-share for holidays, in Disneyland, for example (great for little Iain there), or Portugal (fantastic golf-courses for me) or the Bahamas (for our second honeymoon perhaps). All for free, although there would naturally be the flights to pay for, an exchange fee of £54 per week and maintenance charges of £212 per week on a two-bedroom apartment. And bills. But, give or take a thousand, free. How much the time-share itself would cost we still didn't know. We'd be coming to that, Terry assured us each time we asked. Meanwhile, there was the Four Seasons complex to tour.

First on the itinerary was the Four Seasons Country Club, with its unrivalled bar, squash court, computer golf facility, television, snooker tables and buffet. Would we feel comfortable here? Terry asked us. Why, yes we would. Then out we trooped past the various plaques acknowledging the excellence of the Four Seasons Country Club (all awarded, interestingly, by Interval International), through the lush grounds of the Four Seasons' first phase, until we arrived at the tennis courts and beach club, actually the property of the Don Carlos Hotel but available to Four Seasons time-sharers. Sorry, Country Club members. Would we feel comfortable living in such exclusive, five-star luxury? We said we'd try not to let the side down.

The presentation would definitely take no more than ninety minutes, we'd been told, so we'd reckoned on spending two hours here. But an hour and a half had already gone by and Terry had yet to show us an apartment. Or make any mention of money. Iain had fallen asleep in the buggy I was pushing in a fatherly fashion, but I knew Margaret was getting worried about him. Kind of a telepathic thing I suppose. Besides, whenever Terry turned his back, she'd taken to pointing at Iain, me, her watch and the exit. Then running an index finger along her throat. Okay, okay, I mouthed. She rolled her eyes. Terry led on obliviously to a sample flat.

We were shown everything in that flat. Marble en-suite cludgie, dishwasher, balcony, walk-in utilities cupboard, satellite TV, cutlery, crockery, even the damned corkscrew. Forgetting for a moment her anxiety about her first-born, Margaret pursued a new role of not being impressed, grimacing at the sofa-bed, wrinkling up her nose at the soft furnishings. I had a nightmarish vision of my sister degenerating into one of those people who spend their weekends criticizing show-houses.

Ominously, Iain began to stir as we made our way back to the reception area for the real hard sell to begin. Terry told us to make ourselves at home while he went off to find his accomplice. Margaret seized the opportunity to assuage the awakening Iain and tell me to make this quick.

I did try, but Terry and his besuited accomplice were hell-bent on more small talk. Were we, asked the accomplice, on holiday with anyone who might also be interested in the sun-kissed luxury of Four Seasons?

'Only my brother,' said Margaret, while calming Iain's whimpers.

'Would he like to come to look at a flat as well?' asked the accomplice.

'I don't think so,' she said. 'He won't listen to anything I say.'

'Here on holiday with his family too, is he?'

'Oh, no. Shoosh now, Iain. No, he's very much a confirmed bachelor, if you know what I mean.'

The accomplice flapped his wrist. 'One of them?'

'Difficult to tell,' mused Margaret. 'You're all right, Iain, we'll be home soon. You see, my brother had a bad accident, you know, down there. He annoyed someone very badly once and got beaten up. Mind you, I'm not saying he didn't deserve it. A strange, warped man. We hoped this holiday would help him but . . .'

'Well, when you have your time-share, you could bring him out here with you, couldn't you?'

'Oh, I think this'll be the last time we go on holiday together.'

'Ahah. Still, the thing is about being a Four Seasons Club member, you can use your membership to give anyone you want a fortnight here. And what better investment could you both have for little Iain than guaranteed holidays for life? And Iain can pass it on to his children and his grandchildren.'

The future grandparent was now pitting his jovial nature against hunger. Hunger looked to be winning and he looked to be winding up for a long, puce-faced howl. Margaret spooned some pink gunk into his mouth and told us we had better get a move on because that was the last of the strawberry yoghurt.

There followed a flurry of propaganda as Terry and his accomplice moved into top gear. Look at this sheet listing the personalities who were Four Seasons Club members – George Michael, Rory Bremner, Jimmy Greenhof, Harvey Goldsmith, Sir Edwin Nixon, James Last . . . We too could be part of this star-studded holiday club for the paltry fee of, well, it was all quite complicated, but here were some variables. Say we bought two weeks in a two-bedroom apartment, that'd be sixteen thousand, but seeing as how we had a lump sum, that could be reduced to, oh, fourteen and a half. A quick tap of the calculator showed that payments, through Four Seasons' own finance company, would then be 270 quid a month for ten years. Less than ten quid a day! A mere nothing! No, we couldn't see the brochure or paperwork until we paid a deposit, fully refundable if we were foolish enough to ignore this wonderful offer, of a thousand pounds. And that deposit would also hold the price of the flat which was due to increase *any minute now* when a fax arrived from the Dublin head office.

I wanted that brochure. 'I don't have a thousand for a deposit,' I said, truthfully. 'I'm about a hundred off my Visa limit.'

'That'll do fine,' said the accomplice. How very accommodating he was, to be sure.

And on and on the persuaders continued to persuade, until, almost an hour of their eulogizing and nagging later, another outbreak of dismay from Iain spurred Margaret to insist that we really did have to leave. Now. Or else.

Back on the patio in Calahonda, Margaret fed a ravenous Iain, and I puzzled over some curious economics. Counting the 5,000-peseta inducement, taxis, coffees, and the cost of the lunch we'd had to refuse, the Four Seasons Country Club was forking out £60 per visiting family. On the other hand, Margaret had earned 5,000 pesetas for having completed the tour, but I had paid £100 to look at a brochure. (As I feared, the money was never refunded. Cheers.) And if we had taken up the offer, my irate sibling-wife and I would be paying 120 times £271, over £32,000, for something worth £16,000. And just what would that buy? With mentions of 'your property' and 'your home', the brochure glided over the fact that we would have had no such thing. What we'd actually own was a unit of holiday capacity. We'd have bought the right to try to arrange to book an apartment in a block which was, in fact, in the process of being built, for two weeks a year. For a sum that could buy us outright our very own cottage inland. And on top of the monthly payments of £271, we'd pay up to £700 a year in additional charges.

If that didn't make too much sense, the sums from the company's point of view did. Say each apartment cost £60,000 to build. Twenty-five holiday units per apartment at £17,000 a throw would mean Four Seasons raking in over seven times that £60,000. I realize it might not be quite as simple as that, but that's the basic arithmetic behind the time-share idea. Time-sharers pay a fraction of the building cost, but a much greater fraction than the 2 or 4 per cent their one or two weeks would account for. Same idea with the maintenance charges. Over two hundred a week, ten grand a year?

That would, you'd have thought, cover a laundry service and a thrice-weekly maid, even if every Four Seasoner shat on their sheets nightly and the woman as did was Princess Di.

But maybe I'd got it all wrong. The Four Seasons represents excellent value for money. Rory Bremner is a truly great man who can hold his head high for having his name on the Four Seasons celebrity list. George Michael really does have a Four Seasons time-share because he can't afford his own villa.

I have to confess that I pursued my investigations into the plight of the time-share victim no further. I could explain that this was because I considered one such episode enough to write and read about, but that's not the reason. Actually, I couldn't be bothered. I was on holiday, wasn't I? And doing nothing is what most people do on holiday, especially in Calahonda, so I devoted myself to researching just that. And the fact that I was doing nothing in a family unit, albeit one acquired for the occasion, just went to make the doing-nothing experience all the more authentic.

The family-unit aspect of things also made for early starts in the morning. I speak as one who, in workaday life, can be counted on to regain the power of speech by eleven or so. Having Iain to guarantee my being roused from slumber by seven every morning was, therefore, a . . . new experience for me. I fantasized briefly about spiking his yoghurt with Valium but soon realized the idiocy of that. You had to get a prescription for the stuff.

And, in fairness to Iain, I should add that he was up against stiff competition in the reveille stakes. There was the early-morning grass-cutter who inspired disturbed dreams about Flymos and strimmers. A Spanish car-driver across the road who parped his horn for quarter of an hour every day at half-six. A chainsaw gang who worked very hard on a nearby deforestation project, for shifts that lasted from seven to seven-thirty every morning. (Perhaps they had been trained by a British Gas roadworks team.) And there was the light-switch craftily placed above my pillow, which meant that an arm flung out in sleep would have me waking up floodlit by the overhead lamp.

I persevered with the late-night telly sessions; there were too many football programmes and dubbed films to marvel at, as well as Gibraltar TV's splendid loop-tape of adverts, and there was plenty of time during the day to catch up on lost sleep. Naps, lie-downs and siestas were punctuated by exciting walks to the supermarket and nights out on the town. I say nights, but these started about six and were over by nine or ten, depending on how benevolent Iain was feeling about the idea of us having a meal in public.

It wasn't a labour-intensive time, I admit, but it was my last week in Spain and I deserved a bit of a rest. It had been a hard summer. The sunbathing and the eating and the drinking I had taken in my stride and volleyed in the top right-hand corner of the net, but look at all the hardships I'd had to endure . . .

Okay, so it was difficult to name them just like that, but my scam hadn't worked out at all as planned. Burnished bimbettes had not flocked to my side, and the aim of cultivating a glorious tan had been scuppered by my still-white underarms. I had anticipated two months of rest and recreation but these holidays had often been too much like hard work. I'd been too single for Fuengirola, too old for Torremolinos, too poor for Marbella. But that second week in Calahonda was just right.

Except for the minor problem that I sensed that there was something irritatingly familiar about Calahonda. The comparison was there at the back of my head but, try as I might, I couldn't wrench it forward. This bugged me as such things – the misplaced words to the crappy tune that insists on being whistled throughout the day,

the name of the scorer of that free kick in the Cup Final
– have a way of bugging. It was only well into the
second week that the simile abruptly wandered towards
the front of my head to be articulated. I was walking to
the supermarket, looking downhill past bungalows with
neat, tended gardens and catching glimpses of the sea.
And there the simile was. Kirkcaldy. Calahonda reminded me of home.

Of course, there were differences. The flora, fauna,
architecture and infrastructure, to name but four. Also
the clear blue skies and the blazing sun: I'd be surprised
if Kirkcaldy had seen a temperature above twenty-five
degrees since before the last Ice Age; sunbathing was
possible one day a year back in Fife and then you still
had to cope with midges, gales, rain, hail . . . In addition,
the Mediterranean, the sight of which had done much to
urge the likeness its last few millimetres forward, was not
the Firth of Forth. For a start, you couldn't see Edinburgh from here. And, unpleasant though the experience
could be at times, you could swim in the Mediterranean
without (a) an all-over smearing of goose fat to protect
against instant, fatal exposure or (b) an astronaut-style
suit hired from Sellafield to protect against instant, fatal
exposure to pollution (the filth of Forth making the Med
look like a vast channel of distilled water). Nor did any
pub in Kirkcaldy serve draught San Miguel at 85p a
pint. Not even the Penny Farthing. Or even the Novar.

But apart from all that, the comparison somehow
passed muster. Particularly when the peace and quiet
(there really weren't many Spanish here) was accompanied by the sound of the wind through the trees or children
yelling in the distance or Mister Whippy's chimes, Calahonda revealed its true nature – as a leafy outskirt with
Proustian potential for anyone from an estate with
thematically christened streets and a twice-weekly fish van.

So it felt the same as home and the differences only
made it far better. In a novel by Michael Frayn called

Sweet Dreams, the hero dies for an extended moment and finds himself in a place which miraculously provides Parisian boulevards, yellow cabs, Oxbridge colleges and the kind of restaurants where vines inevitably shade the tables and the proprietor always comes out to chat and offer a brandy on the house. Calahonda, I was shocked to realize, not Soho or Edinburgh's Old Town, far less Fuengirola, Torremolinos or Marbella, had come closest to my paradise. Scotland weren't about to win the World Cup at a nearby stadium and the young Sophia Loren wasn't my enraptured soulmate and sex slave. But it is the only place I've ever known where, mucking about in the pool or padding across the marble floor of the sitting-room to the already-warm patio for my first coffee and fag of the day and a chat with wee Iain, I could imagine having arrived via a flash of light, some tinkling ambient music and an effusive welcome from deceased loved ones wearing long, flowing robes.

So uneventfully blissful was that second week that I felt, for the first time, envious of the people whose holiday here extended not for a fortnight but for the rest of their lives. You may wonder why this jealousy of the expatriates hadn't bedevilled me before. Well, it hadn't, and that's a measure of how quickly and thoroughly I'd formed the impression that the British residents on the Costa are, by and large, not the targets of envy they assume they are – lucky devils downing pina coladas for breakfast before eighteen holes, a spot of lunch and then an afternoon spent tackling a jug of sangria and the hausfrau next door – but a truly sorry bunch.

There are an estimated 250,000 Britons living in Spain, the majority on the Costa del Sol, so I must have come across as many as 0.02 per cent of them. It follows that my assessment of this community reflects my own engrained prejudice rather than extensive research. But it was a useful and enjoyable prejudice to cultivate, and one borne out with welcome reliability when I tried out expat watering-holes, most recently The Dickens Bar. Perhaps I caught the expat bars on off-days when they weren't humming with their customary parry-and-thrust of eager debate and merry banter. I suspect not.

However, The Dickens Bar apart, Calahonda sometimes threatened to offer exceptions to my rule. Maybe it was the pensionability of most of the town's full-time British residents, as well as my new-found rosy contentment, that made me think that the expats here were relatively brimming with zip and vim. Certainly, Tony Meredith, though getting on a fair bit, was experiencing a dynamic retirement helping to run the place, but other oldsters in Calahonda appeared to be making something of their life here too. Many of them frequented the Club Naranje, a British Legionish social centre with bingo, whist, bridge and quiz nights, outings, and special Sunday lunches. Okay, so it wasn't the most happening place I've ever seen, but if I reach the age of some of the club's members and I'm still playing whist without dribbling down my shirt or addressing long-dead school chums, I'll count myself lucky.

The average age of the 4000 expats in Calahonda is sixty-five. I learned this at another of the town's popular social centres – the European Medical Centre on the Avenida España. To be more accurate, I learned this fact at the neighbouring Red Lion where I fell in with a couple of the Medical Centre's Spanish employees. They were chain-smoking Winstons so I knew they were doctors. They were both very amicable, despite their reluctance to provide me with any slimming tablets, and eager to deny all the horror stories I'd heard and read. No, that case in the papers of the British resident who was turfed out of intensive care ten days after his heart attack and then dumped, though paralysed, by ambulancemen on his front lawn was not typical. No, clinics did not overcharge or arrange expensive organ transplants as soon as you complained of hay fever. And they claimed that they really liked the Brits – give them twenty British patients for one German any day. And don't even mention the French.

One coffee and four Winstons later, the doctors' sunny appraisals darkened as we moved on to the topic of the elderly. Did I know that up the road the Dutch were investing 10 million pesetas in a hospital for geriatrics? And what about the Danes, who flew out some of their oldsters for a long winter break in Benalmadena? All those old people's homes being developed? 'In five or ten years' time,' observed one of the doctors between puffs, 'this place will be like Florida.' Europe's playground was being turned into Europe's hospice. The Costa Geriatrica. Cigarette?

The third social centre for Calahonda's expats is the supermarket at El Zoco. It's not that the aisles are blocked by chattering Brits, but the supermarket bar certainly is. Try getting a drink there after a hard morning's shopping and you have to make your way through the massed ranks of octogenarians tackling their first *cervezas* of the day. Polite but firm use of elbows to the midriff and kidney punches will finally secure you a place at the bar where, I guarantee, the conversation will soon have you ordering a succession of very large brandies.

'. . . got them cheaper at Marks and Sparks in Gibraltar.'

'. . . at which point I said to the doc, bloody well get her into the hospital and pronto.'

'Fair's fair, you have to admit the bunkers need a bit of attention.'

'Bulk-buy them and you recoup the cost of the petrol.'

'. . . thought she was in the bloody swimming-pool. Well, of course she wasn't, she was in a bloody ward in Malaga, drips hanging out of her arms.'

'Difficult? I've played the Postage Stamp at Troon but that fourteenth is the hardest par three I've seen.'

'. . . although any fool but that bloody doctor would have seen it wasn't just a bloody allergy.'

'. . . and there's C & A as well.'

'. . . forty-three years together then she's gone just like that . . .'

However, most of my own social encounters with Calahonda's residents were notably untraumatic. So much so that it was often hard not to fall asleep or start screaming with boredom. These folks had time on their hands, and didn't they let you know it. Experts, they were, at wittering on about absolutely bugger all. Take a subject, any subject, and talk about and around it for as long as possible – that beat bridge and quiz nights hands down as their favourite pastime. Save for their fondness for repetition, they would be maestros on *Just a Minute*. A minute? Piece of piss. Sixty seconds on the leaves in the pool? Make that six hundred seconds. Dan-Air from Gibraltar versus British Midland from Malaga? Sit down, make yourself comfortable and ensure you've got a pillow handy.

I suppose it makes sense, if the number of years you have left on the planet doesn't reach double figures, to live them in slow motion. But at least the permanent inhabitants of Calahonda showed a bit of get-up-and-go, even if they were only getting up to go to the bereavement workshop at the supermarket bar. Too often, elsewhere, I found expats nurturing their tedium with glum dedication.

Which brings me to the bit where I have to describe my most depressing encounter with Brits on the Costa del Sol. I'm wary of identifying the pub in question, so I'll stick at saying that it was not far from Calahonda, near a promenade, and it wasn't called The Cardiff Arms. There were two people in the pub when I made the mistake of visiting it, to make the even bigger mistake of engaging them in chat. My best conversational gambits went down like a cup of sick, so I resorted to telling

the barman and his sole customer that I'd appreciate
their help for a book I was writing. Not the best line in
the world, I knew only too well, but it was delivered in a
spiel of such relentless charm it would have seduced
starlets. During which time the barman and the sole
customer inspected me with unblinking stares that had
me wondering for a moment if I'd accidentally gobbed
on the Swansea City pennant beside me.

'From the *Sun*, are you?' asked the barman, after a
pause even Harold Pinter would have thought auda-
cious.

'No, no. Like I said, I'm here to write a book. Honestly.'

'The *Sun* was here two years ago,' said the barman. He
was a tall chap aged, I would guess, between twenty-
eight and forty. 'I'n' that right?' he asked the sole customer, a gap-toothed, strawberry-nosed gent who may
well have been in his fifties. He took time off from
demolishing his gin to nod back at the barman.

'Two years ago they was here,' the barman reassured
the sole customer. 'The *Sun*. Lies they wrote. Fucking
lies.'

Something about the way the conversation was going
told me that the *Sun* might have queered my pitch. Our
social interaction had developed to the stage that I
reckoned I just might make eye-contact with this pair if
I were beautiful, female and offering inventive oral sex.

'Honestly, I'm writing a book,' I pleaded. 'And, okay,
I have a day job as a journalist, but I'm definitely not
from the *Sun*. Look.' I proffered my *Sunday Times* press
pass.

This the barman examined with great diligence.

'You've got no specs on in this photo,' he observed to
his customer.

I removed my glasses and grinned vulnerably.

'You still don't look like this photo,' the barman
accused the customer.

'Well, he doesn't, but I do, ha ha ha,' I quipped to an obstreperous silence. 'Please, truly, I'm not from the *Sun* and I just want an impression or two of your life out here. For example, how long have you lived on the coast?'

Having eventually decided this wasn't a trick question, the barman replied. 'Eleven years,' he informed the customer, who nodded sage agreement.

In fact, what he said was 'leaven yeersh', and in doing so, lit the wrong end of his cigarette. It was midday, but both of them, I now realized, were quietly, professionally, out of it.

I went through the motions. And you never knew. Perhaps they had been best mates with Max Boyce.

'So do you enjoy your life out here?' I asked.

The barman examined his flaring cigarette and tried to throw it in the sink, but succeeded only in throwing it into a plate of peanuts.

'I'll tell you something,' he told his friend. 'You've got to work hard, see?' He grew abruptly animated, stressing his points with a finger jabbing at his customer. 'You can't just lie back and expect to have a holiday for the rest of your life. You work hard, and you have to, see? It's not like you come here for a holiday. No, you have to work hard. It's not like I'm some black back home walking up to you and saying, "Hey, mon, give me a job." No, you have to work hard out here. I'm behind this bar all the hours God sends. No, you have to work. Hard,' he explained.

I swilled my *cerveza* around the glass, hoping that my sudden absence of furious nodding had signalled strong disapproval of his Jim Davidson tribute. 'Course it didn't. A howitzer up his arse he might have registered, but not a lack of nodding.

'But I don't have no choice, see? If I go back to Britain now, I won't get a job, will I? I'm not black, see? If it was me going for a job against some coloured or

Pakistani, they'd choose the wog or the Paki, wouldn't they? Look at London Transport, now. Run by nig-nogs, that is. How many of them in our country now? Fucking millions. No, give me Spain every time. Britain? Ruined, that is. Ruined by fucking niggers.'

While he looked off into the distance, nostalgic for the good old days of 1981 when Britain was strong and proud and white, I decided to risk the most obvious rejoinder in the book. 'It's interesting you should say that,' I said. 'Because my wife's West Indian.'

For the first time since the *Sun* hove into conversational view, the barman turned in an attempt to focus on me. 'Ah, no disrespect, mind,' he said.

The trouble with melodrama is that you have to keep it going. Having delivered my white lie, I put down my glass of beer, like, really fiercely, gave him one of my looks, swivelled round and walked out. Just like that. I bet he was scared witless.

I'd been on the Costa long enough by that time not to be too surprised at finding expats with addictions to glib fascism and alcohol. The latter, especially, is a feature of expat life on the coast. In the same way that money is a feature of the Stock Exchange. That El Zoco's supermarket had a bar was only to be expected because every expat institution you care to think of has a bar – social centres, hospitals, the English Library in Marbella, even the church for British Catholics. Okay, not the church itself, but after a spot of kneeling and praying and so forth, the congregation and the priest repair to the nearest local for a session on the San Miguel.

Which helps explain the burgeoning popularity of the Costa's many branches of one particular social club – Alcoholics Anonymous. The 'Club News' section of *The Entertainer*, the local English language weekly newspaper, hardly has room for the British Legions, Rotary Clubs and Square Dance Societies, what with all the AA meetings it has to advertise. In fact, the Costa del Sol is AA's best recruiting ground in the world. Cheap booze, money to spend and nothing to do – add all three ingredients together and you come up with the recipe for alcoholism. Yes, if you want to become a lush, the Costa del Sol is the place to live.

There are a few activities, such as going to a Catholic service, for those who want to work up a thirst. *The Entertainer* and the weekly edition of *Sur* in English carry reports of matches in the coast's cricket league (Combined Colleges gave Sotogrande a hammering in August, despite Mike Noonan's battling forty-five), as well as ads for the likes of shiatsu classes, slimming programmes, and home visits from 'BOYS young, between 18 and 21 years old, videos, discretion, hygiene' or 'SUSIE attractive, massages, SM speciality, 12–8'.

For a short time I thought that the existence of the expats' newspapers and magazines – however hilariously bad – together with the coast's two English-language radio stations (Coastline and OCI), besides the bridge tournaments and cricket leagues, were signs that the resident Brits had formed a healthy and supportive community. That might be so, but my governing prejudice soon led me away from that opinion and towards the working assumption that the various free-sheets, phone-ins and limited-overs matches were signs of nothing more than the fact that there were people living there with money to attract the attention of advertisers and with a liking for cricket.

For how could it be otherwise? They hadn't been here long enough to establish any convincing simulacrum of community spirit. I came across one old boy who had retired here in 1963, as well as a few survivors of T-Town in the sixties, but almost everyone else had been living on the Costa for five years, ten years maximum. Because most of the expats had made their money either from the property boom in London and the Home Counties or from being bought out of suddenly desirable small businesses, both economic phenomena which can be dated to the period when Thatcherism seemed to be working – i.e., about three weeks in the summer of 1988.

Having said that, I would bet that in twenty years' time the expatriate scene will be as ramshackle and fragmented as it is now, because so many of the Brits who've retired here are lazing about on a permanent holiday – and are permanently pissed. And what networks and microeconomies they have established are usually based on booze. Many of them spend all day every day in the expat pubs (never, *ever* any Spanish place), staring at the gantry, engaged in their only hobby, interest, job or task, which is to sip San Miguel and stub out another cigarette. Others vary this by being employed in little jobettes sipping San Miguel and stubbing out cigarettes while 'working' part-time behind the bars. Witness The Cardiff Arms.

And having said all that, I thought I did detect slight variations on the expats' theme of glazed boredom. Just as the residents in Calahonda were older and livelier than elsewhere, so the expats in Marbella showed promise in living up to their reputation on the coast as dodgily snobby, especially if they appeared a bit down-at-heel. 'You've no idea,' Jimmy of Jimmy Tramps told me, 'how handy the BCCI crash was for people in this town. Gave them a good excuse for all the money they didn't have.' 'What's the difference between a Marbella man and a mirror?' Carmel, the endearing owner of the Tu Casa bar in the town's old quarter, asked me. 'You can't see through a mirror. And what's the difference between a Marbella man and a sloth? One smells and sleeps all day. The other one's a sloth.'

The competition was stiff but the most appalling expats were the most pathetic – the posh bohemians who lingered on in Torremolinos. These once-raffish upper-middle-class relics of T-Town, desperate spurners of bourgeois convention, now found themselves eking out their lives in a town that had long ago turned into the kind of place they utterly despised. That they had been trapped there for as many as thirty years was an indication of how desperately they lacked money or gumption or both.

All they had left were a few hazy memories of the good old days, when Binkie was sick over the policeman, when Spiffy fell off the train, when whatsisname, you know, the chap who could have been a sculptor if he hadn't been an alcoholic, had that beach party when he tried to cook his shoe in a mustard sauce . . .

Ah, how enviable those good old days sounded, when Spiffy drank away his ball-bearing legacy and Binkie was always just a bit too sozzled to start on the great novel he planned to write. 'It was all such fun,' lamented one T-Town survivor over a beer I bought him in a back-street café. 'And now look at it.' He shook his head in disgust at a British family passing by, eating slices of pizza. 'You know what I'm going to do?' I shook my head, taking the opportunity to avoid staring at his ludicrously stained, last-days-of-the-Raj cream suit. 'I'm going to write a book about it.' Sure. As soon as he'd had another drink.

Aaaaaarrrgh. I seem to have rediscovered my Presbyterian roots. To redress the balance, I would like to describe one of several expats I met whom I really liked, all of them, by no coincidence whatsoever, energetically employed at jobs rather than propping up bars.

Nicola was a working girl in both senses of the phrase, though I didn't realize this when we first met in a bar in Calahonda. 'Have you got a light?' she asked, then cupped her hands round mine as I lit her cigarette. I estimated her to be thirty-four and knew her to have stupendous, conical breasts because she was wearing a crochet vest. Struggling to shift my gaze up to her neck at least, I listened to her chat away about the weather.

Then she handed me her business card. 'Massage', it said. I must confess that, cliché though it is, I was about to tell her about my spot of back trouble, before she went on to tell me about the chap she was meeting here, a fellow-expat who made hard-core porn.

We met again, at my stumbling request, the next day at her place. Well, brothel. I'd stressed I wanted to interview her for a book, and, thank goodness, she believed me instead of thinking this the prelude to a peculiar sexual penchant. Heart-rendingly, she'd dressed up for the occasion in her best frock because, as she told her madam and the couple of clients who called her on her mobile phone that afternoon, she was being *interviewed*. She may have been putting on a great performance but she came across as – second cliché in two paragraphs – a kind, generous-hearted woman. To remind myself and you that my judgment can be, er, barkingly wrong, I should confess that the first thing she told me was her age – forty-two. She'd come out to Spain four years before after the break-up of her marriage of twenty years, taught English, made no money, then, in some desperation, had answered an ad for girls to work in a club. 'It sounded interesting. Romantic. Serving drinks, being chatted up, being paid to look great. How naïve can you get? I remember the first *entrada*, as they call it, I was so nervous, and I told the gentleman it was my first time – well, what a great line, I used it all the time after that. Got great tips that way.

'I used to cry myself to sleep, but I got through that phase, mainly by telling myself I had to do it to survive out here. Because there was no way I was going back to Bolton and that bastard. I'm lucky in that I have quite a decent body. I'm able to do something to earn money. Not huge amounts, but enough.'

Most of her clients were Spanish, she said, especially this year which had been really tough; a sure sign of the recession was the falling proportion of British holiday-

makers among her clientele. 'I don't know what I'd do
without my regulars, the bank manager, the lawyers
who visit me once a week. There's a couple of men who
say they're in love with me but that's because they're
like most of my customers.'

'What do you mean?'

'Inadequate, I suppose. It's funny – they're all a bit
strange. Most in a vague kind of way you can't quite
describe. And of course there's the kinky ones. Men who
want me to punch them, swear at them, piss on them. I
had a man in Puerto Banus recently wanted that – you
know, golden showers. I'm getting a bit fed up with it
all. You know what I want to do? Get on one of those
phone lines. The pay's quite good, I'd do quite well
because the Spanish like my accent, and you don't have
anyone touching you. That's why I do porn as well. I
mean, if it's just photographs, for two or three days'
work I can get . . .' she paused to do her mental arithmetic '. . . well, with the exchange rate now, it'd work out
at about £650. And there's a big porn scene down here.
A lot of money involved. Quite a mafia. I don't want to
do too much of that, though, in case anyone from back
home recognizes me. None of my family knows what I'm
doing out here. But it's a lot better than Bolton and a
husband cheating on me.'

All the working expats shared that one significant
characteristic. Unlike the people who'd retired here to
spend their remaining years (or often decades) stinking
in the sun, the working expats had all come here –
obviously enough, I suppose – to escape. Just what they
were escaping from varied wildly: failed marriages, boredom, dead-end jobs, rain . . . One woman working for an
estate agent told me at length that the reason she'd
thrown all her belongings into her Beetle and driven
south for a new life was the dreadfully formal dinner-
parties that had constituted her social life in Teesside,
whereas the easy-going ambience of the Costa meant

everyone was happy to eat alfresco and off their laps. (It seemed impolite to ask her why she hadn't saved herself the upheaval by selling her place-settings and finding less nerdy friends, but maybe that wasn't the whole story.) Barry Hands, who works for the OCI radio station, was adamant that he'd moved to Andalusia to escape the twin evils of 'VAT and Wellington boots'. Nick and John, a twentysomething gay couple I befriended in Calahonda where they worked in a restaurant, came out here to escape the tedium of working for Travellers' Fare in Lancashire and the homophobic bigotry that surrounded them. They'd arrived eighteen months ago with two sleeping-bags, a tent, two rucksacks and £500 between them, struggled to survive for several months, and were now enjoying, for the first time in their lives, a nice flat, money, jobs they liked, and the ability to hold hands in public occasionally without being beaten senseless.

The last three words fail to do justice to the incident that encouraged the emigration to the Costa of one of its most extraordinary characters. Nobby Clark now runs Ladybirds music bar in Fuengirola, having retired here for the sake of his health. That had suffered a tad in his previous job as a prison officer in Lewes, where he'd been attacked by sixty-four inmates during a riot. They'd strung him up by his heels, hit him zealously with an iron bar and thrown him down a metal staircase. 'I was pronounced dead at the hospital. And on the TV,' he claimed, after vacuuming a bacon sandwich into his mouth (I didn't think it appropriate to warn him about cholesterol levels). Eighteen months in and out of hospital later, he upped sticks for Spain. The attractions for him of running a bar on the Costa were unarguable – it was a long way from Lewes, he had friends and now his family out here, and besides, his doctor had told him that if he didn't move to a warm climate he'd be in a wheelchair within five years.

Nobby has a wide and varied range of friends on the Costa. One of his closest chums was Stuart Hutchinson, an oil engineer of independent means who had retired in his very early forties to live in some style in Mijas. Living proof of Ritchie's First Law of Expatriate Life — doing nothing very much will get to you in the end — Hutchinson is now serving a twenty-four-year prison sentence for killing his wife. He'd bludgeoned her to death, cut her body into thirty-eight pieces, impaled her severed head on a stake and chopped it in two with an axe, then disposed of the bits by burning them and putting the remains in rubbish bags. The reports I read of this crime relayed Hutchinson's claim that he thought he'd committed the perfect murder. Which is odd, because he was rumbled (by Nobby's daughter, as it happens) after first claiming his wife had vanished, then that she'd gone to London (without her clothes, jewellery and passport, which were all on view at his villa), then that she was mad and prone to taking off on mysterious trips. How this explained the blood-stained duvet, fingernail scratches on the wall and patches of blood he couldn't say. Not quite the perfect murder, I'd have thought, but then the man had a lot on his mind. In prison Hutchinson claimed he killed his wife because she taunted him about the many lovers she'd had in her life — 300, she estimated — and about how she recorded the performance of each one, and about his own standing in her extended sexual league table. He was in 300th place.

The British have established quite a reputation for violent death on the Costa del Sol. The tabloids back home can rely on a steady production every summer of blazing pile-ups on the N340 and death-plunges from high-rise hotel rooms. Almost as frequent are the professional killings that affect that section of the British community that has taken a particular liking to the coast — the criminals.

The Costa del Sol's first celebrated fugitive was Judah

Brinstock, a financier who fled here in the mid-sixties when the police decided to interest themselves in his financing activities. By the mid-eighties, these activities involved currency irregularities amounting to an estimated £2 million. The reason the police couldn't catch Mr Brinstock, and the reason the coast has proved so appealing to many like-minded citizens, is that Spain tore up its extradition treaty with Britain during a full and frank exchange of views on the ownership of Gibraltar.

This loophole in international law went more or less unnoticed by the public until 1984, when the men wanted for questioning in connection with the £6-million Security Express robbery turned up on the Costa, put their thumbs in their ears and waggled their hands at the police. Their leader was the infamous Freddie Foreman, chum of the Krays, and the most celebrated of the remaining five was Ronnie Knight, then married to Barbara Windsor. Foreman was eventually arrested in 1989 and jailed for nine years, but Knight has had much better luck, having stayed on the Costa, where he now owns a couple of restaurants and a club in Fuengirola. As if to show the extent to which he needs to keep a low profile, Knight has called his club Knight's. Popular with karaoke fans and, I am told, holidaying policemen.

Spain introduced a new Alien Law in 1985, which meant that fugitives from British justice either left the country within forty days or were, supposedly, stuck there for good. Proof that this was hardly the draconian measure the hundreds of expat crims feared might be a selection of the more prominent members of their profession who were sunning themselves two years later: the bank robber Michael Green, part-owner with the coke-smuggler Brian Doran of a night-club in Puerto Banus; the Great Train Robber Gordon Goody; Mad Frankie Fraser; Soho pornsters Joey Wilkins, Tommy Hayes and

Christopher Holloway; Robert Chatwin, a jeweller who turned up on the Costa after he and £3 million worth of jewels went missing from his chain of shops; and, my favourite, Alan Brooks, the king of the dope-smugglers, who was ambushed by police after a surveillance operation lasting two years, together with Sarah, his unsuspecting fiancée, who'd previously found brief fame after caning Prince Andrew at that daft restaurant, School Dinners. And of course there was Charlie Wilson, the Great Train Robber, who was killed in a gangland dispute at his villa outside Marbella.

The Alien Law and a bit of co-operation between British and Spanish police forces mean that the crims no longer flaunt their presence as they once did. Time was when you couldn't throw a maraschino cherry at a marina-side restaurant in Puerto Banus without hitting a gangster. But now they keep their heads down a bit, and the centre of the action has moved to Fuengirola, where their acolytes and apprentices can be found in pubs like the Tall Man and the Queen Vic.

But police interest in the Costa del Sol, though as ineffective as ever, has far from declined. As Nicola confirmed, the porn industry is booming down here; for example, villas up in the hills above Marbella have become popular settings for mock-snuff movies (mock only because they have been discovered to be more realistic than the real thing). And, encouraged by a much more lucrative market, links between the firms in Britain and Fuengirola are stronger than ever, because the coast's resident bank-robbers and murderers have branched out, overcoming a traditional distaste for the activity to muscle in on the drugs scene. Especially the hash scene, with veteran smugglers lending their skills to the more brutish holders-up of building societies and bullion warehouses.

And importing marijuana from the Rif mountains in Morocco is not difficult. The Costa del Sol is awash with the stuff, providing Europe with most of its spliff material. Couriers in hash gangs (often recruited from the ranks of the time-share touts who want a more respectable job) strap dope to themselves and waltz through Customs unchecked. The ferries that land at Algeciras carry many artics whose spare tyres and refrigerated walls are lined with bricks of the stuff, which is stored or repackaged on the coast. And then there are the yachts and speedboats that zip across the Mediterranean to land at secluded bays, often guided there by one apparently respectable expat whose bar closes uncommonly early every day, to allow him to have a rest before resuming his evening job operating guidance systems for night-time landings. And now, with open borders in the EC, the incentive to get hash over and into the Costa del Sol is greater than ever, since distribution is so much less a problem. Thank goodness for that.

The profit margins on hash smuggling being what they are, a firm needs only to supervise the importing of two big loads a year to keep its members happy and prosperous. Theirs is not an arduous lifestyle, in work terms at any rate; the daily schedule of one leading crim is none the less demanding – get up at noon, have three coffees laced with brandy, snort a line of coke, snort another line, smoke a joint, and only then will it be time to tackle the day head-on by sunbathing and popping over to the local to get well and truly hammered. It is because the crims spend an enormous proportion of their time hanging out, around and loose that they blend in so successfully with other expats on permanent, pointless holiday.

Benevolent though that final week in Calahonda had made me, I reckon there was never any real danger of my lapsing into sympathy or admiration for the majority of the British residents on the Costa del Sol. Just in case there was, my last night provided me with a useful reminder that my prejudice was one to be cherished.

We'd dined in Alan's Plaice in El Zoco, early, as usual, before Iain became knackered and grizzly. Come eight, Margaret divined the early-warning signs that, unless we skedaddled pretty soon, we'd have one unhappy child on our hands. Or, rather, she and Ken would. This was my final fling. I was going to make a night of it. Off they went on another nerve-racking journey pushing the buggy up a pavementless hill, leaving me to an hour's solitaire pinball in the amusement arcade and, earning replays being thirsty work, a beer or two in a local. That was the plan, anyway, but I knew it to have backfired as soon as I marched into the pub of my choice. There were three people at the bar, two silent customers with the leathery skins of the expat and one mute barman. Leaning on the counter must have been exhausting work for the latter, for it took him a long, long time to rouse himself to serve me. That achieved, he slumped back for another shift being mute. Eventually, one of the customers spoke.

'Anyone seen Roger?'

Too exhausted to speak, the barman pursed his lips and, after some considerable thought, shook his head.

'Ah,' said Roger's pal, then resumed his silent appraisal of the bar towel under his elbows.

Amazing how quickly you can drink beer sometimes, isn't it? I tore myself away from that palace of fun and trudged up the hill to join Ken and Margaret for a session on the San Miguel back in the house.

Which, as far as I was concerned, didn't make for a happy morn. At least my flight was in the evening, so I had time to recover, unlike the other three whose taxi was due at the house at ten. By quarter to ten they looked to be on schedule. Then Iain got hold of the toy holdall and tipped out, with no little aplomb and all over the kitchen, his collection of gaudy balls, daddy, mummy and baby bears, squeaky men and picture-books, not forgetting the smiley green dinosaur. Margaret started to repack the lot, but this only added to the sudden mayhem, for Iain was not to be persuaded of the necessity of such a move. I tried to distract him by bouncing him up and down and singing 'Fascinating Rhythm' by Bassomatic. A fine piece of music, I think you'll agree, but it failed to appease my nephew, whose crying reached authentically Spanish levels.

At this point the doorbell rang. Ken answered it, preparing to mime to a taxi-driver the message that, despite appearances, he and his family would be ready in only a few minutes. But no. At the door was a clean-cut English chap equipped with a suit and a clipboard. Not a Mormon but a salesman. Having taken Ken by surprise, he was able to start acclaiming the benefits of some health insurance policy for residents. He handed Ken a leaflet and repeated its slogan: 'Is Your Family Worth 15,000 Pesetas?'

Ken told me later that he considered it too much trouble to explain that we were not expats but tourists with a combined total of ten hours left on the Costa del Sol. Instead, he looked round at the three of us in the kitchen – me bouncing his son up and down and chanting, 'Give me some of that bass line on your ster-ee-oh', Margaret cursing the smiley green dinosaur as she failed to cram it into the holdall, Iain exploding with the trauma of it all.

Ken turned back to face the salesman. 'No,' he said, 'they're not.'

Ten minutes later, their taxi arrived, and five minutes after that I was waving them bye-bye. I went upstairs to pack, tidy up and shower. I stood in front of the bathroom mirror, arms raised, like a centre-forward pleading for a high ball. It was no good. My underarms were still white.

I spent my final five hours in Calahonda prone on the lawn, desperate to use up my last ration of hot sun.

Thence, by way of taxi, bus and train, I hauled myself and my suitcases to Malaga. The journey allowed me a brief and nostalgia-free sighting of the hotel in Fuengirola, and then a pangful glimpse of the flat in Benyamina. And here was the turning for the airport. And now the Albert Speer Memorial terminal. And now the truly preposterous queue at my check-in desk.

Aeons afterwards, I was mooching in the Departures Lounge, stomach trying to cope with a hamburger as undercooked as it was expensive, arms aching from carrying my holdall and a poly-bag bulging with duty-free, nose pressed against the window as I looked out at the view. Still no sign of any plane docking at my gate, so the check-in woman had kept her promise of a long delay.

A large orange sun was setting over the jagged peaks of the sierras in the distance. Spain. It looked a beautiful country. Some day, I thought, I really must go there.